Lecture Notes in Computer Science 1173

Edited by G. Goos, J. Hartmanis and J. van Leeuwen

Springer
Berlin
Heidelberg
New York
Barcelona
Budapest
Hong Kong
London
Milan
Paris
Santa Clara
Singapore
Tokyo

William Rucklidge

Efficient Visual Recognition
Using the Hausdorff Distance

Springer

Series Editors

Gerhard Goos, Karlsruhe University, Germany

Juris Hartmanis, Cornell University, NY, USA

Jan van Leeuwen, Utrecht University, The Netherlands

Author

William Rucklidge
Xerox Palo Alto Research Center
3333 Coyote Hill Road, Palo Alto, CA 94304, USA
E-mail: rucklidge@parc.xerox.com

Cataloging-in-Publication data applied for

Die Deutsche Bibliothek - CIP-Einheitsaufnahme

Rucklidge, William:
Efficient visual recognition using the Hausdorff distance /
William Rucklidge. - Berlin ; Heidelberg ; New York ;
Barcelona ; Budapest ; Hong Kong ; London ; Milan ; Paris ;
Santa Clara ; Singapore ; Tokyo : Springer, 1996
  (Lecture notes in computer science ; Vol. 1173)
  ISBN 3-540-61993-3
NE: GT

CR Subject Classification (1991): I.5, I.2.10, I.3.5

ISSN 0302-9743
ISBN 3-540-61993-3 Springer-Verlag Berlin Heidelberg New York

© Springer-Verlag Berlin Heidelberg 1996
Printed in Germany

Typesetting: Camera-ready by author
SPIN 10549103   06/3142 – 5 4 3 2 1 0   Printed on acid-free paper

*To my parents, who taught me a love of knowledge and
a desire to see a job well done.*

Preface

This book describes a method that I have developed that uses the minimum Hausdorff distance to visually locate an object in an image. This method is very reliable, and fast enough for real-world applications.

A visual recognition system takes an image and a model of an object which may occur in that image; these images and models are composed of features (points, line segments, etc.). The system locates instances of the model in the image by determining transformations of the model which bring a large number of model features close to image features. One of the unique strengths of the Hausdorff distance is the *reverse distance* which reduces the frequency of erroneous matching between a model and a cluttered portion of the image.

The Hausdorff distance is a measure defined between two point sets representing a model and an image. Its properties make it attractive for model-based recognition; one of these properties is that the Hausdorff distance is a metric. The *minimum* Hausdorff distance is used to find a transformation of the model which brings it into *closest* correspondence with the image. This can be done by searching over a space of allowable transformations. In some cases, the minimum Hausdorff distance is also a metric. The Hausdorff distance can be modified so that it is reliable even when the image contains multiple objects, noise, spurious features, and occlusions.

I construct lower bounds which show that finding the exact transformation that minimises the Hausdorff distance may be quite expensive. I develop a rasterised approach to the search and a number of techniques which allow this search to be performed efficiently. The principal search technique used is *transformation space subdivision*. The space of transformations is searched in a tree-like fashion: a large region is examined as a unit, and if the results of this examination are good, it is subdivided and each of the subregions examined in turn; if the results are not good, then the region is discarded.

I discuss some implementations of this approach, together with their applications to practical problems such as motion tracking and mobile robot navigation.

This book describes the work I did for my Ph.D. dissertation at Cornell University. For my first four years at Cornell, I was supported in part by a Natural Sciences and Engineering Research Council (Canada) 1967 Scholarship, and I gratefully acknowledge this support. I was also supported in part by NSF grant IRI-9057928 and Air Force Contract AFOSR91-0328.

I thank my Ph.D. committee, Dexter Kozen, Rich Zippel, and Geoff Brown, for their guidance and helpful comments. I especially thank my advisor, Dan Huttenlocher, for his invaluable instruction, supervision, and collaboration.

Portions of the work described in this book were originally done in collaboration with Dan Huttenlocher, Greg Klanderman, Jae Noh and Michael Leventon.

The people who have mostly been voices at the other end of a long distance phone line, and whom I have seen less than I would have liked during the last few years, have all been wonderful: my parents, my brothers Alastair and Andrew, my sister Julia, Dr. Jenn Brasch, Micki and Harald Koch, Bruce Macintosh, Larry and Christy de Souza,

Elizabeth d'Anjou, and many more. Crispin Cowan could always be relied on for a good night's drinking and talk whenever we got together.

Finally, there are the fellow students who made my time at Cornell much more enjoyable. James Allan, Brad Glade (and Cindy, of course), Jim Jennings, Judith Underwood, Paul Stodghill and Sam Weber have all given me many more lunchtime conversations and companionship than I can count. The members of the Computer Science department hockey team have worn me out, bruised and cut me, and otherwise physically abused me, and I would like to thank them all for it. Karen Middaugh has given me many enjoyable outings, biking, watching movies, and so on. Rhonda Reese has been a great support (among many other things) through much of this time. Russell Brown has been a great friend, and we have had innumerable conversations, from productive ones about work to unproductive ones about Muppets. He can also be counted on for a bad pun whenever you most expect it.

The quote at the beginning of Chapter 1 is Copyright © 1990 Liu-tunes, and is used by kind permission.

Table of Contents

List of Tables

List of Figures

Chapter 1

Introduction

I am Joe's eyes
Between the vision and the light
I am Joe's eyes
Between the image and the sight...

What is *practical computer vision*? Computer vision itself is the study of methods that take an *image* (usually just an array of numbers, representing the light intensity at each pixel of a camera), and extract some information from the image: what objects are present in it, where they are, their shapes, and so on. *Practical* computer vision methods not only solve such problems, but they also solve them in particularly reliable ways, as well as particularly fast ways. In this book, I describe such a practical method of computer vision, based on the Hausdorff distance. This method is reliable, due to the intrinsic properties of the Hausdorff distance (when some suitable modifications are made); it is also quite fast, due to the efficient search techniques I have developed.

Emerging desktop multimedia computers, with cameras, digital video, and significant computing power, are becoming more and more common. Using them simply to input and output video data completely ignores the possibilities of doing something with that data while it is stored in the computer's memory. Scanners are also falling in price and increasing in availability; this is opening up an arena for document processing applications.

Using computers to extract *useful* information from the world requires algorithms and systems for computer vision that are

- reliable: they must deal with images from unstructured scenes, natural objects, and uncontrolled environments, and
- efficient: they must be able to extract some information from the incoming images in a timely fashion, while it is still relevant.

In other words, such practical computer vision systems must be able to compute a good answer in the presence of uncertainty, occlusion, and noise; they must also compute it quickly enough that the user still cares about the result.

One problem in computer vision for which such a practical solution would be useful is that of *model-based recognition, image search*, or *visual recognition*. This is the problem of locating an object, of which the computer has a model, in an image. For example, the computer might be given the task of finding a certain book on a cluttered desk, or of tracking an object as it moves about, by locating it in each frame of a video sequence.

The problem of model-based recognition is usually posed as:

Given a model: a set of features of some kind (points, segments, curves etc.), representing an object, and another set of features representing an image, locate the model in the image. That is, determine the *pose* of the object: its location, orientation, size, or other parameters of the pose.

The computer's task is to determine a set of parameters for a transformation of the model such that the transformed model is in close correspondence with the part of the image containing the object. I will use "transformation" interchangeably with "pose", as the pose of the object determines where in the image its features should appear. Figure 1.1 shows this recognition procedure. The model is located in the image at a certain position, rotated and scaled by some amount. The located model is shown overlaid in bold on the image.

This figure illustrates many of the reasons why model-based recognition is hard. Not only must the search find the pose of the object, but this task is complicated by

– multiple objects and extraneous features: there are many things in the image which are *not* the thing being looked for; some of these are other objects, and some of them are noise,
– occlusion: part of the object is hidden behind something else in the image,
– misdetection: part of the object was not detected by the process which generated the set of image features, and
– position error: the positions of the features that were found are slightly perturbed.

There is also no obvious way to build a one-to-one correspondence between the model and the image: even if the image consisted only of the transformed model, it would not be correct to say "this part of the model's contour corresponds exactly to this part of the image's contour", due to the perturbations in the detected features.

One reason that features are used to represent the model and image, rather than just using intensity (grey-level) images to represent them, is that certain features are more stable than intensities in the presence of lighting variations, occlusion, and changes of pose. Also, using features allows the use of a number of efficient search techniques based on the Hausdorff distance; these techniques (and, indeed, the Hausdorff distance itself) do not apply when the model and image are not based upon features.

Model-based recognition is applicable to many practical task domains. A few such domains are automated industrial assembly, document processing applications, optical character recognition gesture recognition, motion tracking, and landmark recognition for navigation. Clearly, a practical, reliable, efficient model-based recognition system would be quite useful. However, any method intended to solve the model-based recognition problem must be able to handle the complications listed above, all of which occur in real-world situations.

Model-based recognition systems generally solve one of two types of problems: determining the three-dimensional position of a three-dimensional model, given a two-dimensional image, or determining the two-dimensional position of a two-dimensional model in a two-dimensional image. These are called "3D-from-2D" and "2D-from-2D" respectively. While the second type is operating essentially in a two-dimensional world, it is possible to put a three-dimensional interpretation on the transformations it finds. For example, if the model is located in the image at half its nominal size, this could be interpreted as a three-dimensional object being twice as far away. This three-dimensional

Image

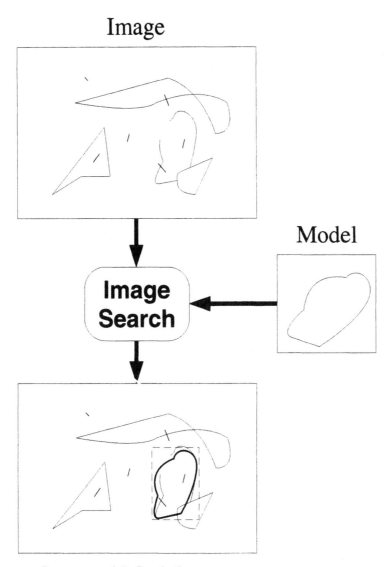

Model

**Image
Search**

Located Model
Rotation: 30 degrees
Size: 75%
Position: (203, 136)

Fig. 1.1. An example of model-based recognition.

interpretation of two-dimensional transformations is the approach that I follow in this book.

I have developed an image search system which addresses the issues raised in the preceding discussion. I have also developed some applications using this system which prove that it is useful in real-world situations. This system

- Can handle dense feature sets, containing many features
- Reliably deals with multiple objects, occlusion, outliers, and positional error
- Computes its answer very efficiently

1.1 The Hausdorff Distance

The method that I have used for model-based recognition is based on the Hausdorff distance. The Hausdorff distance is a distance defined between two sets of points, and is briefly described in this section. It is presented more formally in Chap. 2.

Using the Hausdorff distance for visual recognition is nice in a number of ways. The Hausdorff distance encodes an intuitive notion of the concept of "looking like". It does not try to build any one-to-one correspondences. It performs 2D-from-2D recognition; however, some of the transformation groups that it searches have three-dimensional interpretations. It may also be possible to develop it in a manner so that it could be used in 3D-from-2D recognition. It can handle models and images which contain many features (thousands to tens of thousands). It ensures that not only does the model look like a portion of the image, but that that portion of the image itself looks like the model; this reduces some of the problems caused by cluttered images. It handles the complications described above in natural ways, which degrade gracefully in the presence of increasing noise, occlusion, error, and so on.

I have also developed techniques that enable *efficient* image search using the Hausdorff distance: these techniques can rapidly rule out portions of the space of transformations, by proving that they cannot contain any transformations of interest.

Figure 1.2 shows an example of the application of this method. Figure 1.2(a) shows an intensity (grey-level) image of a scene; Fig. 1.2(b) shows the edges extracted from this scene; these edges are what the Hausdorff distance method uses, rather than the intensities. Figure 1.2(c) shows the model of the object which is to be located, a Coke can. Finally, Fig. 1.2(d) shows the located model, overlaid on the input image edges.

These efficient search techniques are highly effective: using these techniques, this problem took approximately one fifth of a second to solve; without them, on the other hand (using the Hausdorff distance, but in a naïve manner), it took about seventy seconds. In this example, the transformation group searched was the simplest one (translations of the model only). Speedup factors for other, more complex, transformation groups are much higher.

1.1.1 Introduction to the Hausdorff Distance

Suppose that we have two sets of points, representing a model and an image. The Hausdorff distance between these two point sets is small exactly when every point in the

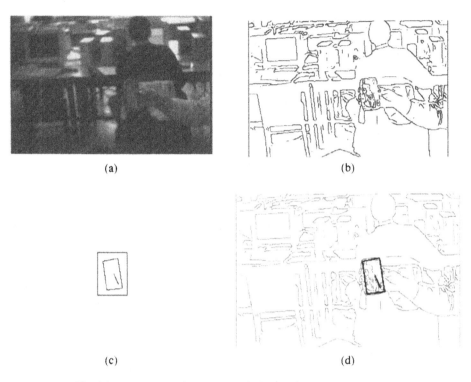

(a) (b)

(c) (d)

Fig. 1.2. An example of the Hausdorff distance image search method.

model is close to some point in the image, and every point in the image is close to some point in the model. Intuitively, this is a good property to have for model-based recognition: it defines a measure of how much the sets look like each other. Also, the Hausdorff distance is a metric. That is, the distance function is everywhere positive, and has the properties of identity, symmetry and the triangle inequality. These properties correspond to our intuitive notions of shape resemblance, namely that a shape is identical only to itself, the order of comparison of two shapes does not matter, and two shapes that are highly dissimilar cannot both be similar to some third shape. This final property, the triangle inequality, is particularly important in pattern matching applications where several stored model shapes are compared to an unknown shape. Most shape comparison functions used in such applications do not obey the triangle inequality, and thus can report that two highly dissimilar model shapes are both similar to the unknown shape. This behavior is highly counterintuitive (for example, reporting that some unknown shape closely resembles both an elephant and a hatrack is not desirable, because these two shapes are highly dissimilar). In [ACH+1], Arkin et al. present related arguments about the desirability of using metrics for shape comparison.

Since the Hausdorff distance is based on proximity between features, perturbing the model and image features slightly affects the Hausdorff distance slightly. Thus, it is robust in the presence of positional errors, which is certainly desirable.

The Hausdorff distance is actually composed of two asymmetric distances: the *forward distance*, which is the distance from the model to the image, and the *reverse distance*, the distance from the image to the model. (As these are asymmetric, they are not strictly distances). The forward distance is small when every point in the model is close to some point in the image (but some points in the image may be far from any point of the model), and the reverse distance is small when every point in the image is close to some point in the model. In other words, the forward distance indicates when the model looks like some subset of the image (but not necessarily vice versa) and similarly for the reverse distance. When both are small, then the image and model look like each other, and the Hausdorff distance is small. I will sometimes call the Hausdorff distance the *undirected distance*, as it incorporates both the forward and reverse directed distances.

1.1.2 Image Search Using the Hausdorff Distance

The Hausdorff distance is defined only between point sets at fixed positions. The image search problem, however, involves finding the transformation (pose) of the model which minimises the distance between the transformed model and the image. The search can be thought of as hypothesising a large number of possible poses of the model, computing the forward and reverse distances for each one, and using these evaluations to choose the best pose by minimising the distances. This minimum Hausdorff distance is, under some circumstances described in Chap. 2, also a metric.

While the Hausdorff distance can be applied to point sets in any number of dimensions, this work concentrates only on problems where both the image and model are two-dimensional point sets. In particular, it concentrates on the three transformation groups of

- Translations
- Translations and independent (x, y) scaling
- Affine transformations (of positive determinant)

While these transformations are defined on two-dimensional point sets, they can also correspond to the change in the appearance of a three-dimensional object moving rigidly in three dimensions, under the weak-perspective projection model. This model is equivalent to orthographic projection, with an added overall scale factor inversely proportional to the depth of the object. It is equivalent (to within a good approximation) to the true perspective projection model when the object is relatively shallow (its depth, or thickness, is small relative to its distance from the camera).

The group of two-dimensional translations corresponds to the change in appearance of a three-dimensional object as it translates within a plane parallel to the camera's image plane; this could be because the camera is looking down on a flat surface, on which objects are moving (for example, a camera looking down on a road). The group of translations also matches document processing applications well, as this really is a two-dimensional world. The group of translations and (x, y) scalings corresponds to the change in appearance of a planar object as it translates in three dimensions and rotates about a vertical axis: its appearance in the camera image translates about, and grows and shrinks; the rotation causes the object to shrink in width, but does not change its height. The group of affine transformations corresponds to the change in appearance of a planar object as it translates and rotates rigidly in three dimensions. These last two groups also closely model the change in appearance of a nonplanar object, as long as it is relatively shallow.

Some subgroups of these translation groups are also of interest. The group of two-dimensional translations and rotations is a subgroup of the group of affine transformations. The commonly-used group of two-dimensional translations, rotations, and uniform scaling is also a subgroup of this affine group.

1.1.3 Handling Occlusion, Multiple Objects and Misdetection

In its original unmodified form, the Hausdorff distance is very sensitive to outliers: in order for it to be small, *every* model point must be near some image point, and vice versa, so a single extra point in the image or the model can affect its value to an arbitrary degree. Clearly, this is not robust enough for any practical use, where such outliers are common. However, it is possible to modify the Hausdorff distance so as to have a high degree of tolerance for outliers. In this modified Hausdorff distance (the *partial Hausdorff distance*), the worst-matching portion of the image or model is disregarded and has no effect on the distance. How large a portion to disregard is a parameter of the method, and can be set differently for the image and the model. These poorly-matching portions can arise from a number of causes. The most common cause is occlusion: part of the model does not correspond to anything in the image, because that part of the object is hidden. The feature detector can also generate noise features where no features really exist, or fail to detect features where they do exist.

The presence of multiple objects in the image (apart from the one being located) also causes portions of the image to match nothing in the model. In Fig. 1.1, for instance, over 75% of the image is nowhere near the model object. One approach might be to use the partial Hausdorff distance, setting the parameter so that the worst-fitting 75% of the image is rejected, but this is not a good solution: adding another object causes the fraction that must be rejected to grow, even if the new object is nowhere near the position of the model object. Also, this is stretching the concept of outlier a bit too far. A different way to deal with this problem is to compute the reverse distance from the image to the model using only the portion of the image which is close to the current hypothesised position of the model. The rest of the image, no matter how complex it is, does not affect the value of the reverse distance.

In Fig. 1.1, the image features contributing to the reverse distance are only those within the dotted box: the features that really are part of the object under consideration, along with some noise features, and a small part of the occluding wedge-shaped object. These excess features do not match well and so are disregarded. The rest of the image does not affect the reverse distance at all, since it is not near the position of the transformed model.

The Hausdorff distance retains some pseudo-metric properties even when it is modified as described above. The triangle inequality no longer holds, as it is possible for something to look a lot like both an elephant and a hatrack, if it is in reality an elephant standing by a hatrack: when comparing it against the hatrack, the features belonging to the elephant are disregarded as outliers or background, and vice versa. However, a weaker property does hold: if two sets match to the *same portion* of a third, then the triangle inequality holds between the portions that were not disregarded.

1.1.4 Features and Correspondences

With these modifications, image search based on the Hausdorff distance is quite reliable. However, any feature-based search technique is only as reliable as the features that it uses. The Hausdorff distance deals (in this work) with point sets, and so it works with any feature detector that produces point features. Versions that use linear features (straight line segments), or features with some associated information, such as oriented points, are also possible, but are not investigated here; see [YC1] and [OH1] for some recent work (based on the work presented here) addressing these two issues.

Most current methods of model-based recognition do not handle model and image sets with many (thousands to tens of thousands) features; they are typically restricted to sets with relatively few (tens to hundreds) features. One common reason for this is poor combinatorial properties; this will be discussed further in Section 1.2. This means that these methods must attempt to encode the information present in the image and model in a relatively small number of features. The Hausdorff distance method, however, is much less affected by this, and in fact most of the applications I have investigates have involved large feature sets.

In most cases, the point features that are the input to the Hausdorff distance search method are the edge pixels obtained by passing a grey level (intensity) image through some standard edge detector (such as [Ca1]): every pixel where an edge was detected becomes a point in the image point set. No further processing of these points is done; especially, they are not linked into linear segments. The point sets can therefore be quite large.

The reason that such simple features are used is that they preserve many of the subtleties of the shapes in the image. Linking edge pixels into line segments ensures that curves are not well represented. Corners (places where two linear edge segments meet) are also not as reliable as simple edges. Also, when a model composed of corners is used, even a small amount of occlusion of the object can cause a relatively large fraction of its corners to be occluded. This is not the case when edge points are used: a small amount of occlusion produces a more proportional response, in terms of the fraction of the model features occluded.

Some types of methods have further problems with curves: any linking technique which attempts to approximate curves by chains of line segments does not necessarily break up the curve consistently; it might be broken in widely different places in two images which are quite similar. Figure 1.3 illustrates this situation. Figure 1.3(a) shows a smooth curve; Fig. 1.3(b) and Fig. 1.3(c) show two different approximations to this curve by chains of line segments; these might represent the ways in which the curve was broken up in order to generate the model and the image. Both chains contain seven segments, and approximate the original curve with the same degree of accuracy, but there is no one-to-one correspondence between the line segments in the two chains. Any matching method that relies on feature-feature pairing, like many of those described below, can have problems in this case: any pairing between the two sets of segments is incorrect, as no one segment from either set corresponds, even roughly, with one of the segments

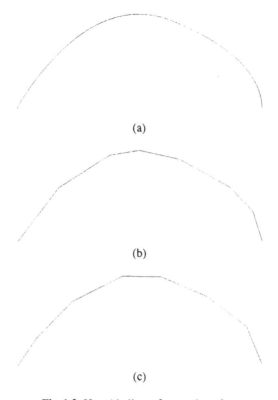

(a)

(b)

(c)

Fig. 1.3. Unstable linear feature detection.

from the other set. One of the strengths of the Hausdorff distance is that it never builds
any such one-to-one correspondences; in fact, it does no explicit pairing between model
and image features: instead of searching the space of all sets of model feature-image
feature pairings (also called *correspondence space*), it searches *transformation space*:
the space of all poses of the model.

If point features (for example, corners) are used, similar problems with building one-
to-one correspondences can occur. Figure 1.4 shows a model in grey and an image in
black. This illustrates one problem with point feature detectors: a single feature might
be detected as a pair, or a pair of close features might be merged. The best translation of
the model (and the one which is found by minimising the Hausdorff distance) is shown in
Fig. 1.4. This best translation might not be found by a method searching correspondence
space, as no matter how a one-to-one pairing is built, the maximum distance between
members of a pairing is large, and the translation minimising this measure is far from the
correct one. Thus, the requirement for a one-to-one pairing between model and image
features has led to a large error.

Some methods which search correspondence space also suffer from the problem of
pinning. Figure 1.5(a) shows the model point set. Figure 1.5(b) shows (in black) an im-

Fig. 1.4. The problem with correspondence and unstable point feature detection.

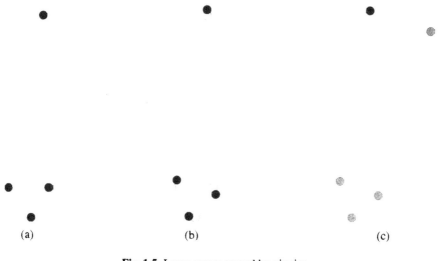

(a)   (b)   (c)

Fig. 1.5. Large errors caused by pinning.

age formed by perturbing the model points slightly, and the true point positions as dashed circles. Note that all of the image points are close to their true positions, representing the effect of a small amount of noise. Suppose that a method searches correspondence space by pairing up three image points with three model points, using this to determine the pose of the model, and projecting the remaining model points to verify this pose. The assumption is that if the pairing is correct (the model and image features really do correspond to each other), and the locations of the three image points are only slightly perturbed, then the remaining model points are projected close to their true locations. However, this is not true: Fig. 1.5(c) shows what happens if the bottom three model points are paired with the bottom three image points, which is correct, and the model pose is recovered from this pairing. The model, in this pose, is shown in grey, overlaid on the image. The three model points that were paired with image points lie, when transformed, exactly on the image points that they were paired with (thus the term "pinning" — they were pinned to specific spots in the image). However, the fourth model point lies a large distance from the fourth image point, showing that even this small amount of error in the position of the pinned points has been magnified significantly when projected to the positions of any of the other model points.

The Hausdorff distance uses all of the model features all of the time, rather than working with some privileged subset, such as the three points above; all of the model and image points are treated uniformly. This allows the matching error (distance from a model point to the closest image point, or vice versa) to be distributed uniformly, rather than being suppressed in some points and exaggerated in others. Because of this, it finds the correct pose of the model, that shown with dotted circles in Fig. 1.5(b).

Another problem that methods using feature pairing encounter is that of increasing the number of pairs. Suppose that a number of pairings have been made, and the method wishes to increase the set of pairings. It must then choose a model feature and an image feature and pair them up. This decision can cause problems if it is made incorrectly: what appears to be the best pairing may cause problems later, as it might actually be incorrect, and make future correct pairings for the points chosen impossible. The problem then essentially becomes one of (possibly weighted) bipartite matching, and can be difficult to solve, requiring an expensive algorithm (see [AMWW1]), or introducing the possibility of error by using a heuristic algorithm.

1.1.5   The Reverse Hausdorff Distance

One way of looking at the Hausdorff distance is similar to a paradigm which a number of other model-based recognition methods have used: that of *hypothesise-and-test* or *guess-and-verify*. Methods using this paradigm typically involve two phases: one generates a number of hypothesised poses; these are then checked by the second phase, to see if they meet some match quality criterion. In the case of the Hausdorff distance, the forward distance could be considered to be the hypothesis-generating phase: all transformations which make the forward distance from the transformed model to the image small are hypothesised as possible matches. The reverse distance is then used to verify these matches. This is more symmetrical than most hypothesise-and-test systems, where often the features used in the hypothesise phase are different from those used in the test phase.

However, this way of looking at the Hausdorff distance does not emphasise one point strongly enough: that other methods do not have anything which acts like the reverse distance. Recall that this distance is small if every image feature (or some sufficiently large fraction of them) in a region of the image is close to some feature of the transformed model. Most methods simply attempt to make sure that many model features are close to some image feature, but not vice versa. I have found the reverse distance to be valuable in rejecting false matches. For example, if a part of the image feature set is quite dense (perhaps in some highly-textured region), then it might be possible to find an incorrect pose of the model so that every transformed model feature is close to some image feature, making the forward distance small. However, unless the model itself is correspondingly dense, many of the image features in the region where the model is placed are not close to any model feature. This means that the reverse Hausdorff distance is large, and so such a pose will be rejected. On the other hand, if the pose is correct, then the number of image features in the region which do not correspond to model features is relatively small. Figure 1.6 shows this application of the reverse distance. Figure 1.6(a) shows a model, and Fig. 1.6(b) shows an image. Figure 1.6(c) shows two possible poses for the model. In both of them, every part of the model is close to something in the image, and so the forward distance is small. However, in the left-hand pose, many of the image features are far from anything in the model, making the reverse distance large; in the

12

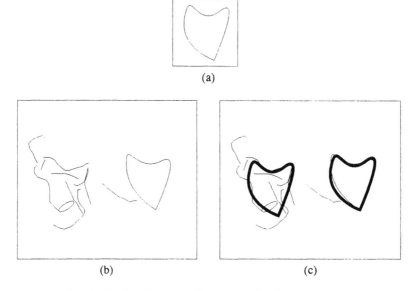

(a)

(b)   (c)

Fig. 1.6. Using the reverse distance to reject incorrect poses.

Table 1.1. Some lower bounds for the complexity of the Hausdorff distance.

Transformation Group	Lower Bound
Translation	$\Omega(n^3)$
Translation and x, y scale	$\Omega(n^7)$
Affine transformation	$\Omega(n^9)$

right-hand pose, the reverse distance is small, and so this is the best pose. Without the reverse distance, this distinction is more difficult to make.

1.1.6 Efficient Search

The previous subsections discussed some of the advantages of searching for the transformation which minimises the Hausdorff distance, but did not mention how this is done. It is possible to use techniques from computational geometry to develop exact algorithms for finding this minimising transformation, but these algorithms may not be practical. Chapter 3 presents some bounds that indicate that such algorithms are likely to have have poor combinatorial properties: while they might be polynomial in the number of features, in many cases the degree of the polynomial can be unacceptably high. These bounds, for the transformation groups mentioned above, are shown in Table 1.1; in this table, n refers to the total number of features in the image and the model.

The approach I have taken instead of using exact algorithms involves imposing a raster grid on the space of transformations, and searching every grid location for the best (minimising) transformations; transformations not lying on the grid are disregarded.

Chapter 4 discusses how this grid should be determined, so as to make the errors due to this approximation as small as possible, and develops bounds on these errors.

As the transformation space can have up to six dimensions (in the cases studied here), searching every location on the grid is clearly impractical. In Chapter 5, I present efficient search techniques which can search this grid without explicitly considering most of the grid locations. I also show how it is possible to accelerate the evaluation of an individual grid location. These search techniques give speedups of one hundred to one, in typical cases, for searching the group of translations. Rough measurements indicate that the speedups due to the efficent search techniques for searching the other, more complex, transformation groups can be over one million to one; see Table 6.4.

One of the main search techniques that I have developed is a multi-resolution search of transformation space. The space is searched in a tree-like fashion: a large region is examined as a block, and if the results of this examination are good, it is subdivided and each of the subregions examined in turn; if the results are not good, then the region is discarded. This is similar, in some ways, to a quad-tree or octree search. Various modifications to this basic technique are possible which increase its overall efficiency, as well as the efficiency of examining a single region. One interesting modification involves the concept of *allowable mistakes*: allowing mistakes to be made at various points in the search, as long as these mistakes are eventually corrected and do not affect the final search result. The advantage of allowing these mistakes to be made is that inexact, but cheaper to compute, heuristics may be used in place of some exact computations; these heuristics can introduce errors, but if they are designed so that all the errors made are *allowable*, there can be an overall performance gain.

It should be noted that the rasterised minimum Hausdorff distance is *guaranteed*: it always produces the correct minimising grid transformation. Although this might not be the exact minimising transformation, it is the transformation lying on the grid which produces the minimum Hausdorff distance. All of the efficient search techniques that I have developed are also guaranteed: incorporating them into the search does not change the results of the search. Some heuristics are used in these techniques, but only in ways such that the outcome is not affected. Many of these techniques rely strongly on some of the properties of the structure of the Hausdorff distance search problem.

Branch-and-bound techniques can also be applied to the Hausdorff distance search. The search tree of regions of transformation space is expanded in a best-first manner, and so the most promising regions are expanded first. Thus, the best transformations, yielding low values for the Hausdorff distance, are likely to be found early on in the search. These transformations can then be used to prune the remaining parts of the search tree: if a branch cannot contain anything better than what has already been seen, then there is no point in expanding it further.

These efficient search techniques make it possible for the minimum Hausdorff distance to be used in a number of practical applications. Chapter 6 describes some implementations of the search, and some examples of its use. Chapter 7 presents the application of the search engines described in Chapter 6 to some real-world problems: tracking nonrigid objects as they move and change shape, and mobile robot navigation using visual landmark recognition. Finally, Chapter 8 presents an overall summary and describes some possibilities for future work.

1.2 Previous Work

A considerable amount of work has been done on model-based recognition. In this section, I describe some of the major approaches. These approaches fall into two classes: the *combinatorial* and the *correlational*, with most of them falling into the first class.

Combinatorial methods are characterised by their emphasis on *pairing* model and image features: they attempt to construct a set of pairings between image features and model features, such that every pairing is, ideally, correct. This set of pairings then determines the model pose. In some methods, a large number of hypothesised pairing sets (not all correct) are constructed, and the poses that these determine are then clustered in some manner, the idea being that the correct pose should generate a large cluster.

In the following discussions, n refers to the size of the image feature set, and m refers to the size of the model feature set.

I will be discussing a number of features of these methods. In particular, I will be discussing

- What type of features does the method use?
- Are the models and images two-dimensional or three-dimensional?
- What transformation (pose) space does it search?
- What projection model is used for 3D-from-2D recognition (orthographic, perspective, weak perspective)?
- Is the method guaranteed: if there is a transformation satisfying the criteria for a model-image match, could it be missed?

A good reference for many of the issues involved in these combinatorial methods is [Gr2].

Correlational methods, on the other hand, do no explicit pairing; in this way, they are similar to the Hausdorff distance. They work by considering the model and image to be functions, or deriving functions from the model and image, and computing a correlation (or some variant of correlation) between these functions; locations where the correlation is large are then considered to be the most likely locations of the model object.

1.2.1 Interpretation Trees

The *interpretation tree* approach to model-based recognition is presented by Grimson and Lozano-Pérez in [GLP1]. This method uses two-dimensional models and images, whose features are line segments, and searches the transformation space of two-dimensional rotations and translations. It can also be applied to three-dimensional models and images; in this case, the features in each are planar, polygonal faces.

The method searches an interpretation tree in order to find a set of pairings between model and image features. The interpretation tree is a n-level tree, where each level corresponds to one of the n image features, and each node in the tree (except the leaves) has a branching factor of $m + 1$, corresponding to the m model features and a so-called "null face" branch.

At every internal node in the tree, the tree search attempts to find a pairing for the image feature corresponding to the level of that node. The path from that node back up to the root corresponds to the pairings that have already been made. The search tries to pair the image feature with each model feature in turn, if that is possible. Each model feature is checked for compatibility with the image feature; it will not be paired with it if they do not match (for example, if their lengths are too different). If they are compatible, then that pairing is checked, pairwise, against all the other current pairings (i.e., the path back to the root). Thus, for each of the pairings in the current set, the new pairing is checked to see if it is consistent with that pairing. Two pairings are consistent if there is a transformation of the model which brings both model features close to their respective image feature. If the new pairing is (pairwise) consistent with all previous pairings, then the subtree rooted at the current node's child corresponding to that pairing is explored. If no model feature can be paired with the image feature, due to incompatibility or inconsistency with the previous pairings, then the null face is paired with the image feature. This represents the image feature matching nothing in the model.

Whenever a leaf is reached, the current pairing set is checked for global consistency. The search to this point has only checked pairwise consistency between pairings; while every pair of pairings is consistent under some pose, there may not be a pose which brings every model feature in the pairing set close to its corresponding image feature. If there is no such transformation, then the leaf is rejected and the search backtracks. Checking global consistency, rather than pairwise consistency, at each node in the tree was investigated, but it was found that it contributed little to the pruning power, and significantly increased the cost of examining each node.

It is possible to apply various heuristics to this search. To begin with, the search can be terminated when a leaf is reached where the set of pairings is of a sufficiently high quality (defined, for example, by number of model features paired, or total edge length of paired features). Branch-and-bound techniques can also be used: a subtree can be pruned if it cannot produce a better match than the best so far seen. Hough clustering (described in detail below) can also be used to reduce the size of the model and image feature set: a coarse Hough clustering is done, and within each Hough bin with a large count, an interpretation tree search is performed. This has the advantage that, within a single bin, features which do not contribute to the count can be disregarded, reducing the size of the interpretation tree.

The principal disadvantage of this method is that its worst-case running time is proportional to the size of the tree, which is exponential. Grimson [Gr1] showed that, if all of the image features correspond to model features, then the expected running time is quadratic, but if the image is cluttered, then exponential time may still be required.

1.2.2 Alignment

The class of *alignment* techniques is characterised by their hypothesise-and-test structure. Essentially, such methods choose a subset (of some size) of the image features and a subset (of the same size) of the model features, and form pairings between these sets. This set of pairings is then used to compute a set of possible poses for the model which bring the chosen model features onto the chosen image features (i.e., the poses *align* the model and image features). The sizes of the feature subsets are chosen so that the number of possible poses is a small constant. For example, if the model and image are two-dimensional point sets, and the transformation space being searched is the space of rotations, translations, and scales, then the subsets will be of size two: only one pose can align two model point features with two image point features. For three-dimensional models, two-dimensional images, weak-perspective projection, and rigid three-dimensional motion, three point correspondences are required to restrict the set of possible poses to a single pose; if the models can also be reflected as part of their transformation, then two poses are possible.

Once the subsets are chosen, and the aligning poses computed, the poses are then verified by projecting additional model features into the image, and seeing if they are close to matching image features. If enough of the model features are sufficiently close to some image feature, then the pose is accepted; if not, another pair of subsets is tried. The methods described in this subsection differ in the type of model and image features, how the subsets are chosen, and how the poses are verified.

The method of Huttenlocher and Ullman [HU1] searches for a rigid three-dimensional transformation of a model, using the weak-perspective projection model. The features in the three-dimensional model are oriented points (points together with associated orientations), and straight-line edge segments. The two-dimensional image is processed to extract similar (though two-dimensional) features. "Virtual corners" formed by the intersection of the extensions of two line segments or point orientations can be added to enrich the model and image sets; these can be unstable if, for example, the extensions of the line segments are too long.

This has been one of the more studied approaches to this problem; some of the extensions to the basic method are described below.

The authors show that if three model points are paired with three image points, a unique (up to reflection) transformation maps the projections of the three model points onto the corresponding image points. Alternately, in some cases two points from each set can be used; the orientation vectors are used to locate a third virtual point in both the model and image. All possible pairs (or triples, if creating virtual points is not possible, or the error in the virtual points is unacceptable) of model points are paired with all possible pairs of image points; each such pairing generates two transformations which must be verified.

The verification step uses the model and image edge segments, which were not used in the pose hypothesis generation step. Each hypothesised pose is tested in two steps; poses which fail the first test are not tested again. The first test transforms and projects the model point features, and determines for each one if it lies close enough, and in a similar enough orientation, to some image point feature. If enough do, the pose is tested further, in more detail. This second test transforms and projects the model segment features, and determines how many lie close enough, and in similar enough orientations, to image segments. As well, a model segment being crossed by an image segment is considered negative evidence for the match. This aspect of this method is one of the few which are similar to the reverse Hausdorff distance.

The principal problem with this method is that of pinning: as shown in Fig. 1.5, slight errors in the positions of the three paired points can lead to large errors in the positions of the remainder of the model points. The use of different features in the hypothesis generation and verification steps also means that the method is not guaranteed: there may be some poses that would pass the verification, but which are not generated. Its time complexity is also quite high ($O(m^3 n^2)$, or $O(m^4 n^3)$ if virtual points cannot be used). A recent result by Olson [Ol1], however, uses randomised methods to reduce the time complexity to $O(mn^3)$ (expected), without using virtual points.

In [GHJ1], Grimson, Huttenlocher and Jacobs derive bounds for the error in the position of a fourth model point due to pinning the first three model points. They show that these errors can be quite large: many times the actual errors in locations of the three pinned points.

Jacobs, in [Ja1], introduces the concept of *error space*. Suppose that three model points are paired and aligned with three image points, and some fourth model point is then paired with a fourth image point. This fourth pairing is unlikely to be exact: the transformed model point is not likely to lie exactly on the image point. However, if the three pinned model points are perturbed within some error bounds, reflecting the presence of positional error in the image points that they are pinned to, then it may be possible to exactly align the fourth points. The perturbations are parameterised by a point in a six-dimensional error space. The constraint that the fourth points must align (possibly to within some tolerance) is translated into a region in error space: the region contains those perturbations for the three pinned points that cause the fourth points to be (approximately) aligned.

The error space can now be examined to find perturbations of the three pinned points (which are no longer really pinned) that bring a large number of the remaining model features close to some image feature. This increases the accuracy of the method by reducing the problems due to pinning. However, it does so at a large computational cost: this examination of error space must take place for every hypothesised pose, greatly increasing the computation required.

Alter and Jacobs [AJ1] extend this error space analysis to handle incrementally increasing the size of the pinned set. They project a fourth model point, and use the possible error in its position to search for a fourth image point to pair it with. Once it has been paired, bounds on error space can be computed which are consistent with that pairing. If a fifth model point is projected into the image, the region which must be searched to locate a matching image point is reduced because of these bounds; similarly, pairing up this fifth point reduces the region which must be searched for a sixth point. However, if there are several possible image points which a single model point could be paired with, given the current bounds on error space, then some choice must be made. An incorrect choice can lead to search failure, or require backtracking, leading to an interpretation tree-like method and further increasing the time required to evaluate a hypothesised alignment.

The method of Ayache and Faugeras [AF1] is somewhat similar to this last approach. Models in its domain are two-dimensional objects, represented as a set of polygons, each one of which is represented as a list of line segments. Images are represented in the same manner. The transformation space under consideration is that composed of two-dimensional translation, rotation and scale.

Pose hypotheses are generated by pairing and aligning one model segment with one image segment. Only some privileged model segments, the longest few, are used for this. While this gives good accuracy for the initial estimate of the pose, the longest segments are exactly those most likely to be broken up in the image, by occlusion or misdetection. However, in most cases at least one privileged segment will be correctly detected. Hypotheses are evaluated by how well the angles between the model segment and its neighbouring segments match the angles between the image segment and its neighbouring segments; only the top hundred or so hypotheses are evaluated further.

These top hypotheses are evaluated by attempting to grow the initial alignment outward along the polygon containing it. The next segment in the model polygon is paired with the image segment closest to it, if their lengths and orientations are similar enough. The transformation parameters are then updated by minimising an error criterion, using a Kalman filter. This process reduces the effect of pinning, since after the first iteration the original segments need no longer be exactly aligned, and the first iteration can use the model segment closest to the pinned segment, where errors in the transformation have the least effect.

Hypotheses are ranked by how much of the model was matched, and how good the segment matches are. The best hypothesis is then re-examined, to attempt to improve the pairing. The growing process is repeated, but using the final transformation estimate produced by the original process as the initial estimate for the new process. This can change which image segment a particular model segment is paired with, hopefully eliminating pairing errors from the first pass. If a different transformation is determined by this re-growing process, it is used to seed another re-growing process; this is repeated until it converges. However, this post-processing cannot correct all the errors due to erroneous pairings in the initial hypothesis evaluation, which could cause a correct initial pairing to be rejected due to a poor evaluation, leading to failure to locate the model.

In [Lo1], Lowe describes the SCERPO system, which has some similarities to the pair-growing method of [AF1] described above. This system attempts to recover the three-dimensional pose of a rigid three-dimensional model, composed of line segments, under full perspective projection (not weak perspective). The image is also composed of line segments. The model and image are both processed to extract *perceptual groups*: groups of line segments that are either (approximately) parallel, collinear, or co-terminating. These groups are then themselves organised into *perceptual structures*, such as trapezoids. The idea is that a perceptual structure in the model forms the same type of perceptual structure when transformed (by a rigid body transformation) and projected into the image. This is not strictly true, as parallel lines do not remain parallel under perspective projection, but they do remain close to parallel when viewed from most reasonable viewing directions.

Once the perceptual groups have been extracted from the image and model, all possible pairings of like groups are examined. Each such pairing generates a pose hypothesis. Since different types of perceptual groups may contain different numbers of segments, some of these poses may be over-constrained, so it may not be possible to align the groups exactly. In these over-constrained cases, and in later processing, the pose parameters are determined using an iterative Newton's method least-squares minimisation. The set of paired segments is then increased: each model segment finds the best-matching image segment, and some pairings are made. A model segment is only paired with an image segment if they are similar enough (in position, orientation, and length) that this similarity is not likely to have arisen by chance. To reduce the possibility of incorrect pairings leading the search astray, the pairing is also made only if it is unambiguous: there are not two image segments with roughly the same similarity to the model segment. Once these additional pairings have been made, the pose parameters are re-estimated, by repeating the minimisation process. This cycle of adding more pairings and re-minimising is repeated until it converges.

While this method works well, its domain is not really full perspective projection: the requirement that parallel lines stay close to parallel after projection means that the projection must be essentially weak perspective, where parallel lines do stay parallel. Also, the perceptual grouping works best with polyhedral (and thus artificial) model objects; extending it to more natural objects is difficult. The pair-growing aspect, as before, also introduces the possibility of not locating the model due to the search being led astray.

1.2.3 Hough Transforms

Hough transform-based methods, also called parameter clustering methods, attempt to determine the parameters of the model transformation by generating a large number of model subset to image subset pairings, determining the set of poses which could generate each pairing (unlike alignment methods, this set need not contain only a few poses; it may be a subspace of the transformation space), and building a histogram in the space of pose parameters: each bin in the histogram which is intersected by this set of possible poses is incremented. If the pairing is correct, then it should increment the bin containing the correct pose. Peaks in the histogram are then taken as the most likely places to search for the correct pose.

Silberberg, Harwood and Davis [SHD1] describe a system which uses Hough clustering to recognise a three-dimensional polyhedral model from a two-dimensional image. The model object is constrained to lie on a ground plane, whose distance from the camera is known. The object can translate on the ground plane and rotate about a line normal to the ground plane; it cannot change the face being used as its base. There are thus three parameters to the model pose.

The image is processed to extract junctions: points together with incident edges; the model is composed of similar points, one for each vertex of the polyhedron. Initially, every junction is paired with every vertex. For each pairing, the incident edges are used to determine a small number of possible poses which bring the vertex's edges close to the junction's edges. The bins containing these poses are then incremented; the amount by which they are incremented depends on the quality of the vertex-junction match.

Once all these pairings have been computed, and the histogram counts accumulated, the histogram is scanned for peaks. All those peaks which have a high enough value are then processed further. The model is projected using an initial pose based on the location of the histogram bin. Pairings between model vertices and image junctions are then built, in such a way that the maximum amount of image data is matched, with the least amount of error, using a simple form of the stable marriage algorithm. The pose parameters are then re-estimated using a least-squares minimisation; this pairing and minimisation is repeated until it converges. The best result from applying this to each of the histogram peaks is then given as the location of the object.

Thompson and Mundy [TM1] study a more general problem: locate a three-dimensional model in a two-dimensional image, under rigid motion and weak-perspective projection. Rather than using model vertices as features, it instead uses *vertex pairs*. A vertex pair is composed of one vertex and two of its incident edges, plus another (possibly distant and unconnected) vertex. Pairing one image and one model vertex pair determines a single transformation which aligns those two features (aligning all the vertices and edges involved). The image is processed to extract junctions, and all possible vertex pairs are formed from these junctions. Each model vertex pair is then paired with each image vertex pair; the transformations thus generated are histogrammed. Since the transformation space is six-dimensional, histogramming them directly is infeasible; instead, they are histogrammed in three independent histograms: one two-dimensional histogram indexed by two of the rotational parameters, one one-dimensional histogram indexed by the third rotational parameter, and one three-dimensional histogram indexed by the three translational parameters. These histograms are cascaded: wherever there is a (sufficiently strong) peak in the initial two-dimensional histogram, a one-dimensional histogram is computed over the transformations lying in that bin; peaks in that histogram then generate a three-dimensional histogram. Finally, peaks in the three-dimensional histograms are used as the location of the model.

Unfortunately, the results of this method are fairly poor: parts of the model are poorly aligned with the corresponding parts of the image. It would probably benefit from a pose refinement step after clustering, as in [SHD1]. Also, the large number of image vertex pairs (quadratic in the number of image junctions) which must be paired with each model vertex pair means that the model can have very few vertex pairs; in the examples given, it had 4 or 5.

Grimson and Huttenlocher have examined the general problem of Hough clustering. In [GH2, GH3] they derive bounds for how large a region in the histogram might need to be incremented for a given pairing. This might be a large area, since even a small amount of error in the locations of the paired features can cause a large amount of error in the pose parameters computed from them. Thus, a large number of bins must be incremented in order to ensure that the correct bin is hit. However, this leads to problems: since every model feature is paired with a large number of image features, and vice versa, and every such pairing generates at least one count in some histogram bin, the total number of counts due to incorrect pairings is much larger than the number of counts due to correct pairings. The chance of a large peak being formed by a random combination of incorrect pairings is thus quite large; in some cases, there can be many such large peaks, larger than any of the peaks formed from correct pairings. This indicates that Hough clustering must be used with care, and in combination with a verification pass to remove these spurious peaks (at additional computational cost), or it may not always yield the correct location of the model.

1.2.4 Geometric Hashing

Geometric hashing relies on the idea that, for a two-dimensional model (composed of points) under affine transformation, knowing the locations of three transformed model points is sufficient to determine the transformation, as well as the locations of the remaining transformed model points. In fact, if those three points are used to define an origin and a basis for the locations of the remaining model points, and the transformed positions of those three points are used to define an origin and a basis for the remaining transformed model points, then the coordinates (in the original basis) of a model point are the same as the coordinates (in the transformed basis) of its transformed position. These *affine coordinates* are thus invariant under application of any affine transformation. Note that any given model point can have a number of different affine coordinates, derived from different initial bases.

Lamdan and Wolfson [LW1] use this invariance of the affine coordinates to locate two-dimensional models in two-dimensional images under the influence of affine transformation. They also search for the models under two-dimensional rotation, translation, and scale; in this case, only two points are needed to define a basis.

The model is pre-processed to produce a hash table. Each possible basis for the model is examined; for each basis, the coordinates of every other model point are determined. These coordinates are entered in the hash table, along with an indication of which basis produced them.

Point features are then extracted from the image. Three image points are chosen, and the affine coordinates of the remaining image points are computed. The coordinates of each point are used to probe the hash table; the model basis entries lying in that bin of the hash table are retrieved. If all the three image points were actually features of the object being searched for, then the basis that they form will be one of the ones used to build the hash table; that basis should be retrieved whenever one of the remaining object features is used to probe the table, and so should occur more often than any other basis. If not all three image points were part of the object (if they were due to noise or some additional object), then no basis should be preferentially retrieved; in this case, another triple is chosen, and this proceeds until a basis is located.

Grimson and Huttenlocher have analysed this method as well, in [GH1], and have found that it performs poorly when the model contains more than about thirty features. Errors in the affine coordinates can be large with even moderate amounts of error in the positions of the three points forming the basis (see [GHJ1]), and so, as in the analysis of the Hough transform, the number of hash bins which need to be checked in any lookup may be large; false positives due to random conspiracies between spurious points can occur.

1.2.5 Computational Geometry

Another class of combinatorial algorithms is that which use techniques from computational geometry. These algorithms generally construct some sort of arrangement of geometric objects in transformation space, and then search this arrangement to determine where good transformations lie. Each pairing between a model feature and an image feature (or between small sets of such features) generates a set in transformation space, which is the set of transformations which align the features to within some tolerance. This set has some geometric form in transformation space: a circle, sphere, polyhedron and so on. The arrangement of all such sets formed by pairings between the model and the image is searched in order to find a location in transformation space where they overlap as much as possible. To avoid the problems in the Hough clustering methods, where bins could contain votes from one model feature matching several separate image features, or vice versa, causing counts to be inflated, the search can scan for locations where many compatible sets overlap: sets corresponding to pairings involving different model features.

Cass [Ca2] studies the problem of locating a two-dimensional model, composed of oriented points (points with associated orientations, as in [HU1]), in an image, also composed of oriented points, under two-dimensional translation and rotation. The idea is to find a translation and rotation of the model which brings as many as possible of the model points to within some tolerance, in both position and orientation, of some image point. In some ways, this work is quite similar to exact algorithms which solve a related Hausdorff decision problem (see Section 3.1).

For a fixed rotation, the plane of translations can be viewed as containing a number of disks: one disk for each model point-image point pairing which is valid at that rotation (i.e., for which, at that rotation of the model, the model point's orientation is similar enough to the image point's orientation). The size of the disks depends on the amount of positional mismatching which is allowed. This plane can be scanned for locations where the coverage by disks associated with different model points is maximal; these are the best translations for that one rotation, aligning as many model points as possible with image points, up to the allowed rotational and translational tolerances.

As the rotation of the model is varied, these disks move about in the translation plane. The method now searches for *critical rotations* of the model; these are rotations at which the topology of the arrangement of disks in the translation plane changes. This change can be due to two of the disks intersecting where they did not before, or the centres of three disks becoming co-circular, or a disk appearing (due to the orientations of the points involved becoming similar enough), or disappearing. If the translation plane is scanned at each of these critical rotations, a transformation which aligns the maximum number of model points with image points will be found; the method is guaranteed to find this best transformation.

The computational complexity of this method is polynomial in the number of model and image points, but the polynomial is quite large ($O(m^6 n^6)$). While this polynomial could certainly be reduced, notably through use of improved plane sweep and incremental update algorithms, some of the constructions from Chapter 3 could be adapted to give a still-high lower bound for the complexity of the space being examined, indicating that reducing the degree of the polynomial below this bound is difficult or impossible.

Cass, in [Ca3], and Hopcroft, in [Ho1], describe a method which searches for an affine transformation of a model consisting of line segments which brings it into close correspondence with an image also consisting of line segments. This is a six-dimensional search space, which renders methods similar to [Ca2] difficult: arrangements in this space are likely to be extremely complex. The method uses a single alignment to reduce the scope of the problem: if one model segment is exactly aligned with one image segment, then the transformation producing such an alignment must lie on a plane in transformation space. The method therefore makes such a pairing, and constructs polygonal sets on this plane which correspond to one of the remaining model segments becoming close to one of the remaining image segments. Standard plane sweep techniques can then examine this collection of polygons to determine the location which brings the maximum number of model segments close to some image segment (or the maximum segment length, or some other measure of match quality). All possible initial pairings are examined, and the resulting plane swept for each; this determines a transformation which maximises the match quality.

Like the alignment method of [HU1], this method always produces an uneven distribution of the match error: one model segment is perfectly aligned, and (most of) the remaining segments are approximately aligned with image segments. This means that pinning can still be a problem.

1.2.6 Transformation Space Subdivision

The RAST (Recognition by Adaptive Subdivision of Transformation space) method, developed by Bruel, is described in [Br3, Br4]. This method is quite similar to some of the techniques that I have developed to determine the minimum Hausdorff distance. In some ways, it is also similar to the computational geometry methods from Subsection 1.2.5. While it has relatively general application, I will be discussing its application to the search for an affine transformation of a two-dimensional model, composed either of points or line segments, in a similar image.

As noted before, each pairing of a model feature with an image feature defines a constraint set in transformation space, containing the transformations which align those features to within some tolerance. The RAST algorithm considers a rectilinear region in the space of transformation parameters, and computes which of these $O(mn)$ constraint sets intersect that region. If enough of them do, and if enough distinct model features are involved in those that do, then it recursively subdivides that region, and considers each of the subregions; otherwise, the entire region is discarded. The requirement that there must be a significant number of model features involved reduces the effect of the problem which led to high counts in the Hough transformation methods: a region of transformation space which is intersected by a large number of these constraint regions, but where only a few model features are involved, cannot contain a transformation aligning many model features.

This method also uses branch-and-bound techniques to prune the search: it does not subdivide a region if it cannot contain a transformation which aligns at least as many model features as one which has already been found. However, the test to determine whether a region should be subdivided or not is quite expensive, as it involves examining all $O(mn)$ constraint regions. In contrast, the Hausdorff distance method uses a much less expensive $O(m)$ test. For this reason, while the RAST method does not suffer from pinning, and is guaranteed not to miss a transformation which meets any quality criteria if one exists, it is not suitable for use when the image or model contain a large number of features.

1.2.7 Correlational Methods

All the combinatorial methods that I have discussed so far involve, at some level, pairing some model feature (or set of model features) with some image feature (or set of image features). Because of this, they suffered from high computational complexity, and so could not be used with large numbers of image and model features; in some cases, this pairing also led to problems with pinning. The methods that I present in this subsection do not involve any such pairing. They can therefore be used with models and images containing a large number of features; they also do not suffer from uneven distribution of the match error.

I will not be dealing with one type of correlational method, namely grey-level correlation, where the image and model are represented as intensity images. The reason for this is that I am concentrating on feature-based image search, rather than intensity-based search.

To introduce these correlational methods, I will first discuss using binary correlation for image search. Suppose that the model and image are both point sets, and that all the points are located on an integer grid (i.e., all the points have integral coordinates), and we want to find the translation of the model which makes as many model points as possible lie on top of image points. If we consider the image and model to be binary arrays A and B respectively, having values of 1 wherever there is a point and 0 everywhere else, then this problem is exactly that of finding the maximum value of the function defined by correlating these two arrays. That is, we want to find (integral) values of t_x and t_y that maximise

$$\sum_{x,y} A[x,y] B[x + t_x, y + t_y]. \tag{1.1}$$

As we shall see later, this problem can be viewed as a special case of the Hausdorff distance search problem.

This method suffers from its all-or-nothing character: if a certain translation causes a large number of the model points to lie very close to image points, but not directly on top of them, then those model points might as well be very far away from image points: their closeness has not increased the measured quality of that translation at all. Thus, if the model and image are exact copies of each other, except that the image points have been perturbed by some small amounts, the maximum binary correlation is greatly degraded. This magnification of small errors limits the effectiveness of binary correlation.

Barrow, Tenenbaum, Bolles and Wolf show, in [BTBW1], how this limitation can be removed by using *chamfer matching*. In this technique, the array A in the summation above is replace by a new array Δ, representing the *distance transform* of A. That is, every location in the array Δ holds the distance to the closest point of the image: it is zero wherever A is 1, and nonzero everywhere else; the farther that a given location is from any point of the image, the larger the value that Δ has at that location. Distance transforms will be discussed further in Section 4.3. The correlation of A and B in (1.1) is then replaced by a correlation between Δ and B:

$$\sum_{x,y} \Delta[x,y] B[x + t_x, y + t_y]. \tag{1.2}$$

In this case, however, we want to find t_x and t_y that *minimise* this value, rather than maximising it as before; this corresponds to finding a translation that makes the points of the translated model as close as possible to the points of the image. With this modification, the method becomes quite tolerant of noise: small changes in the positions of the image points can cause only small changes in this value. Note that there is no pairing going on: it does not matter if many model points are close to one image point, and no explicit linking of a model point and its closest image point is done.

This idea can be extended to deal with other transformations of the model than just translation: search for a transformation of the model, giving a corresponding transformation of B, which minimises the corresponding sum-of-products. In this case, it is no longer true correlation, but I will continue to use the term to refer to this class of methods.

Paglieroni, in [Pa1, PFT1], uses the chamfer matching technique to search for the best translation and rotation of a model, minimising this chamfer distance (actually, a slight variant of the distance is used: instead of a summation of the distance transform values, as in (1.2), the mean distance transform value is computed). Since evaluating the chamfer distance at every possible rotation and translation is impractical, this method derives some bounds on the possible change in the chamfer distance as the transformation changes. These bounds can then be used to accelerate the search: if the distance, evaluated at a certain transformation, is very large, then no transformation close to that one can make the distance small; they can therefore be eliminated. This technique is quite similar, though in a different domain, to the ruling out circles method which I present in Section 5.2.

Some work using chamfer matching has also been done by Borgefors. In [Bo2], the *hierarchical chamfer matching* method is presented; this method is applicable to a wide range of transformation domains. As in [Pa1], a slight variant on the chamfer distance is used. In this case, the summation operator in (1.2) is replaced by an RMS (root-mean-square) operator; the goal is then to find the transformation that minimises this RMS distance value. This method performs an edge detection on the input grey-level image, then forms an edge pyramid by repeatedly decimating it by a factor of two in each dimension: each pixel in one level is formed by ORing together a block of four pixels in the next lowest level; the lowest level of all is just the output of the edge detector. This method ensures that connected edges at one level stay connected in the next higher level. The distance transform of each level is then taken, producing a *distance pyramid*. The model is decimated in a similar manner to that used to construct the edge pyramid.

The method then seeds a number of initial transformations of the model, at the highest (smallest, coarsest resolution) level of the pyramid. Each of these seeds uses steepest-descent to modify its transformation parameters, to find a local minimum of the RMS distance function. The worst of these local minima are rejected. The remaining local minima then proceed to the next, finer resolution, level of the pyramid, where their parameters again are modified to find local minima, and so on. This proceeds until the method has found a number of local minima at the finest level of the pyramid, which corresponds to matching the original model with the original edge image. The smallest of these local minima is then picked as the located position of the model. Of course, this may not be the true global minimum; using more seed positions initially increases the probability of finding the global minimum, but at a cost in speed. It may be possible to develop lower bounds on the number of local minima in the RMS distance as a function of transformation, similar to the bounds in Chapter 3; I conjecture that these bounds, like those for the Hausdorff distance, will show that there can be a very large number of such local minima.

One of the weaknesses of the chamfer matching methods is that they can be sensitive to outliers: a single model point, far from every image point, can increase the mean, or RMS, distance by a large amount. Borgefors and Olsson [BO3] propose a technique which deals with occlusion by looking at the *local* chamfer distance (i.e., computed using only a few model points), around the silhouette of the transformed model. If the model is completely visible, and the transformation is correct, this local distance should remain small all around the silhouette; its amplitude is based solely on the noise in the locations of the image features. If the transformation is incorrect, though, the function should be much more irregular, and have a larger overall amplitude. On the other hand, if the transformation is correct, but the image of the object is incomplete, due to occlusion, then there will be some large local peaks in this function, corresponding to the parts of the model which are not visible in the image, but apart from these peaks, it should also be small. These last two cases might have a similar overall chamfer distance, but inspection of this function might disambiguate them; the large local peaks in the second case might then be discounted, yielding a lower corrected distance value. This method of dealing with occlusion, by discounting the worst-fitting model points, bears some similarity to the partial Hausdorff distance, presented in Section 2.4; the main difference is that this method requires the outliers to have some spatial coherence, which is not a requirement in my method.

1.2.8 Summary

In this section, I have presented brief descriptions of a number of current approaches to feature-based model-based recognition. While all these image search methods, both combinatorial and correlational, each have their good characteristics, none of them combines all of the desirable properties that I presented in Section 1.1 for the Hausdorff distance.

Chapter 2

The Hausdorff Distance

In this chapter, I introduce the Hausdorff distance, the measure I use for visual recognition. It is robust in the presence of uncertainty in position; I will show how it can be made to be robust in the presence of outliers, or noise points. It can be further modified to make it especially suitable for visual recognition tasks: the modified version can essentially ignore objects in the image other than the one being recognised.

I will also show how the Hausdorff distance and the minimum Hausdorff distance under transformation are (in some cases) metrics, and that the modified Hausdorff distance has some pseudo-metric properties. As I noted in Sect. 1.1, it is desirable for a shape comparison function to have metric properties.

2.1 Definitions

Given two point sets A and B, the Hausdorff distance between A and B is defined as

$$H(A, B) = \max(h(A, B), h(B, A)) \tag{2.1}$$

where

$$h(A, B) = \sup_{a \in A} \inf_{b \in B} \|a - b\| \tag{2.2}$$

and $\| \cdot \|$ represents some underlying norm defined on the plane. In this work, this is generally required to be an L_p norm, usually the L_2 (Euclidean) norm. The function $h(A, B)$ is called the **directed Hausdorff distance** from A to B.

For the remainder of this section, suppose that A and B are compact sets, as this simplifies the explanations significantly. In this case,

$$h(A, B) = \max_{a \in A} \min_{b \in B} \|a - b\|$$

and so each point of A finds its closest neighbour from B, and the most mismatched point of A (the point that is farthest from any point of B) determines the value of $h(A, B)$. Intuitively, if $h(A, B) = d$, then each point of A must be within distance d of some point of B, and there also is some point of A (the most mismatched point) that is exactly distance d from the nearest point of B.

The Hausdorff distance can also be considered in terms of disks in the plane. Let A^ε be the set obtained by drawing a disk of radius ε about every point in A. The shape of the disk depends on the underlying norm; it is a circle for the L_2 norm, and a square or a diamond for the $L_\times$ or L_1 norms. A^ε is the set A **dilated** by a disk of radius ε.

The directed Hausdorff distance from A to B, $h(A, B)$, can then be thought of as the radius of the smallest closed disk which can be drawn about each point of A such that each disk contains at least one point of B.

There is another way to look at the Hausdorff distance in terms of disks: $h(A, B)$ is the smallest ε such that $A \subseteq B^\varepsilon$: if every point of A is within ε of some point of B, then dilating B by ε causes the dilated set to completely enclose A. Figure 2.1 illustrates these two ways of looking at the Hausdorff distance. Figure 2.1(a) shows two point sets, A in black and B in grey. Figure 2.1(b) illustrates the directed Hausdorff distance from A to B: each disk drawn around each point of A contains some point of B, and one disk has a point of B on its rim, and contains no closer point; not every point of B needs to be contained in a disk. This corresponds to the first way of looking at the Hausdorff distance in terms of disks. Figure 2.1(c) shows the other way of looking at the Hausdorff distance: B has been dilated until it just contains *all* of A; the radius of the disks is $h(A, B)$ (the same as the disks in Fig. 2.1b). Similarly, Fig. 2.1(d) illustrates the directed Hausdorff distance from B to A, $h(B, A)$, in the same manner. Note that this is quite a bit larger than $h(A, B)$, as one point of B was not close to any point of A, while every point of A was relatively close to some point of B; A therefore had to be dilated by a larger ε before A^ε completely enclosed B.

In general, I use this second interpretation of the Hausdorff distance in terms of disks; in Chap. 3, I show how this interpretation can be very useful.

The **undirected Hausdorff distance**, $H(A, B)$, is the maximum of $h(A, B)$ and $h(B, A)$. It measures the degree of mismatch between two sets by finding the point of A that is farthest from any point of B and vice versa. Intuitively, if the Hausdorff distance is d, then every point of A must be within a distance d of some point of B and vice versa; also, at least one point of A or B must be exactly d away from its closest neighbour in the other set. If $H(A, B)$ is small, then each point of A must be near some point of B and vice versa. Unlike most methods of comparing shapes, there is no explicit pairing of points of A with points of B (for example many points of A may be close to the *same* point of B).

It is well known [Cs1] that the Hausdorff distance, $H(A, B)$, is a metric over the set of all closed, bounded sets. It should be noted that the Hausdorff distance does not allow for comparing portions of the sets A and B, because every point of one set is required to be near some point of the other set. Section 2.4 presents a natural extension to the Hausdorff distance that measures the distance between some subset of the points in A and some subset of the points in B.

2.2 The Minimum Hausdorff Distance under Transformation

The Hausdorff distance measures the distance between two point sets that are at a fixed position relative to each other. For image search tasks, though, one set represents the image, and the other represents the model, and the task is to find a transformation of one set (the model) that brings it into close correspondence with the other set (the image). I will refer to the image point set as I and the model point set as M, and call the directed Hausdorff distance from the model to the image ($h(M, I)$) the **forward distance**; the distance from the image to the model ($h(I, M)$) is then the **reverse distance**.

Let G be some group of transformations. Then for any $g \in G$ define

$$D_G(g) = H(g(M), I) \tag{2.3}$$

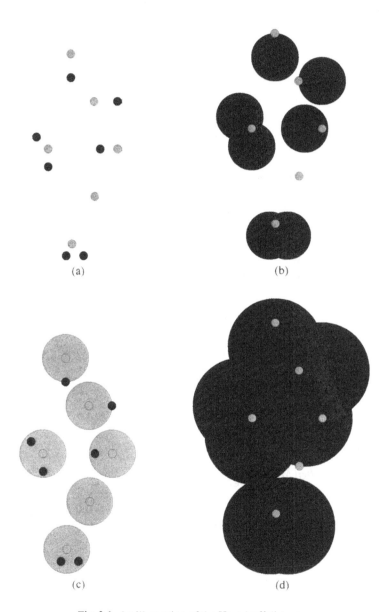

Fig. 2.1. An illustration of the Hausdorff distance.

30

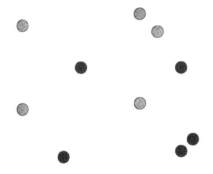

Fig. 2.2. The difference between H and H_G.

(where $g(M) = \{g(m) \mid m \in M\}$ is the result of applying the transformation g to every point in the model M). In other words, M is first transformed by some transformation g; the Hausdorff distance between this transformed set and I is then computed. This operation defines a function of the transformation g, and the transformation that gives rise to the minimum value of this function minimum value is the one bringing M into closest correspondence with I.

It is often useful to look at the two parts of $D_G(g)$ separately: define

$$d_G(g) = h(g(M), I) \tag{2.4}$$
$$d'_G(g) = h(I, g(M)) \tag{2.5}$$

which are the directed distances between the transformed model $g(M)$ and the image I. $d_G(g)$ is the forward distance as a function of the transformation g, and $d'_G(g)$ is the reverse distance as a function of g.

Define

$$H_G(M, I) = \inf_{g \in G} H(g(M), I) = \inf_{g \in G} D_G(g) \tag{2.6}$$

and, correspondingly,

$$h_G(M, I) = \inf_{g \in G} h(g(M), I) = \inf_{g \in G} d_G(g) . \tag{2.7}$$

$H_G(M, I)$ thus measures the minimum Hausdorff between I and M, as M is transformed by all the elements of G. If it is small, then there is some transformation $g \in G$ which brings every point of $g(M)$ close to some point of I, and vice versa. Figure 2.2 illustrates the difference between $H(M, I)$ and $H_G(M, I)$. It shows two sets, I in black and M in grey, for which $H(M, I)$ is relatively large. If G is the group of translations, $H_G(M, I)$ is small: there is a translation which brings every point of M close to some point of I, and vice versa.

An alternate definition for the minimum Hausdorff distance under transformation is

$$\hat{H}_G(M, I) = \inf_{g_1, g_2 \in G} H(g_1(M), g_2(I)) . \tag{2.8}$$

$\hat{H}_G$ is clearly symmetric. The reasons that this definition is not used are

- For some groups, $\hat{H}_G$ is not very useful. Consider the case when G is the group of nonzero scalings of the plane. Then for any bounded point sets I and M, $\hat{H}_G(M. I)$ is zero. This is because both I and M can be shrunk to within an arbitrarily small radius of the origin, making the Hausdorff distance between the shrunken sets as small as desired. H_G does not have this problem.
- The asymmetry in the definition of H_G actually represents an asymmetry in the definition of the problem: one of the point sets represents an image, and the other represents a model of the appearance of some object in that image. Locating the object in the image can be thought of as finding a transformation of the model which brings it into close correspondence with the image; thus, only one of the point sets needs to be transformed.

Note that as a result of this asymmetry in the definition, the function $H_G(M. I)$ is not necessarily symmetric, even though $H(M. I)$ is: let G be the group of nonzero scalings of the plane about the origin, $I = \{(0.0)\}$ and $M = \{(1.0)\}$. Then $H_G(M. I) = 0$, but $H_G(I. M) = 1$, since scaling M by some small value brings its only point arbitrarily close to the point of I, making $H(g(M). I)$ small; on the other hand, scaling I does not affect it, and so $H(g(I). M) = 1$ for any g. (The zero scaling is not a member of G, as it is noninvertible).

However, under some circumstances, the two definitions are identical:

Lemma 2.1. *Suppose that for any $g \in G$ and for any points $p_1. p_2$, $\|g(p_1) - g(p_2)\| = \|p_1 - p_2\|$. Then $H_G = \hat{H}_G$.*

Proof. Let A and B be any two point sets, and $g_1. g_2 \in G$ any two transformations. Then

$$H(g_1(A). g_2(B)) = \max(h(g_1(A). g_2(B)). h(g_2(B). g_1(A)))$$

$$= \max\left(\sup_{b \in B} \inf_{a \in A} \|g_1(a) - g_2(b)\|. \sup_{a \in A} \inf_{b \in B} \|g_1(a) - g_2(b)\|\right)$$

$$= \max\left(\sup_{b \in B} \inf_{a \in A} \|g_2^{-1}(g_1(a)) - b\|. \sup_{a \in A} \inf_{b \in B} \|g_2^{-1}(g_1(a)) - b\|\right)$$

$$= H(g_2^{-1}(g_1(A)). B)$$

and so

$$\hat{H}_G(A. B) = \inf_{g_1. g_2 \in G} H(g_1(A). g_2(B))$$

$$= \inf_{g_1. g_2 \in G} H(g_2^{-1}(g_1(A)). B)$$

$$= \inf_{g \in G} H(g(A). B)$$

$$= H_G(A. B)$$

so $H_G(A. B) = \hat{H}_G(A. B)$; H_G is therefore symmetric. $\square$

When G is the group of translations and $\| \cdot \|$ is any norm, $\|(p_1 + t) - (p_2 + t)\| = \|p_1 - p_2\|$, and so the lemma holds. It holds also when G is the group of rigid motions and

$\|\cdot\|$ is the L_2 norm, since $\|(r_\theta(p_1)+t)-(r_\theta(p_2)+t)\|_2 = \|r_\theta(p_1-p_2)\|_2 = \|p_1-p_2\|_2$ (where $r_\theta(p)$ represents the result of rotating the point p by an angle θ about the origin). Such a norm is said to be **transformation-independent**.

Define a **shape** to be a closed, bounded subset of the plane, modulo the action of some transformation group G. Two (closed, bounded) sets A and B are considered to be the same shape iff $H_G(A,B) = 0$. Note that, for this definition to be reasonable, G must have the property that every $g \in G$ maps closed, bounded sets to closed, bounded sets; this certainly holds if every $g \in G$ is continuous.

This definition of two sets being the same shape meets the criteria for an equivalence relation, when the norm is transformation-independent:

1. For any A, $H_G(A,A) = 0$, because $H(A,A) = 0$, and the identity transformation must be a member of any transformation group.
2. For any A and B, $H_G(A,B) = 0$ iff $H_G(B,A) = 0$, because H_G is symmetric when the norm is transformation-independent.
3. If $H_G(A,B) = 0$ and $H_G(B,C) = 0$ then $H_G(A,C) = 0$. Since $H_G(A,B) = H_G(B,A) = 0$, for any $\varepsilon > 0$ there exists some transformation g_{AB} such that $H(B,g_{AB}(A)) \le \varepsilon/2$. Similarly, $H(B,g_{CB}(C)) \le \varepsilon/2$. Since H is a metric, and thus obeys the triangle inequality, $H(g_{AB}(A),g_{CB}(C)) < \varepsilon$, so $\hat{H}_G(A,C) = H_G(A,C) < \varepsilon$. This holds for any $\varepsilon > 0$, and $H_G(A,C) \ge 0$ by necessity, so $H_G(A,C) = 0$.

Shapes are therefore equivalence classes of point sets. H_G can be extended to shapes in a natural way: let $\mathcal{A}$ and $\mathcal{B}$ be two shapes. Let A and B be any representative examples from each shape, and define $H_G(\mathcal{A},\mathcal{B}) = H_G(A,B)$.

Lemma 2.2. H_G *extended to shapes is well-defined if the norm* $\|\cdot\|$ *is transformation-independent with respect to* G.

Proof. Suppose that A' and B' are two other representative examples from $\mathcal{A}$ and $\mathcal{B}$. Then $H_G(A',B') = H_G(A,B)$: $H_G(A,A') = 0$, so for any $\varepsilon > 0$, there exists a transformation g_ε such that $H(g_\varepsilon(A),A') < \varepsilon$. Now, for any transformation g,

$$H(g(B),A') \le H(A',g_\varepsilon(A)) + H(g_\varepsilon(A),g(B))$$
$$< \varepsilon + H(g_\varepsilon(A),g(B))$$

because H is a metric and so obeys the triangle inequality. Therefore,

$$
\begin{aligned}
H_G(A',B) &= H_G(B,A') \\
&= \inf_{g\in G} H(g(B),A') \\
&< \inf_{g\in G} H(g_\varepsilon(A),g(B)) + \varepsilon \\
&= \inf_{g\in G} H(g^{-1}(g_\varepsilon(A)),B) + \varepsilon \\
&= H_G(A,B) + \varepsilon.
\end{aligned}
$$

Since this holds for any $\varepsilon > 0$, $H_G(A',B) \le H_G(A,B)$; by symmetry, $H_G(A',B) = H_G(A,B)$, and similarly $H_G(A',B') = H_G(A',B) = H_G(A,B)$, so no matter which representatives from $\mathcal{A}$ and $\mathcal{B}$ are chosen, the same H_G value is obtained; $H_G(\mathcal{A}, \mathcal{B})$ is therefore well defined. □

H_G is well-defined on shapes when the underlying norm is transformation-independent; it is furthermore a metric:

Theorem 2.3. *Suppose that for any $g \in G$, g is continuous, and for any points p_1, p_2, $\|g(p_1) - g(p_2)\| = \|p_1 - p_2\|$. Then H_G is a metric on shapes.*

Proof. A metric ρ must satisfy the following four properties

1. $\rho(A, B) = \rho(B, A)$
2. $\rho(A, B) = 0$ iff $A = B$.
3. $\rho(A, B) \geq 0$ for all A, B.
4. $\rho(A, B) \leq \rho(A, C) + \rho(B, C)$.

Let A, B and C be three point sets which represent three shapes $\mathcal{A}$, $\mathcal{B}$ and $\mathcal{C}$.

1. Lemma 2.1 shows that $H_G(A, B) = H_G(B, A)$, so $H_G(\mathcal{A}, \mathcal{B}) = H_G(\mathcal{B}, \mathcal{A})$.
2. This follows from the definition of shapes: $H_G(\mathcal{A}, \mathcal{B}) = 0$ iff $H_G(A, B) = 0$, and so A and B are members of the same shape and $\mathcal{A} = \mathcal{B}$.
3. Since the value of $H_G(\mathcal{A}, \mathcal{B})$ is, at some level, the result of evaluating H on two sets, it must always be nonnegative.
4. Since $H_G(A, C) = \inf_{g \in G} H(g(A), C)$, for any $\varepsilon > 0$ there is some transformation $g_{AC} \in G$ such that $H(g_{AC}(A), C) < H_G(A, C) + \varepsilon/2$. Similarly, there is a $g_{BC} \in G$ such that $H(g_{BC}(B), C) < H_G(B, C) + \varepsilon/2$. Then

$$H_G(A, C) + H_G(B, C) > H(g_{AC}(A), C) + H(g_{BC}(B), C) - \varepsilon$$
$$\geq H(g_{AC}(A), g_{BC}(B)) - \varepsilon$$
$$\geq H_G(A, B) - \varepsilon$$

so for any $\varepsilon > 0$, $H_G(A, B) < H_G(C, A) + H_G(C, B) + \varepsilon$. Thus, $H_G(A, B) \leq H_G(A, C) + H_G(B, C)$ and so $H_G(\mathcal{A}, \mathcal{B}) \leq H_G(\mathcal{A}, \mathcal{C}) + H_G(\mathcal{B}, \mathcal{C})$. □

In general, however, H_G may not be a metric. Nonetheless, the transformation groups for which it is a metric are quite important ones, so this result is a good indication that the minimum Hausdorff distance under transformation has good properties.

2.3 Transformation Groups for Visual Recognition

In the image search problem, we are given a model and an image, and told to locate the model in the image, by determining a transformation which brings the model into close correspondence with the image. Different tasks involve searching different transformation groups. I discuss searching three specific transformation groups; these groups correspond to some of the transformations that the two-dimensional image of a three-dimensional object can undergo as that object moves in the three-dimensional world.

This is still 2D-from-2D recognition: the image and model are both two-dimensional point sets, but the transformations that the model undergoes can be thought of as the two-dimensional result of a three-dimensional motion followed by projection.

These transformation groups accurately support such a three-dimensional interpretation under the assumption that the image was produced using **weak-perspective projection**. This projection model assumes that the distance from the object to the camera is much greater than the depth of the object. Suppose that that the camera is set up with the image plane in the plane formed by the x and y axes, with the z axis pointing away from the camera. In this coordinate frame, the perspective projection equation is

$$(x, y, z) \longrightarrow \left(f\frac{x}{z}, f\frac{y}{z} \right)$$

where f is the focal length of the camera. In the weak perspective model, this projection equation is modified to be

$$(x, y, z) \longrightarrow (\sigma x, \sigma y)$$

where σ is some *global* scaling factor (i.e., the same value of σ is used in the projection of every point (x, y, z) in the object). If the z values of all these points are similar, then this is a good approximation to the true projection of the object. σ is thus usually $1/Z$, where Z is the (aggregate) distance from the object to the camera. This projection system is midway between the perspective projection system and the orthogonal (or orthographic) projection system (where $(x, y, z) \rightarrow (x, y)$, and the distance from the object to the camera is not considered at all).

Document processing applications involve searching for a shape in a scanned document, which is really a two-dimensional world. In this case, the image and model are truly two-dimensional objects, and there is no three-dimensional interpretation of the transformation; no projection model is needed.

2.3.1 Translation

The first, and simplest, transformation group that I consider is the group Tr of all translations of the plane. If an object moves in the three-dimensional world in a plane parallel to the image plane, then its projected image appears to undergo a planar translation. This is the case, for example, when the camera is positioned looking down on some flat surface (e.g., a table or a road) on which objects are moving, as long as the objects themselves do not change shape or aspect too much.

The minimum Hausdorff distance for this transformation group is

$$H_{Tr}(I, M) = \inf_{t_x, t_y} H(A, B \oplus (t_x, t_y))$$

where $\oplus$ represents the Minkowski sum,

$$B \oplus (t_x, t_y) = \{(b_x + t_x, b_y + t_y) \mid (b_x, b_y) \in B\} .$$

When the image is a scanned document, many applications rely on searching for a model at a fixed orientation and scale. For example, optical character recognition is typically done on images which have been de-skewed so that all the lines of text are horizontal. If the style and size of the typeface being recognised are known, then the images of the characters will be of known sizes, and so only their locations and identifications need to be determined. Thus, an OCR application might search for all locations where the image matches the model of an "a", then a "b", and so on; it would do so by finding translations of the current model where the Hausdorff distance is small. Note that this requires the ability to tolerate the presence of extraneous points; see Sects. 2.4 and 2.5.

2.3.2 Translation and Scale

Finding the best translation of the model suits applications where the camera is fixed and the motion of the object is restricted, or when the size of the object in the image is known beforehand. It can tolerate some amount of size change in the object, but beyond a certain point the approximation that the size is known breaks down. In order to overcome this, it is necessary to handle searching for not only the position of the object, but also its size. I do this by searching over a group Sc where every element of Sc is a quadruple (s_x, s_y, t_x, t_y) representing a translation and scaling of the plane,

$$(x, y) \to (s_x x + t_x, s_y y + t_y).$$

s_x and s_y are restricted to be positive, since otherwise the mapping would not be invertible, or would represent a reflection or rotation of the model, rather than a straightforward scaling. The minimum Hausdorff distance under the action of this group is then denoted by H_{Sc}.

As before, suppose that a camera is set up with the image plane in the (x, y) plane, and the z axis pointing away from the camera. As an object moves toward the camera (or, equivalently, the camera moves toward the object), its distance to the camera reduces, and its apparent size increases. Under the weak perspective assumptions, the object can be considered to be flat, and so this is the only change in its image (i.e., variable self-occlusion is not an issue).

Slight camera rotations can also be modeled as changes of size: suppose now that the camera rotates about the y axis by some small angle θ. Before the rotation, a point (x, y, z) on the object projected to the location $(x/Z, y/Z)$ in the image plane (recall that Z is the aggregate depth of the object, and so $z = Z + \delta z$ where δz is small). After the rotation, its aggregate depth is $Z \cos \theta$, and so this point projects to

$$\left(\frac{x \cos \theta - z \sin \theta}{Z \cos \theta}, \frac{y}{Z \cos \theta} \right) \approx \left(\frac{x}{Z} - \tan \theta, \frac{y}{Z} \sec \theta \right)$$

Thus, the primary effects of this rotation on the image of the object are

1. The object has translated in x.
2. The object's size has increased in the y direction, but has not changed in the x direction.

Alternately, the object could rotate about a line parallel to the image y axis, passing through the object's centroid. The primary effect of this rotation on the image of the object is a slight reduction in the size of the object, measured along the x axis of the image plane; its size in the y direction does not change. Thus, as the camera moves forward and pans, or (equivalently) the object moves toward the camera and rotates around an axis parallel to the image plane, the object's image translates in x and y, and scales independently in x and y. The group Sc captures this form of change in the object's appearance.

In some applications dealing with scanned documents, it is necessary to locate some model no matter what size it appears at. For example, given engineering drawings for some part, the computer might locate all the holes to be drilled by finding circles of various sizes. An example of this type of application is given in Sect. 6.2.

2.3.3 Affine Transformation

The third group that I consider is the group Aff of all nondegenerate, noninverting affine transformations of the plane: transformations which preserve parallel lines. An element of Aff can be represented as a 2×2 matrix T, of positive determinant, together with a translation (t_x, t_y), representing a mapping of the plane

$$(x, y) \rightarrow (t_{00}x + t_{01}y + t_x, t_{10}x + t_{11}y + t_y)$$

when T is the matrix

$$T = \begin{bmatrix} t_{00} & t_{01} \\ t_{10} & t_{11} \end{bmatrix}.$$

Suppose that an object consists of a number of points lying on a plane in space. First, project (using weak-perspective projection) each point of the object onto an image plane, creating one image point set. Next, change the pose of the model (or, equivalently, the location of the image plane) and repeat the projection. Then there exists an affine transformation that maps every point in the first image point set onto the corresponding point in the second image point set; also, every affine transformation of the first image point set can be generated by appropriate choice of the second pose. Thus, given a (two-dimensional) model of a planar object, and an image containing that object, I search for an affine transformation of the model that brings it into close correspondence with a portion of the image; finding this two-dimensional transformation is essentially equivalent to finding the three-dimensional pose of the object. The "close correspondence" just mentioned is measured using the Hausdorff distance. The object does not need to be perfectly planar, as the change in its appearance as its pose changes is close to an affine transformation as long as the object is relatively shallow (its thickness is small relative to its distance from the camera).

Degenerate transformations (where the determinant of T is zero), which are not part of Aff as they are noninvertible, correspond to positions of the object where it is viewed edge-on.

This group is most useful in three-dimensional object recognition applications when the position of the object in three dimensions is unconstrained. Also, the group Aff has some subgroups which may be of interest; Tr and Sc are certainly subgroups, as is the group Rig of two-dimensional translation and rotation (i.e., two-dimensional rigid motion). The group of similarity transformations (translation, rotation and scale) is also a subgroup; some of the methods in Sect. 1.2 used this subgroup.

2.4 The Partial Hausdorff Distance

As I mentioned in Sect. 1.1, I use sets composed of point features as the inputs to the image search task. These sets are the output of some feature detector, and so contain a finite number of points. Let $p = \#(I)$ be the number of features in the image I, and $q = \#(M)$ be the number of features in the model M.

Since M and I are finite, and thus compact, $h(M, I)$ and $h(I, M)$ can now be redefined as

$$h(M, I) = \max_{m \in M} \min_{i \in I} \|i - m\| \tag{2.9}$$

$$h(I, M) = \max_{i \in I} \min_{m \in M} \|i - m\| \tag{2.10}$$

The nearest neighbour function $\Delta(m)$, defined by

$$\Delta(m) = \min_{i \in I} \|i - m\| \tag{2.11}$$

is often quite useful. For each location in the plane, it gives the distance to the closest point of I. The forward Hausdorff distance $h(M, I)$ can then be defined as

$$h(M, I) = \max_{m \in M} \Delta(m).$$

Sect. 4.3 discusses how the time required to compute the Hausdorff distance can be significantly reduced by computing Δ.

The Hausdorff distance, as I have been treating it to this point, compares all of one set to all of another set, and is large if some portion of one set does not correspond well with *any* portion of the other set. In many machine vision and pattern recognition applications, it is important to be able to recognise instances of an object which are not fully visible: some features of the object may not be represented in the image, due to occlusion or sensor failure. The Hausdorff distance is not robust with respect to this type of error: if I and M are quite similar, except that a single point of M is far from every point of I, then $h(M, I)$ and thus $H(M, I)$ is quite large. This is not acceptable in practical recognition tasks: this single outlier point could be a noise point that crept into the model, or it could be a part of the model that, through occlusion or failure of the feature detector, is not present in the image; in any case, it should not be allowed to significantly change the distance between M and I. It is therefore necessary to extend the definition of the Hausdorff distance to allow for the comparison of *portions* of two shapes. This extension increases the generality of the search: it can now deal both with objects that are partially hidden from view, and scenes that contain multiple objects.

2.4.1 Partial Distances Based on Ranking

The Hausdorff distance can be naturally extended to the problem of finding the best *partial* distance between a model set M and an image set I. For simplicity, I first consider just the directed Hausdorff distance from M to I, $h(M, I)$. The computation of $h(M, I)$ simply determines the distance of the point of the model M that is farthest from any point of the image I. That is, each point of M is *ranked* by the distance to the nearest point of I, and the largest ranked point (the one farthest from any point of I) determines the distance.

A natural way to modify the directed Hausdorff distance to take care of the problem of outliers problem is to replace (2.9) with

$$h^f(M,I) = f^{\text{th}}_{m \in M} \min_{i \in I} \|m - i\| \qquad (2.12)$$

where $f^{\text{th}}_{x \in X} g(x)$ denotes the f-th quantile value of $g(x)$ over the set X, for some value of f between zero and one. For example, the 1-th quantile value is the maximum and the $\frac{1}{2}$-th quantile value is the median. Let f be some value between zero and one, and $K = \lceil fq \rceil$. $h^F(M,I)$ is computed by determining $\Delta(m)$ (the distance to the closest point of I) for each model point $m \in M$, and ranking these values. The K-th ranked value, d, indicates that K of the points of M are no further than d away from some point of I; d is the f-th quantile of these distance values. This f-th quantile value can be computed in $O(q)$ time using standard methods such as those in [AHU1]. In practice, it takes about twice as long as computing the maximum. This modified Hausdorff distance is called the **partial directed Hausdorff distance**. When $f = 1$, it is the same as the unmodified directed Hausdorff distance. This definition of the distance has the nice property that it *automatically selects* the K best matching points of M, because it identifies the subset of the model of size K that minimises the directed Hausdorff distance; the other $q - K$ points are considered to be outliers.

In general, in order to compute the partial directed forward distance, I specify some fraction $0 \le f_F \le 1$ of the points of M that are to be considered. Each of the q points of M is ranked by the distance to the nearest point of I. The f_F-th ranked such value, given by (2.12), then gives the partial distance. If this value is d, then the fraction of the points of M that are within d of some point of I is at least f_F.

This partial distance measures the difference between a *portion* of the model and the image: the K points of the model set which are closest to points of the image set. One key property of this method is that it does not require pre-specification of which part of the model is to be compared with the image. This is because the computation of the directed Hausdorff distance determines how far each model point is from the nearest image point, and thus automatically selects the points of the model that are closest to image points. In Chap. 6 I illustrate this partial matching capability, and contrast its performance with that of correlation. I have found that the directed partial Hausdorff distance works well for partial matches on images where correlation does not.

The **partial undirected Hausdorff distance** is now naturally defined as

$$H^{f_F f_R}(M,I) = \max(h^{f_F}(M,I), h^{f_R}(I,M)) \qquad (2.13)$$

where f_F and f_R control what fraction is used when evaluating the forward and reverse distances respectively; these are called the **forward fraction** and **reverse fraction**. $H^{f_F f_R}(M,I)$ is less than d when the fraction of points of I closer than d to some point of M is at least f_R, and the fraction of points of M closer than d to some point of I is at least f_F.

The function $H^{f_F f_R}$ clearly does not obey metric properties. However, it does obey weaker conditions that provide for intuitively reasonable behavior. These conditions are, in effect, that metric properties are obeyed between given subsets of I and M. In order to specify these properties more precisely, it is necessary to understand something about the subsets of I and M that achieve the minimum partial distance:

Theorem 2.4. *Suppose that* $H^{f_F f_R}(M.I) = d$. *Let* $K = \lceil f_F q \rceil$ *and* $L = \lceil f_R p \rceil$. *There exist sets* $I_L \subseteq I$ *and* $M_K \subseteq M$ *such that* $H(M_K.I_L) \le d$. *Each of* I_L *and* M_K *has exactly* $\min(K.L)$ *elements.*

Proof. The "neighbours" of an image point i are the points in M within d of i, and vice versa. Let I' be the points in I for which there is some point in M within d (i.e., those points in I having at least one neighbour):

$$I' = \{i \in I \mid \exists m \in M \text{ such that } \|i - m\| \le d\} .$$

Similarly, let M' be the points in M for which there is some point in I within d. Then $\#(I') \ge L$ and $\#(M') \ge K$, since $h^{f_R}(I.M) = f_R^{\text{th}} {}_{i \in I} \min_{m \in M} \|i - m\| \le d$ implies that there are at least L points in I that are closer than d to some point in M (and similarly there are K points in M that are closer than d to some point in I). Also, since $\| \cdot \|$ is symmetrical (i.e., $\|i - m\| = \|m - i\|$), all the neighbours of any point in I' must be in M' and vice versa.

The problem now reduces to finding $I_L \subseteq I'$ and $M_K \subseteq M'$ having $\min(K.L)$ points each such that $H(M_K.I_L) \le d$. I show that this is possible by building I_L and M_K one element at a time, while maintaining the invariant that $H(M_K.I_L) \le d$ (i.e., that for each element of I_L there is some element of M_K within d and vice versa).

Base case: Pick any point i from I'. Put it into I_L. Find any point m in M' such that $\|i - m\| \le d$. There must be at least one. Put m into M_K. Then $H(M_K.I_L) = \|i - m\| \le d$.

Induction step: Suppose that I_L and M_K each have $n < \min(K.L)$ elements and that $H(M_K.I_L) \le d$. There are now two cases:
- Suppose that there exist $i \in I' - I_L$ and $m \in M' - M_K$ such that $\|i - m\| \le d$. Then adding i to i_L and m to M_K increases the size of each set to $n + 1$ while maintaining the invariant.
- Suppose that no such i and m exist. Then pick any point $i \in I' - I_L$ and consider its neighbours: points in M' within d. It is a member of I', so it must have at least one such neighbour. All the neighbours must be in M_K already, so it has at least one neighbour in M_K. Similarly, every point $m \in M' - M_K$ has at least one neighbour in I_L. Picking any point in $I' - I_L$ and any point in $M' - M_K$ and adding them to I_L and M_K respectively increases the size of each set to $n + 1$ and maintains the invariant, since every point in the new I_L has a neighbour in the new M_K and vice versa.

Since there are at least L elements in I' and K elements in M', it is not possible to run out of elements in $I' - I_L$ and $M' - M_K$ before achieving $\min(K.L)$ elements in I_L and M_K.

This process builds I_L and M_K by ensuring that whenever a pair of points are added, they each have neighbours in the augmented sets, thus maintaining the desired invariant. $\square$

There are also large subsets of I and M which exactly achieve the distance d:

Theorem 2.5. *If $H^{f_F f_R}(M, I) = d$ then there exist sets $I'_L \subseteq I$ and $M'_K \subseteq M$ such that $H(M'_K, I'_L) = d$, with $L \leq \#(I'_L) \leq \max(K, L)$ and $K \leq \#(M'_K) \leq \max(K, L)$.*

Proof. This proof uses I', M', I_L and M_K from the proof of Theorem 2.4 to construct I'_L and M'_K. Suppose (without loss of generality, because I and M are treated symmetrically here) that $K \geq L$. Now, pick any $K - L$ points from $M' - M_K$ (there must be at least this many points since $\#(M_K) = \min(K, L) = L$ and $\#(M') \geq K$). Let M'_K be the union of M_K and these points. For each of the new points, pick one of its neighbours from I'. Let I'_L be the union of I_L and these neighbouring points. I'_L contains at most K points and at least L points, because $\#(I_L) = L$, and all these neighbours might have been members of I_L. Thus, $L \leq \#(I'_L) \leq K = \max(K, L)$. Since every point in M'_K has a neighbour (within d) in I'_L and vice versa, $H(M'_K, I'_L) \leq d$. However, equality must hold: if $H(M'_K, I'_L)$ were strictly less than d, then $H^{f_F f_R}(M, I)$ would also be strictly less than d, since I'_L and M'_K would then be minimising subsets of sizes at least L and K respectively. $\square$

It follows immediately that the identity and symmetry metric properties hold with respect to I'_L and M'_K, because $H(\cdot, \cdot)$ obeys these properties. Intuitively, this means that for the partial distance with some given f_F, f_R, the order of comparison does not matter, and the distance is zero exactly when the two minimising subsets I'_L and M'_K are the same.

For the triangle inequality metric property, the minimising subsets may be different when comparing A with B than when comparing B with C. Thus in general the triangle inequality can be violated. In the restricted case that the same subset $B'_K \subseteq B$ is the set of inliers both when B is compared against A and when B is compared against C, then the triangle inequality holds. Intuitively, this means that if two sets are compared with the *same portion* of a third set (denoted B'_K above) then the triangle inequality holds. For practical purposes this is a reasonable definition: if two models both match the same part of a given image then we expect the models to be similar to one another. On the other hand if they match different parts of an image then we have no such expectation.

2.5 The Box-Reverse Hausdorff Distance

The modifications to the Hausdorff distance discussed in the previous section make it more tolerant of imperfections in the model and image: it is not greatly affected by some portions of the model being missing in the image, or some portions of the image not corresponding to the model. In many instances, though, the model is considerably smaller than the image: a single image can contain several objects, so a single instance of the model might occupy only a small portion of the image, and so account for only a small fraction of the image's points. If there are many other objects in the image besides the object of interest, then the vast majority of the image points do not have anything to do with the object of interest, and so the reverse Hausdorff distance is large, unless the fraction of the points of the image which are allowed to be considered outliers (f_R) is set very low.

In an ideal situation, the points that do not belong to the target object should be ignored in the computation of the Hausdorff distance. This is not in general possible, and so some allowance must be made for their presence. Their effect can be reduced by modifying the computation of the reverse (image to model) distance so that it considers only those points of the image lying near the target object, as points far from the target object are part of other, unrelated, objects in the scene. I do this by considering a box which encloses all of the points of the model. Suppose that the model is contained in a box ($x_{min} \cdots x_{max}, y_{min} \cdots y_{max}$) in the plane. The reverse Hausdorff distance from the image to the model is then computed based only on the points which lie inside this box; this defines the **box-reverse Hausdorff distance**:

$$h_{box}(I, M) = \max_{\substack{(i_x, i_y) \in I \\ x_{min} \le i_x \le x_{max} \\ y_{min} \le i_y \le y_{max}}} \min_{m \in M} \|(i_x, i_y) - m\| \qquad (2.14)$$

Thus, any points in the image which are not close to the model's position are ignored. This is a reasonable approach, since they probably have nothing to do with the image of the target object.

This formula describes the computation in the case that $f_R = 1$: the maximum distance of all the applicable image points determines the reverse Hausdorff distance. It is possible to extend this to a partial distance in the same manner as was done in the preceding discussion: rather than taking the maximum of all the distances of applicable image points, instead take the f_Rth quantile. Some portions of extraneous objects might overlap the box, and so f_R may have to be set lower than if only the target object were present, in order to reduce the effect of these extra points. However, this is preferable to setting it absurdly low because all the points outside the box must be considered to be outliers.

Equation (2.14) is applicable to computing the reverse distance between an image and a fixed model. If the reverse distance is to be computed between the image I and a transformed model $g(M)$, then the image points contributing to the reverse distance should be those lying under the transformed model box. In other words, for a given transformation g, the forward Hausdorff distance from the transformed model $g(M)$ to the image is computed as usual; the reverse Hausdorff distance from the image to the model is computed ignoring any image points lying outside the location of the transformed model box. Under translation, the box has the same size, but its position changes along with the model; under translation and scale, it remains an axes-aligned box, but at any position and size. Under affine transformations, the model box can be transformed into any parallelogram; only image points lying under the parallelogram are used in evaluating the reverse distance for the transformation generating that parallelogram.

The basic Hausdorff distance was not suitable for practical applications, due to its instability and inability to ignore background clutter. However, the partial Hausdorff distances defined in Sect. 2.4, and the (partial) box-reverse distance defined in this section are much more tolerant to outliers, occlusion, and clutter. In general, in what follows I will be using d_G and d'_G to refer to the partial forward distance and partial box-reverse distances, implicitly parameterised by f_F, f_R, and the size of the model. The following chapter, dealing with exact algorithms, is an exception to this, but in the remaining chapters, only these modified distances will be used.

2.6 Summary

In this chapter, I have presented the Hausdorff distance, and modified it to make it more useful to image search tasks. Image search can be performed by finding the transformation of a model which minimises the Hausdorff distance between it and an image. The basic Hausdorff distance has good metric properties, and I have shown how, in some cases, these properties are carried through to the minimum Hausdorff distance under transformation.

The Hausdorff distance is, in its basic form, quite brittle in the presence of outliers, caused by image or model corruption or occlusion. Modifying it to use a quantile-based ranking rather than a maximisation operation reduces this brittleness, by allowing some fraction of the image or model points to be ignored if they match poorly. If the image contains other objects than the one being searched for, then the Hausdorff distance can be modified further to ignore large portions of the image lying far from the position of the model object. I also showed that even after these modifications the Hausdorff distance retains some pseudo-metric properties.

Chapter 3

Exact Computation

Thus far, I have discussed how the minimum Hausdorff distance under transformation might be used in performing image search. However, I have not presented any algorithms for actually determining the transformation minimising the Hausdorff distance. In this chapter, I briefly discuss some of the work which has been done in developing such algorithms, and then develop some lower bounds which imply that these exact algorithms are not appropriate for most practical image search applications.

The work in the area of exact algorithms has been done on two types of sets: sets consisting of a finite number of points, and sets consisting of a finite number of points and nonintersecting line segments. (Any set made up of finitely many points and line segments can be transformed into a set of points and nonintersecting line segments by splitting the segments at their intersections). Algorithms have been developed to find the minimum Hausdorff distance under translation and two-dimensional rigid motion (translation and rotation) in the plane. I will develop lower bounds both for these groups, and also the other two transformation groups discussed in the previous chapter.

In this chapter I will principally be using the "complete" Hausdorff distance, rather than the partial or box-reverse variants developed in the previous chapter. Section 3.11 discusses how some of the constructions can be extended to the partial Hausdorff distance.

3.1 Summary of Methods

In this section I briefly describe some of the algorithms which have been developed to determine the minimum Hausdorff distance under transformation by members of some group G, $H_G(A, B)$.

One of the first algorithms is that of Huttenlocher, Kedem and Sharir, described in [HKS1]. This algorithm solves the problem of finding the minimum Hausdorff distance under translation (i.e., the global minimum of $D_{Tr}(t)$), for both sets of points, and sets of points and line segments. It first constructs a number of Voronoi diagrams, such that the Voronoi edges of these diagrams must contain all the local minima of $D_{Tr}(t)$. It then enumerates these local minima, and thus determines the global minimum of $D_{Tr}(t)$. The running time of this algorithm is clearly bounded below by the complexity of the graph of $D_{Tr}(t)$, as it must examine each local minimum.

All of the more recent algorithmic results are obtained using a different technique. First, they develop an algorithm for solving the minimum Hausdorff distance *decision problem* over some transformation group G. Such an algorithm solves queries of the form: given a value ε and two sets A and B, is $H_G(A, B) \leq \varepsilon$ (i.e., does there exist some transformation $g \in G$ such that $H(A, g(B)) \leq \varepsilon$)?

Once an algorithm which solves the decision problem has been obtained, it can then be converted to an algorithm to solve the corresponding optimisation problem: find the smallest value of ε for which the decision algorithm returns "yes". This smallest value is then the value of $H_G(A, B)$. This conversion is generally done using Megiddo's parametric search technique ([Me1]). See [AST1] for a description of this search technique, and a number of examples of its application.

These Hausdorff distance algorithms do not depend as explicitly on the complexity of the graph of D_G. The decision problem algorithms generally have their time complexity determined by some aspect of constructing, updating or sweeping an arrangement of lines and arcs in the plane. The number of topological events that may have to be dealt with in this process limits the time complexity of these algorithms (an event might be, for example, four points of $g(B)$ becoming co-circular as the transformation g is varied; such an event requires special processing, increasing the time complexity of the algorithm). In fact, the algorithm of Chew and Kedem, in [CK1], achieves its low time complexity by being able to *implicitly* process a large number of events simultaneously, in a small amount of time, due to the peculiarities of the L_1 and L_∞ norms.

3.2 Lower Bounds

Recall from Sect. 2.1 that the directed Hausdorff distance from A to B, $h(A, B)$, is small exactly when every point in A is close to some point in B; $h(B, A)$ is small when every point in B is close to some point in A, and $H(A, B)$ is small when both of these are true. In particular, $h(B, A) \leq \varepsilon$ exactly when for any $b \in B$ there is some $a \in A$ such that $\|a - b\| \leq \varepsilon$. Let $A^\varepsilon = A \oplus D(\varepsilon)$ where $D(\varepsilon)$ is the disk of radius ε (the set of all points x such that $\|x\| \leq \varepsilon$) and $\oplus$ is the Minkowski sum. A key observation [AST1, CK1] then is that $h(B, A) \leq \varepsilon$ iff $B \subseteq A^\varepsilon$: B is contained in the set obtained by dilating each point of A by ε.

Finding the transformation of the model B (drawn from some transformation group G) which brings it into closest alignment with A is equivalent to finding the transformation $g^* \in G$ of B which minimises $H(A, g^*(B))$. This is also equivalent to finding the global minimum of the function $D_G(g) = H(A, g(B))$, as defined in (2.3). Some approaches to determining this minimising transformation are based on searching the graph of this function (for example, by enumerating the local minima, as in [HKS1]). It is therefore of interest to know what the geometric complexity of this graph may be. Upper bounds have been determined for some transformation groups, but few lower bounds were known [HKS1, CK1]. I also consider the graph of the function $d_G(g)$, as defined in (2.4), the directed Hausdorff distance from the transformed set $g(B)$ to A.

I exhibit lower bounds for the complexity of such graphs as follows. Each construction is parameterised by two values, ε and n (and possibly other parameters). For each construction, I fix some values for ε, n, and any other parameters, and construct sets A and B having kn elements each, for some constant k depending on the problem. I then show that the set $\{g \mid d_G(g) \leq \varepsilon\}$ has $\Omega((kn)^l) = \Omega(n^l)$ complexity, for some constant l depending on the problem. I do this by showing that this set has $\Omega(n^l)$ distinct connected components. Since each one must contain some local minimum of $d_G(g)$, this shows that there are $\Omega(n^l)$ local minima in the graph of $d_G(g)$. In some cases, I also

Table 3.1. Lower bounds for the complexity of the Hausdorff distance between two sets of size n. The only previously known lower bounds were those by Chew and Kedem [CK1] for the directed distance under translation (for both sets of points, and sets of points and line segments).

Transformation Group	Point Sets Results for $d_G(t)$ and $D_G(t)$ except $\ddagger$ for $d_G(t)$ only			Points and Segments Results for $d_G(t)$ only	
	L_1	L_2	L_∞	Any L_p	L_2
Translation	$\Omega(n^3)$	$\Omega(n^3)$	$\Omega(n^3)$	$\Omega(n^4)$	
Rigid motion		$\Omega(n^5)$			$\Omega(n^6)$
Translation and x, y scale	$\Omega(n^7)$	$\Omega(n^7)$	$\Omega(n^7)^\ddagger$	$\Omega(n^8)$	
Affine transformation	$\Omega(n^9)$	$\Omega(n^9)$	$\Omega(n^9)$	$\Omega(n^{12})$	

show that the graph of $D_G(g)$ may have this complexity. Previous constructions, such as those in [HKS1, CK1], have been for the directed Hausdorff distance alone. I also discuss how these bounds can be extended to apply to the partial Hausdorff distance. For the most part, however, I will be discussing only the complete Hausdorff distance, when $f_F = f_R = 1$.

The constructions for the undirected Hausdorff distance and the constructions for the directed distance on which they are based may have high complexity in a small space: for a fixed ε, it is possible to make $D_G(g)$ have $\Omega(n^l)$ complexity in an arbitrarily small region of transformation space (i.e., this does not depend on just shrinking ε). This is motivated by the observations in [ABB1] and [Ro1] that for some groups G, if $D_G(g) \leq \varepsilon$, then g must lie in a small region in transformation space. If the undirected Hausdorff distance could have only small complexity in a small area, even though it might have high complexity overall, it might be possible to obtain efficient algorithms: if the global minimum of $D_G(g)$ is restricted to lie in a small area, then searching only this area of its graph can take less time than searching the entire graph. The constructions here show that, in some cases, this is not possible.

Table 3.1 shows the problems for which I present lower bounds; Table 3.2 shows the running times of the algorithms which solve those problems. It can be seen that in most cases, the running times are nearly tight with the lower bounds. The exception is the bound for point sets under translation with the L_1 and L_∞ norms in [CK1], where an algorithm was given which uses the structure of the problem under these norms to avoid explicitly searching the entire graph. It may be possible to develop algorithms using similar techniques for some of the other problems, and so it should be emphasised that the lower bounds presented here are for the complexity of the graph of the Hausdorff distance, and do not necessarily give lower bounds for algorithms that determine the optimal transformation.

3.3 Point Sets under Translation

Let t be a translation. Define

$$D_{Tr}(t) = H(A, B \oplus t) \tag{3.1}$$

Table 3.2. Time bounds for finding the exact minimum Hausdorff distance under transformation between two sets of size n.

	Point Sets		Points and Segments	
Problem	L_1, L_∞	L_2	L_1, L_∞	L_2
Translation	$O(n^2 \log^2 n)$	$O(n^3 \log n)$	$O(n^4 \alpha(n))$	$O(n^4 \log^3 n)$
	[CK1]	[HKS1]	[HKS1]	[AST1]
Rigid motion		$O(n^5 \log^2 n)$		$O(n^6 \log^2 n)$
		[CGH+1]		[CGH+1]

$$d_{Tr}(t) = h(B \oplus t, A) \tag{3.2}$$

as the (undirected and directed respectively) Hausdorff distance between A and B as a function of translation. This section describes two constructions of point sets A and B, each containing $O(n)$ points, for which $D_{Tr}(t)$ and $d_{Tr}t$ have $\Omega(n^3)$ local minima within an arbitrarily small area. The first construction is for the L_1 or L_∞ norm; the second is for the L_2 norm.

3.3.1 The L_1 and L_∞ Example

I use the L_∞ norm throughout; rotating the point sets by $45°$ gives the construction for L_1.

Let A consist of two diagonal rows, each of n points spaced σ apart (i.e., σ apart in both x and y). The rows are $2\varepsilon + \delta$ apart, where $\delta < \sigma/n$. A and A^ε are shown in Fig. 3.1. The area left uncovered by A^ε contains a staircase of $\Omega(n)$ steps, in the gap between the two sides. The width of this gap is δ. Note that by reducing σ, the two rows can be compressed inwards, thereby making the stairsteps (and thus the total length of the staircase) as small as desired.

Let B consist of two diagonal rows of points, each of n points, as shown in Fig. 3.2. The points in each row are slightly more than δ apart, and are placed so that one row lies around the horizontal part of a stairstep, and the other lies around the adjacent vertical part. Since the stairstep lengths are all σ, and $\delta < \sigma/n$, each row of B is shorter (in height and width) than a stairstep segment.

Consider translating B slightly upwards or downwards. The points around the vertical stairstep remain inside A^ε or outside it, as they were before, but the points around the horizontal stairstep move into and out of A^ε as B moves. Similarly, as B moves left or right, the points around the vertical stairstep move in and out of A^ε, but the points around the horizontal stairstep do not. There are thus $\Omega(n^2)$ different configurations of B with respect to this one stairstep, since it is possible to independently choose where the gaps lie in the two rows of B. B can also be translated so that it straddles any of the other stairsteps, each of which gives rise to $\Omega(n^2)$ configurations, for a total of $\Omega(n^3)$ configurations. I only consider configurations where there is at least one point of each row of B on either side of the gap. Each one of these configurations can be labeled with three numbers from 1 to $n - 1$: the number of points in the bottom row of B that are inside the upper/left component of A^ε (i.e., to the left of the gap), the number of points

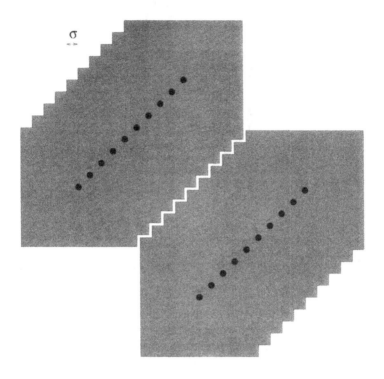

Fig. 3.1. The sets A and A^ε for the $L_\times$ lower bound for point sets under translation.

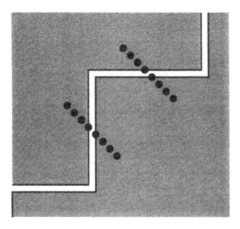

Fig. 3.2. The sets A^ε and B for the $L_\times$ lower bound for point sets under translation.

48

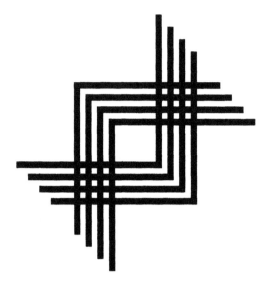

Fig. 3.3. Part of $S(A, \varepsilon, B)$ for the L_∞ lower bound for point sets under translation.

in the top row of B that are to the left of the gap, and the number of the stairstep which is straddled by B. $\Omega(n^3)$ such labels are possible. Suppose t_1 and t_2 are translations representing configurations with distinct labels. Then $d_{Tr}(t_1) \leq \varepsilon$ and $d_{Tr}(t_2) \leq \varepsilon$, since each translation places B entirely inside A^ε, but any path from t_1 to t_2 must pass through a translation t where $d_{Tr}(t) > \varepsilon$: either some point in one of the rows of B must cross the gap, in which case $d_{Tr}(t) > \varepsilon$ when t is a translation placing that point inside the gap, or B must be moved so as to straddle another stairstep, in which case again at least one point of B must move through the gap. All these labels therefore label distinct regions.

Another way to visualise this is similar to that used in [CK1]: define $S(A, \varepsilon, b)$ for some $b \in B$ to be $A^\varepsilon \oplus -b$. Then $t \in S(A, \varepsilon, b)$ exactly when $b + t \in A^\varepsilon$. This set is therefore the set of all translations which map b into A^ε. Now define $S(A, \varepsilon, B) = \cap_{b \in B} S(A, \varepsilon, b)$. Then $t \in S(A, \varepsilon, B)$ iff $B \oplus t \subseteq A^\varepsilon$, or $d_{Tr}(t) \leq \varepsilon$; $S(A, \varepsilon, B)$ is therefore the set of all translations t which make $h(A, B \oplus t) \leq \varepsilon$.

$S(A, \varepsilon, B)$ can be constructed by making a copy of A^ε for every point in B, translating these copies and forming their intersection. It can also be construced by making a copy of the *complement* of A^ε for every point in B, translating these copies, and forming their *union*. This union has a hole for every connected component of $S(A, \varepsilon, B)$. Figure 3.3 shows part of such a union. Each jagged line represents one segment of the gap staircase of some translation of A^ε (i.e., portions of one copy of the complement of A^ε). There are two sets of translations of this staircase, corresponding to the two rows of B. These two sets intersect in $\Omega(n)$ crosshatches, each having $\Omega(n^2)$ holes; Fig. 3.3 shows two of the crosshatches.

Now, note that δ can be made as small as desired, thereby narrowing the staircase gap and reducing the lengths of the rows of B, and the staircase itself can be compressed as much as is desired by reducing σ (as long as δ stays smaller than σ/n). This means that, for a fixed n and ε, the $\Omega(n^3)$-complexity region can be compressed down into an arbitrarily small area, bounded by a square $n\sigma$ on each side, since that is the length of the staircase.

The area where the undirected Hausdorff distance $D_{Tr}(t)$ is no greater than ε can also have large complexity in a small space. Set $\sigma < \varepsilon/n$ so that the rows of A have length less than ε, and add two points to B, one in the middle of each row of A. Then if the main body of B is translated anywhere on the staircase, these two extra points remain close to the rows of A. Since the rows have length less than ε, there is always some point of B within ε of any point of A, for any translation in the complex region. Thus, $H(A, B \oplus t) > \varepsilon$ exactly where $h(B \oplus t, A) > \varepsilon$ (at least in this region of interest), since $h(A, B \oplus t)$ is always at most ε. The undirected Hausdorff distance $D_{Tr}(t)$ therefore has complexity $\Omega(n^3)$.

3.3.2 The L_2 Example

In this subsection, I show how the previous example can be modified so that it works with the L_2 norm. The set A consists of two vertical rows of n points, spaced σ apart; the two rows are staggered by $\sigma/2$ (see Fig. 3.4). The distance between the rows is set such that the circles of A^ε are δ apart at their closest approach; the gap between the left and right sides is not of constant width.

The set B again consists of two rows of n points. These rows are horizontal, and spaced $\sigma/2$ apart. The points in each row are slightly more than 2δ apart. They are shown superimposed on A^ε in Fig. 3.5. The idea is that, no matter what values σ, ε and n have, if δ is small enough, then it is possible to choose n_1 and n_2 independently, and position B such that $B \subseteq A^\varepsilon$, there are n_1 points of the top row on the left side of the gap, and n_2 points of the bottom row on the left side of the gap. This gives $\Omega(n^2)$ possible configurations of B around a single wobble in the gap; as there are $\Omega(n)$ such wobbles, there are $\Omega(n^3)$ different configurations of B with $B \subseteq A^\varepsilon$. A labeling argument, similar to that in the previous subsection, shows that these configurations are all distinct.

This is difficult to visualise, so again look at $S(A, \varepsilon, B)$. As before, this is constructed by taking the union of $O(n)$ copies of the gap, translated by various amounts, and showing that this union has $\Omega(n^3)$ disjoint holes.

Since the actual gap has such a complicated shape, I deal only with a small part of it. In particular, I consider only the regions where the gap's width is between δ and 2δ (recall that δ is the width of the narrowest part of the gap). There are $\Omega(n)$ regions where this is true, each one centred around a place where the gap is at its narrowest. Each such region is bounded by a rectangle; these rectangles are 2δ wide by λ long, where λ is determined by ε and δ, and is equal to $\sqrt{4\varepsilon\delta - \delta^2}$. See Fig. 3.6 for an illustration of this region. Now, note that $\lambda/\delta = \sqrt{4\varepsilon/\delta - 1}$. Thus, for any fixed ε, λ/δ can be made as large as necessary by making δ small enough: as δ decreases, the rectangles get both narrower and shorter, but their length to width ratio increases.

The gap is narrowest exactly where a line from one point in the left row of A to one of its neighbours in the right row crosses it. The interesting rectangles are oriented perpendicular to such lines. There are two sets of such rectangles, one leaning to the left

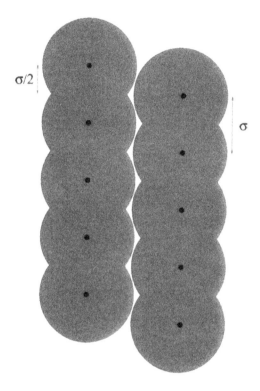

Fig. 3.4. The sets A and A^ε for the L_2 lower bound for point sets under translation.

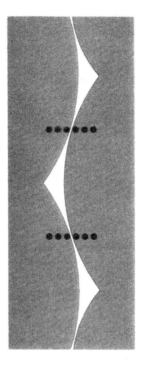

Fig. 3.5. The sets A^ε and B for the L_2 lower bound for point sets under translation.

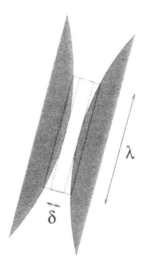

Fig. 3.6. A closeup of the interesting region of the gap.

and the other leaning to the right. The angle between these two sets decreases as σ decreases, but is not significantly affected by δ. Consider taking n right-leaning rectangles, and positioning them slightly more than 2δ apart (the same spacing as the points of B), so that the right edge of one rectangle almost touches the left edge of the next. Then, for a small enough value of δ, λ/δ is large enough that one left-leaning rectangle can intersect all n of these right-leaning rectangles.

$S(A, \varepsilon, B)$ is constructed by making n copies of the gap stacked slightly more than 2δ apart (corresponding to one of the rows of B), and having these intersect with another n copies, shifted down by $\sigma/2$ (corresponding to the other row), giving $\Omega(n^3)$ intersections: each left-leaning rectangle from one of the copies intersects n right-leaning rectangles from other copies, and vice versa. Figure 3.7 shows part of such an arrangement. There are $\Omega(n^2)$ holes in the crosshatch, and $\Omega(n)$ such crosshatches in the complete arrangement. As in Subsect. 3.3.1, it is possible to independently choose n_1 and n_2, and position B in such a way that n_1 points from its top row lie in the left half of A^ε, and n_2 points from its bottom row lie in the left half. There are $\Omega(n)$ such placements for any n_1 and n_2 ($1 \le n_1, n_2 < n$), one around each wobble of the gap, for $\Omega(n^3)$ different configurations. Going from some configuration to another with a different n_1 or n_2 involves some point crossing the gap. Also, since the points of B are spaced about 2δ apart and the gap becomes wider than this between two adjacent wobbles, it is impossible to translate B from one configuration to another with the same n_1 and n_2 without some point moving outside A^ε. Thus, all these $\Omega(n^3)$ configurations all belong to different connected components of the complement of $S(A, \varepsilon, B)$. These components are all contained in an area which is $O(n\sigma)$ high by $O(n\delta)$ wide, and so by a suitable choice of σ, this region of high complexity can be made arbitrarily small.

As in Subsect. 3.3.1, if $n\sigma < \varepsilon$, B may be augmented by two points, one each in the middle of the two rows of A, such that $h(A, B \oplus t) \le \varepsilon$ for all translations in the complex region; this construction therefore similarly shows that the undirected Hausdorff distance can have large complexity in a small area.

3.4 Sets of Points and Line Segments under Translation

This section describes a construction of two sets A and B, each consisting of $2n$ points and nonintersecting line segments, for which the graph of the directed Hausdorff distance as a function of translation $d_{Tr}(t) = h(B \oplus t, A)$ has $\Omega(n^4)$ complexity.

Fix ε and n and pick δ such that $\delta < \varepsilon/n$. Now let A consist of a group of n horizontal segments, each of length $(n-1)(2\varepsilon + \delta)$, spaced $2\varepsilon + \delta$ apart, plus a similar group of n vertical segments. Under any L_p norm, A^ε consists of n horizontal bars and n vertical bars, with gaps of width δ between adjacent bars; the shape of the caps on the ends of the bars depends on the exact norm. Now, let B consist of a vertical row of n points, spaced 2δ apart, located at the bottom-left corner of the group of horizontal lines in A, plus a similar horizontal row located at the bottom-left corner of the group of vertical lines. Figure 3.8 shows B overlaid on A and A^ε.

There are $\Omega(n^4)$ different configurations of B with respect to A: the vertical row of B can be straddling any of the $n - 1$ gaps, and from 1 to $n - 1$ points can lie below the gap; similarly, the horizontal row can be placed in any one of $\Omega(n^2)$ different

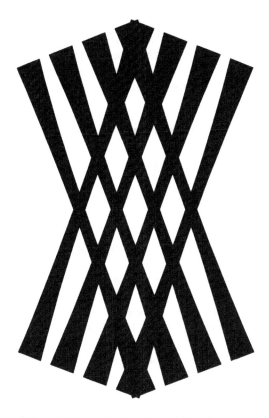

Fig. 3.7. Part of $S(A, \varepsilon, B)$ for the L_2 lower bound for point sets under translation.

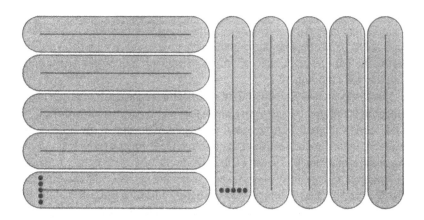

Fig. 3.8. The sets A, A^ε and B for points and segments under translation.

configurations with respect to the vertical segments of A. Sliding B horizontally does not affect the configuration of the vertical row, and sliding it vertically does not affect the configuration of the horizontal row (as long as these rows remain within limits); the configurations of the two rows may thus be chosen independently, for a total of $\Omega(n^4)$ different configurations. These are all clearly distinct, since any two differ in the number of points of B contained in one of the connected components of A^ε.

3.5 Point Sets under Rigid Motion

Let t be a translation and θ an angle. Define

$$D_{Rig}(t,\theta) = H(A, r_\theta(B) \oplus t) \tag{3.3}$$

$$d_{Rig}(t,\theta) = h(r_\theta(B) \oplus t, A) \tag{3.4}$$

where $r_\theta(B)$ denotes the set obtained by rotating B by θ counterclockwise about the origin.

I use the L_2 norm when dealing with rotation, since it is the only rotationally symmetric L_p norm.

The following construction shows that there can be $\Omega(n^5)$ distinct connected components in (t,θ) space where the undirected Hausdorff distance $D_{Rig}(t,\theta)$ between two sets of $\Omega(n)$ points is less than ε. It is based on an augmentation of A and B from Subsect. 3.3.2. For clarity, I refer to the sets A and B constructed for the translational lower bounds as A_{Tr} and B_{Tr}.

First, note that it is possible to rotate B_{Tr} from that construction by some very small angle $\theta_{\min}$ about its centroid while still maintaining the $\Omega(n^3)$ complexity of $h(B_{Tr} \oplus t, A_{Tr})$. This is because there must be, in the $\Omega(n^3)$ arrangement of connected components of $S(A, \varepsilon, B)$, some minimum distance between features, and so any rotation that does not move any feature of the arrangement more than half this distance cannot change the overall topology of the arrangement: none of the connected components merge, nor do any vanish.

The augmentation to A_{Tr} consists of n points along a vertical line, spaced less than $\varepsilon/(2n)$ apart. Placing a disk of radius ε about each gives a shape with two vertical scalloped edges: the left and right sides are close to vertical, but have n slight bulges or lobes. Call this row of points A_2.

Now, if A_2 is located sufficiently far away from the origin, and perpendicular to the line joining it to the origin, then it is possible to pass a circular arc (centred at the origin) through the inner scalloped edge so that it passes through each of the n lobes and the gaps between them. The arc does not pass through these lobes evenly, but cuts deeper into some of them than others. However, the magnitude of this effect may be controlled by moving the row farther away and thus increasing the radius of the arc, since the arc approaches a straight line as A_2 moves away. Slightly adjusting the radius of the arc also controls the ratio between the arc length contained inside the lobes and the arc length contained in the spaces between the lobes. Then A_2 should be placed, and the circular arc positioned, such that the ratio between the arc length contained in any lobe and the arc length contained in the space next to that lobe is greater than $8n : 1$. Let the shortest

Fig. 3.9. The interaction between A_2^ε and B_2.

---

of the arc lengths contained in the lobes be l (see Fig. 3.9). As the arc becomes closer to a straight line (as A_2 is moved away from the origin), the lengths of the arc segments contained in the lobes become more similar (and, at the limit, are all equal). A_2 should be positioned far enough away that they are all within a factor of two of each other. The widest gap is then smaller than $l/(4n)$.

I now describe the construction of B_2. B_2 consists of n points positioned $l/(2n)$ apart along this circular arc, initially located in the lowest lobe of A_2^ε. B_2 also contains an extra point, initially located at the lower end of A_2. Now, as B_2 rotates about the origin, this row of points moves along this circular arc. Since the spaces between lobes along this path are all less than $l/(4n)$ across, and the entire arc of points fits into a single lobe, only one point passes through a gap at a time, and there are $\Omega(n^2)$ different configurations of B_2 with respect to this part of A_2^ε: there are $n-1$ gaps to be straddled, and for each gap, between 1 and $n-1$ points of B_2 can be above the gap. Note that all of these configurations have the property that all of the points of A_2 are within ε of some point of B_2, specifically the extra point.

Pick θ, the amount by which B_2 is rotated about the origin, such that the points of B_2 are straddling one of the spaces between lobes, and such that this straddling is even: the two points closest to the gap are equal distances away from the edges of the gap. They are at least $l/(8n)$ away from these edges. Now, consider translating the points of B_2 vertically up or down by up to $l/(16n)$. If the arc along which the points lie is close enough to a straight vertical line, then they will stay inside A_2^ε. Let d be the minimum horizontal depth inside A_2^ε achieved for any point of B_2 at any point in this translational range. Figure 3.10 shows this situation; the vertical bars are $l/(8n)$ high ($l/16n$ above and below the centre). Let $d_{\min}$ be the smallest such d value achieved for any of the $\Omega(n^2)$ possible such straddling configurations. Also, let w be the minimum distance between the circular arc and the bottom of the space between two lobes.

The next step in the construction is to construct A_{Tr} and B_{Tr} as in Subsect. 3.3.2 by choosing σ and δ so that the $\Omega(n^3)$ complexity region of $D_{Tr}(t)$ is at most $l/(16n)$ high by $\min(d_{\min}/2, w/2)$ wide, and so that the centroid of B_{Tr} is at the origin. Let $A = A_{Tr} \cup A_2$ and $B = B_{Tr} \cup B_2$. Let θ produce one of the straddling configurations described above. Then, if $|\theta| < \theta_{\min}$, there are $\Omega(n^3)$ different connected components in t space where $D_{Rig}(t, \theta) \le \varepsilon$. This is because a slight translation of B_2 with respect to A_2 does not move any of the points of B_2 out of A_2^ε, and B_{Tr} and A_{Tr} have been

56

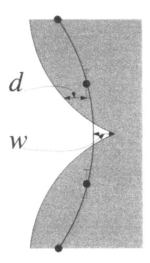

Fig. 3.10. The minimum depth of the points of B_2.

constructed so that the range of translations required is very small. Note that $D_{Rig}(t, \theta)$ is determined by $d_{Rig}(t, \theta)$ for all transformations in the range under consideration, as the directed distance from A to the rotated and translated B is always less than ε.

A labeling argument similar to that in Subsect. 3.3.1 now shows that there are $\Omega(n^5)$ different connected components in (t, θ) space where $D_{Rig}(t, \theta) \leq \varepsilon$, $\Omega(n^3)$ corresponding to each of the $\Omega(n^2)$ such values of θ. A key point in the argument is that it is not possible for one of the points of B_2 to sneak around the space between the lobes (through the main body of A_2^ε), since it would have to translate at least w away from the original circular arc, which would force at least one point of B_{Tr} to cross some gap. Thus, any two configurations which differ in how the points of B_2 are straddling the gaps of A_2^ε must belong to different connected components.

There is a problem with this construction as it has been presented: A_2 must subtend an angle of less than θ_{min}, which depends on σ and δ, which depend on l, d_{min} and w, which depend on the circular arc along which B_2 is placed, which must have a larger radius for a smaller θ_{min} and thus depends on θ_{min}; the parameters are thus interdependent. However, as A_2 and B_2 are moved farther out, l, d_{min} and w approach limit values, as the circular arc becomes closer to a straight line. Thus, A_2 and B_2 can initially be placed where l and w are within some small factor (say, within 1%) of their limit values; next, determine σ and δ which work for any values of l and w between their original values and their limit values, and thus determine θ_{min}. This gives a minimum value for the radius of the circular arc, and A_2 and B_2 can be moved farther out if necessary without affecting the validity of the construction.

3.6 Sets of Points and Line Segments under Rigid Motion

This example is a modification of the example from Sect. 3.4, using the techniques from Sect. 3.5. Again, I will refer to the sets A and B constructed in Subsect. 3.4 as A_{Tr} and

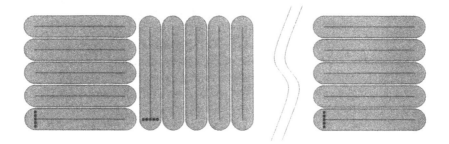

Fig. 3.11. The sets A, A^ε and B for points and segments under rigid motion.

B_{Tr}. As before, I observe that the set B_{Tr} may be rotated by some small angle $\theta_{\min}$ about its centroid without changing the topology of the arrangement.

Place B_{Tr} so that its centroid is at the origin (the centre of rotation). Augment A_{Tr} by a group of segments A_2 identical to the left-hand group of A_{Tr}. A_2 is placed so that it subtends a total angle of less than $\theta_{\min}$ to the origin, and lies directly to the right of it. Let $A = A_{Tr} \cup A_2$. Now, add n points to B_{Tr} in a vertical row, in the same relative position to A_2 as the first vertical row of B_{Tr} was to the left-hand group of A. Call this new row B_2 and let $B = B_{Tr} \cup B_2$. A, A^ε and B are shown in Fig. 3.11.

Now, any translation t for which $B_{Tr} \oplus t \in A^\varepsilon_{Tr}$ also has $B \oplus t \in A^\varepsilon$. Fix such a t and consider values of θ where $|\theta| < \theta_{\min}$. As θ changes through this range, the points in B_2 sweep across the gaps in A^ε_2. Their spacing is such that only one point crosses a gap at a time. Thus, as θ varies, the points of B_2 achieve $\Omega(n^2)$ different configurations with respect to the gaps of A^ε_2. For this choice of t, there are thus $\Omega(n^2)$ values of θ for which $d_{Rig}(t, \theta) \leq \varepsilon$, since any rotation in this range keeps $r_\theta(B) \oplus t$ inside A^ε. t can be chosen to represent one of the $\Omega(n^4)$ distinct configurations of B with respect to A, and so this gives $\Omega(n^6)$ different configurations of B with respect to the gaps of A^ε for which $d_{Rig}(t, \theta) \leq \varepsilon$. These configurations are not connected in (t, θ) space, since any path from one to another must cause at least one point to cross some gap.

3.7 Point Sets under Translation and Scale

In this section, I discuss the complexity of the graph of the Hausdorff distance between two sets of points as one set is translated and scaled with respect to the other. This scaling is with respect to fixed x and y axes. I present three different lower-bound constructions: one each for the L_1, L_2 and L_∞ norms. They are all similar in concept, and are based on the constructions in Sect. 3.3, using techniques from Sect. 3.5. The L_1 and L_2 constructions show lower bounds for both the directed and undirected Hausdorff distance; the L_∞ construction, however, shows a lower bound for the directed Hausdorff distance only.

Define the undirected and directed Hausdorff distance as functions of a translation t and two scale parameters s_x and s_y as

$$D_{Sc}(t, s_x, s_y) = H(A, S_{s_x s_y}(B) \oplus t) \tag{3.5}$$

$$D_{Sc}(t, s_x, s_y) = h(S_{s_x s_y}(B) \oplus t, A) \tag{3.6}$$

where $S_{s_x s_y}(B)$ denotes the set $\{(s_x x, s_y y) \mid (x, y) \in B\}$ (i.e., the set obtained by scaling B by a factor of s_x in the x direction and s_y in the y direction).

The central idea behind these constructions is that changing s_x slightly has very little effect on points which are near the y axis, while it has a largely translational effect on groups of points which are located a large distance along the x axis ("large" here means that the distance of the group from the origin is large relative to the size of the group).

3.7.1 The L_2 Example

This example is very similar to the example for point sets under rigid motion. Again, a key observation is that the construction of A_{Tr} and B_{Tr} in Subsect. 3.3.2 can be perturbed slightly without affecting the topology of the graph. In this case, this perturbation takes the form of a slight scaling of B_{Tr} in x and y. Suppose that the origin is placed at the lower left corner of B_{Tr}. Then let $s_{\min}$ be the valid range of such scaling: if $1 - s_{\min} \leq s_x, s_y \leq 1 + s_{\min}$, then there are $\Omega(n^3)$ translational configurations of B_{Tr} with respect to A_{Tr} for which replacing B_{Tr} by $S_{s_x s_y}(B_{Tr})$ does not change the configuration (i.e., the same points are on the same sides of the gap of A_{Tr}^ε). $s_{\min}$ clearly depends on the n, ε and σ used to construct A_{Tr} and B_{Tr}.

First, construct A_2 as in Sect. 3.5, and place it so that the y axis cuts through the left-hand scalloped edge in a manner similar to that described in Sect. 3.5: each lobe of the scalloped edge contains a length l of the y axis, the smallest depth of any of the gaps is w, and the ratio between the axis length contained in any lobe (i.e., l) and the length contained in the space next to that lobe is greater than $8n : 1$. Note that this construction does not depend on the location of this copy of A_2 along the y axis.

Next, construct A_{Tr} and B_{Tr} as in Subsect. 3.3.2 such that the region of $\Omega(n^3)$ complexity occupies a region less than $\min(w/2, l/(8n))$ square, and position them so that the lower left corner of this region in translation space is located at $t = (0, 0)$, and the lower left corner of B_{Tr} is at the origin. This determines a value for $s_{\min}$. Position the copy of A_2 a distance of $2\varepsilon/s_{\min}$ above the origin, with the y axis cutting through it as described above. Also, make a copy of A_2, rotated by $90°$, to the right of the copy of A_{Tr}, with the x axis cutting through the lower scalloped edge in the same manner. A consists of A_{Tr} together with these two copies of A_2. B then consists of B_{Tr} plus two rows of n points plus an extra point per row, as described in Subsect. 3.5; one row and its extra point are positioned along the y axis inside the uppermost lobe of the first copy of A_2; the other row and its extra point are in the corresponding position on the x axis, in the second copy of A_2. Call these two rows B_2.

Now, it is possible to independently choose seven numbers $n_1, \ldots, n_7$ from 1 to $n - 1$ and determine a translation t and scale s_x, s_y of B with respect to A so that $d_{Sc}(t, s_x, s_y) \leq \varepsilon$:

1. n_1, n_2 and n_3 determine the translation. They are used to position n_1 of the points of the lower row of B_{Tr} to the left of the gap in A_{Tr}^ε, n_2 of the points of the upper row to the left of the gap, and with the rows straddling the n_3th wobble of the gap.

2. n_4 and n_5 determine s_y. They are used to position n_4 of the points of the row of B_2 lying on the y axis below one of the gaps in the scalloped edge of the upper copy of A_2. n_5 selects the gap. Note that changing s_y acts as (essentially) a translation of this row, as its distance from the origin (and therefore its y coordinate) greatly exceeds its length. It is possible to do this no matter what translation was chosen above, since the range of translations is small. Also, any s_y chosen in this manner does not exceed the range determined by $s_{\min}$.

3. n_6 and n_7 similarly determine s_x, by positioning the points of the row of B_2 lying on the x axis with respect to its copy of A_2.

If two such configurations are generated with different n_i values, then it is not possible to move from one to the other without some point crossing a gap, and so they must belong to different connected components in transformation space where $d_{Sc}(t, s_x, s_y) \leq \varepsilon$. Also, due to the extra points added to the various parts of B, $h(A, S_{s_x s_y}(B) \oplus t)$ is no greater than ε for all such configurations; D_{Sc} therefore has $\Omega(n^7)$ distinct local minima. These can occur in an arbitrarily small region of transformation space for a fixed ε.

3.7.2 The L_1 Example

This example is quite similar to the example in the previous subsection. The construction uses a copy of A_{Tr} and B_{Tr} from Subsect. 3.3.1 (the translational example for L_∞), rotated $45°$. Instead of A_{Tr} being augmented by two rows of points, each generating a scalloped edge, it is instead augmented by two rows of points, each generating a saw-tooth edge; however, these augmentations are used in the same manner.

3.7.3 The L_∞ Example

This example must be constructed differently from the previous two, since a vertical row of points, when dilated by ε, generates a straight vertical edge, with no irregularities that can be exploited. Let A_2 be a vertical row of n points spaced $2\varepsilon + \delta$ apart, lying on the the y axis, far away from the origin. A_2^ε is then a row of n squares with a δ-wide gap between adjacent squares. Let B_2 be a vertical row of n points spaced just over δ apart, lying close to A_2. As s_y varies, B_2 moves mostly translationally, and its points therefore move through the $n - 1$ gaps in A_2^ε, one point at a time. $\Omega(n^2)$ configurations of the points of B_2 relative to the gaps of A_2^ε are therefore possible.

Let A be a copy of A_{Tr} from Subsect. 3.3.1, plus A_2 as described above, plus a similar horizontal row of n points lying along the x axis. Similarly, let B be a copy of B_{Tr} plus B_2 plus a row of points on the x axis. First, choose a translational configuration of B_{Tr} with respect to A_{Tr}, and initially set s_x and s_y to 1. Next, choose one of the $\Omega(n^2)$ configurations of B_2 with respect to A_2, and adjust s_y so that this configuration is achieved. Similarly, choose one of the $\Omega(n^2)$ configurations of the parts of A and B lying along the x axis, and set s_x accordingly. Thus, there are $\Omega(n^7)$ different configurations of B with respect to A; d_{Sc} therefore has $\Omega(n^7)$ distinct local minima.

Unlike the other constructions for point sets, it is not possible to augment B by a few points so that $h(A, t(B))$ is always below ε for the region of transformation space of interest. This construction is therefore valid for the directed distance only.

3.8 Sets of Points and Line Segments under Translation and Scale

This example is quite similar to the examples in the previous section: make a copy of A_{Tr} and B_{Tr} from Sect. 3.4, shown in Fig. 3.8, and place these copies near the origin, together with a copy of the right-hand group of each (the group exploiting vertical gaps) placed some distance away along the x axis, and a copy of the left-hand group of each placed some distance away along the y axis. This construction gives $\Omega(n^8)$ distinct local minima for d_{Sc} ($\Omega(n^4)$ from A_{Tr} and B_{Tr}, and $\Omega(n^2)$ from each of the additional groups). As before, the exact norm being used is not relevant, since it does not affect the gaps between the segments.

3.9 Point Sets under Affine Transformation

This section discusses the Hausdorff distance as a function of members of the affine transformation group Aff: transformations that map B to $T(B) \oplus t$, where T is a non-singular 2×2 matrix defined by

$$T = \begin{bmatrix} t_{00} & t_{01} \\ t_{10} & t_{11} \end{bmatrix}$$

and $t = (t_x, t_y)$ is a translation. In other words, each point $(b_x, b_y) \in B$ is mapped to $(t_{00}b_x + t_{01}b_y + t_x, t_{10}b_x + t_{11}b_y + t_y)$. As before, define

$$D_{Aff}(t, T) = H(A, T(B) \oplus t) \tag{3.7}$$
$$d_{Aff}(t, T) = h(T(B) \oplus t, A) \tag{3.8}$$

The key observation here is that if B consists of three groups of points, one near the origin, one located a large distance along the x axis, and one located a large distance along the y axis, then

- Changing t_{00} slightly causes the second group in the transformed B to translate in x, but has little other effect.
- Changing t_{10} slightly causes the second group to translate in y, but has little other effect.
- Changing t_{01} or t_{11} slightly similarly causes the third group to translate in x or y, and has little other effect.
- If T is sufficiently close to the identity matrix, then $T(B)$ is essentially the same as B, with the relative positions of the three groups shifted around somewhat.

The magnitude of these translational motions with respect to their other effects can be increased by moving the corresponding group farther away from the origin along the appropriate axis. Thus, this is a six-parameter system (two translational and four linear parameters), which can be decomposed into three two-parameter translational systems, plus a small amount of slop, which can be made as small as required. In order to build a $\Omega(n^9)$ example, simply take three copies of the appropriate A_{Tr} and B_{Tr}, and arrange them as described above. Again, copies 2 and 3 of A_{Tr} and B_{Tr} can be moved out from the origin until all nontranslational effects are not significant, since as they move farther out, the amounts by which the t_{ij} values need to be adjusted are reduced. Since all the copies of A_{Tr} and B_{Tr} have $\Omega(n^3)$ complexity under translation, for both the directed and undirected Hausdorff distance, and are essentially independent, this construction gives $\Omega(n^9)$ complexity for both d_{Aff} and D_{Aff}.

3.10 Sets of Points and Line Segments under Affine Transformation

This example is constructed identically to the previous example: take three copies of A_{Tr} and B_{Tr} from Sect. 3.4 and position one at the origin, one out along the x axis, and one out along the y axis. This gives $\Omega(n^{12})$ local minima of d_{Aff}, from three essentially independent $\Omega(n^4)$ translational examples.

3.11 Extension to the Partial Hausdorff Distance

All of the constructions involving point sets can be easily extended to apply to the partial Hausdorff distance. Suppose that the forward fraction f_F has some positive value, less than 1. I will show that the forward partial Hausdorff distance for point sets under translation, using the L_∞ norm, has $\Omega(n^3)$ complexity. Fix ε and n and construct A and B as in Subsect. 3.3.1. In this construction, B has $2n + 2$ points. Add $\lfloor (2n + 2)(1/f_F - 1) \rfloor$ points to B, far away from all the other points in the construction. Call this larger set B'. B' contains $\lfloor (2n + 2)/f_F \rfloor$ points.

Now note that any translation t of B' where the original B is contained in A^ε causes the partial Hausdorff distance from B' to A, $h_{Tr}(B' \oplus t, A)$, to be no greater than ε, and any translation t where $B \oplus t \not\subseteq A^\varepsilon$ causes $h_{Tr}(B' \oplus t, A) > \varepsilon$. Thus, the partial forward Hausdorff distance from B' to A has the same complexity, as a function of translation, as the complete forward Hausdorff distance from B to A had, namely $\Omega(n^3)$. B' contains $O(n)$ points, and so the partial forward Hausdorff distance under translation has $\Omega(n^3)$ complexity, no matter what the value of f_F is.

This also applies to the undirected partial Hausdorff distance: the construction already had $h_{Tr}(A, B \oplus t) \leq \varepsilon$ for any t of interest, so that the value of the undirected distance was determined by the forward distance. Adding points to B, or lowering the reverse fraction f_R below 1 can only lower the value of the reverse distance, which has no effect in the region of interest.

This same technique of adding outliers to B also works for all the other constructions involving point sets. It is also not affected if the box-reverse distance is used, since the reverse distance cannot be increased by restricting the points of A which contribute to it, and so can never be the determining factor in the undirected distance.

The definition of the partial Hausdorff distance can be extended to sets of line segments by defining it in terms of the fraction of one set's total segment length, instead of the fraction of points, closer than ε to something in the other set. This same technique can then also be used to extend the lower bounds for the Hausdorff distance between sets of points and line segments to the partial Hausdorff distance.

3.12 Summary

I have presented constructions which give lower bounds on the complexity of the directed (and, in many cases, the undirected) Hausdorff distance in several different contexts, summarised in Table 3.1. In a number of the cases, I have shown that the directed and undirected Hausdorff distances can have large complexity in small space; I have also shown how some of these bounds can be extended to apply to the partial Hausdorff distance. The large exponents in these bounds imply that, to solve these problems, either one will have to approximate the Hausdorff distance, or come up with algorithms that can somehow get around them.

I have demonstrated the complexity of the Hausdorff distance as a function of transformation by constructing cases where it has a large number of local minima. A related question is the number of *global* minima that it can have. In some cases, such as the constructions for point sets under translation with the L_1 or L_∞ norms, it is possible to make the function have equal values at all of the local minima that I have constructed, so that they are all (equal) global minima; in other cases, the number of global minima is an open question.

The problems for which lower bounds on the complexity of the undirected Hausdorff distance were not shown were those involving sets of points and line segments, plus the problem of point sets under translation and scale with the L_∞ norm. A remaining open problem is that of determining bounds for these cases. For example, can the *undirected* Hausdorff distance under translation between sets of points and segments have any complexity greater than $\Omega(n^3)$? Also, is it possible to develop algorithms such as those in [CK1] which find the minimum Hausdorff distance under the action of some transformation group in less time than that given by the complexity of the graph of the Hausdorff distance function?

The $\Omega(n^4)$ example shown in Sect. 3.4 is due to Paul Chew and Klara Kedem. Much of this chapter has been previously published as [Ru3].

Chapter 4

Rasterisation

In the previous chapter, I showed that exact combinatorial algorithms that compute the transformation minimising the Hausdorff distance are likely to be prohibitively expensive to compute, not to mention difficult to implement; implementations of such algorithms are unsuitable for many real-world applications. Since using exact algorithms is infeasible, I have developed algorithms that compute an approximation to the minimum Hausdorff distance under transformation. In this chapter, I present such approximate algorithms, and develop bounds on the approximation errors introduced. I will show in Chap. 5 how these algorithms may be computed efficiently, with no further loss in accuracy.

In many applications, the input image and model point sets do not contain points at arbitrary locations, but instead contain only points located on some integer grid. Such a point set is essentially a binary array: every location on the integer grid, within some bounds, is either a member of the set or not; any location outside these bounds is not a member of the set. This restriction to integer coordinates is generally because the point sets are the result of some feature detector that produces a binary array as output. For example, a thresholded scanned document is such a binary array, as is the output of many commonly used edge detectors. More arbitrary point sets could also be rounded to lie on an integer grid, with as small a loss of precision as desired. I restrict the model and image point sets to be such bounded, finite, integer point sets. I also assume that the image and model point sets lie only in the first quadrant: all the image and model points have integral, nonnegative x and y coordinates. This assumption can be made without loss of generality if the transformation group includes a translational subgroup, which is true for the three translation groups under consideration.

Since the model and image point sets are rasterised, one approach to finding an approximate minimum Hausdorff distance algorithm is to extend this rasterisation. I impose a grid on the transformation group being searched, and consider only the transformations lying on this grid, rather than any transformation in the (presumably continuous) space, as is done by the exact algorithms mentioned in Sect. 3.1. The resolution of this transformation grid is determined by the resolution and sizes of the input arrays: the grid's fineness (or **pitch**) is determined by the pitch of the image and model grid. This chapter discusses such a rasterisation of transformation space, as follows: Section 4.1 shows how to develop such a grid once the image and model are known, Sect. 4.2 shows how to compute the minimum Hausdorff distance for all transformations lying on this grid, Sect. 4.3 discusses the distance transform, a technique used to perform this computation, and Sect. 4.4 discusses how large an error can be introduced by this rasterisation.

The lower bound constructions presented in the previous chapter for point sets all had the property that the minimum spacing between points had to be very small with respect to the overall size of the sets, and with respect to the value of ε, the allowable uncertainty. In practice, the minimum spacing between points in the image is not many orders of magnitude smaller than the overall size of the image, as the smallest distance between points is one step on the image grid, and the image's size is unlikely to be larger than a few thousand pixels, even when the image is a high-resolution scan of a page. Also, in many of the lower bound constructions, all of the local minima lay in a very small region of transformation space. These potential regions of high complexity in the graph of the Hausdorff distance do not cause problems in the rasterised case, as every transformation in such a complex region is approximated by the same transformation, lying on the grid of transformations.

4.1 How To Rasterise

It is possible to impose a grid on the space of transformations only if it is a vector space of some form, where a transformation is determined by the settings of some number of real-valued parameters. This is the case for the three transformation groups discussed in Sect. 2.3: they are vector spaces of two, four, and six dimensions respectively. The rasterisation techniques and error bounds given in this chapter do not apply only to these three groups, but are more general in scope.

As the input data sets (the image and model) are bounded sets of points with integral coordinates, lying in the first quadrant, they can be considered to be binary arrays (arrays of zeros and ones), with "1" pixels representing feature points. Here, I discuss the case where one dimension of the image array corresponds to the x axis, and the other to the y axis of the image plane. If the image and model arrays lie in some other space (for example (r, θ)), some of the techniques presented in this chapter may be applicable, but this has not been investigated in detail. It may also be possible to apply these techniques to problems involving higher-dimensional images (for example, where the image and model are three-dimensional binary arrays). The basic assumption, then, about the image and model is that there is an underlying grid, called the image grid, in the space containing the image; all points in the image and the model lie on this grid (all points have integer coordinates).

How should the transformation space be rasterised, given a particular pair of image and model arrays? This rasterisation is equivalent to by choosing a parameterisation of the transformation space (as several different parameterisations may be possible), and a basis for the transformation parameter space. The unit vector in each basis direction determines the grid pitch in that dimension (i.e., how finely the corresponding parameter is quantised). The idea here is to make this as uniform a quantisation as possible. Suppose that two transformations g and $\hat{g}$ are directly adjacent on the grid of transformations: they have identical parameters, except in one dimension, in which they differ by only one grid step. This small change in the transformation parameters should produce only a small change in the transformed model. Thus, for any model point $m \in M$, $g(m)$ and $\hat{g}(m)$ should be neighbours on the image grid: their coordinates differ by at most one grid step, and they differ only in one dimension.

This implies that the basis vectors should be divided into two types: the x-linked basis vectors and the y-linked basis vectors. Changing a transformation by some amount in an x-linked dimension causes the transformed model points to change only in x; changing a y-linked dimension causes the transformed model points to change only in y. A transformation g in a transformation space with n_x x-linked dimensions and n_y y-linked dimensions (so $n_x + n_y$ total dimensions or parameters) consists of a tuple

$$\left[g_{x.1}, \ldots, g_{x.n_x}, g_{y.1}, \ldots, g_{y.n_y} \right].$$

If all the $g_{x.i}$ and $g_{y.i}$ are integers, then g lies on the grid in transformation space. The set of x-linked coordinates $g_{x.1}$ through $g_{x.n_x}$ is referred to collectively as g_x; similarly, g_y refers to the $g_{y.1}$ through $g_{y.n_y}$ coordinates of g.

A more formal way to state that neighbouring transformations should produce neighbouring transformed points is the following condition, called the **transformation uniformity condition**. Let $1 \leq i \leq n_x$. Suppose that g and $\hat{g}$ are identical in every coordinate except that $\hat{g}_{x.i} = g_{x.i} + 1$. Let m be any point of the model M, $\mu = g(m)$ and $\hat{\mu} = \hat{g}(m)$. Then the transformation uniformity condition states that

$$\mu_x \leq \hat{\mu}_x \leq \mu_x + 1$$
$$\hat{\mu}_y = \mu_y$$

must be true. A similar condition must also hold for any of the y-linked dimensions. In other words, changing the parameters of a transformation by one unit in one x-linked dimension moves the transformed model points in x only, and by at most one unit. Also, the direction that the transformed points move in is the same as the direction that the transformation parameter changed in: if some x-linked parameter increased, then the x coordinates of the transformed points cannot have decreased. This condition only applies if m is a point of the model M; if a point p is, for example, far outside the bounds of the model M, then $g(p)$ and $\hat{g}(p)$ can be far apart.

A further issue in determining the rasterisation is that the identity transformation should lie on the grid: it must be an integral linear combination of the basis vectors. This is usually not hard to achieve.

The grid should also not be made finer than is necessary. The transformation uniformity condition says that no transformed model point should move by more than one unit as the transformation changes by one unit. Also, some transformed model point should move by *exactly* one unit as the transformation changes by one unit. If this is not the case, then two distinct transformations might produce identical transformed models, once the model points have been rounded; this is wasteful.

These constraints allow me to prove some very useful results about the effects of restricting transformations to those lying on the grid. These are presented in Sect. 4.4.

Typically, the transformation space has some natural, or commonly-used, parameterisation. Either this natural parameterisation can be discretised in some fashion, giving a set of basis vectors which satisfy the transformation uniformity condition, or it can be transformed and then discretised. To avoid confusion, I use square brackets to denote the parameters of a transformation in the discretised parameterisation (the parameterisation obeying the transformation uniformity condition). Thus, if the natural parameterisation of a certain transformation g in a three-dimensional transformation space is $g = (a, b, c)$, and $g = pe_1 + qe_2 + re_3$ (where e_1, e_2 and e_3 are the three basis vectors of the rasterisation), then g can also be denoted as $g = [p, q, r]$. The transformation lies on the raster grid exactly when its parameters in this new basis are integers.

Applying these principles to rasterising the three transformation groups described in the previous chapter yields the following parameterisations:

Translation The transformation space is the space of all translations (t_x, t_y). This is rasterised by simply restricting t_x and t_y to be integers; there is one x-linked dimension (t_x) and one y-linked dimension (t_y). The transformation uniformity condition clearly holds: increasing t_x by one simply increases the x-coordinate of every transformed model point by one. The identity transformation is just the translation $(0, 0)$, which lies on the grid.

Translation and scale The basic parameterisation has four parameters: s_x, s_y, t_x and t_y; the transformation (s_x, s_y, t_x, t_y) maps any point $m = (m_x, m_y) \in M$ to $(s_x m_x + t_x, s_y m_y + t_y)$. Quantising this parameterisation involves determining four basis vectors e_1 through e_4 such that the transformation uniformity condition holds. Each vector must be classified as x-linked or y-linked.

Let $M_x = \max_{m \in M} m_x$ and $M_y = \max_{m \in M} m_y$. The points in the model are bounded by $0 \le m_x \le M_x$ and $0 \le m_y \le M_y$ for all $(m_x, m_y) \in M$. Then the four basis vectors are $e_1 = (1/M_x, 0, 0, 0)$, $e_2 = (0, 1/M_y, 0, 0)$, $e_3 = (0, 0, 1, 0)$ and $e_4 = (0, 0, 0, 1)$. e_1 and e_3 are x-linked; e_2 and e_4 are y-linked. The transformation uniformity condition clearly holds for e_3 and e_4, as they are purely translational components. For e_1 and e_2, it holds also, since if g is a transformation and $m = (m_x, m_y)$ is some point of the model, then $(g + e_1)(m) - g(m) = (m_x/M_x, 0)$, which is a displacement in the positive x direction of no more than one unit, as is required by the condition. The identity transformation, $(1, 1, 0, 0)$ clearly lies on the grid, at $[M_x, M_y, 0, 0]$, since it is $M_x e_1 + M_y e_2$, and M_x and M_y are integral. The transformation $[a, b, c, d]$ (in the raster basis) is the same as the transformation $(a/M_x, b/M_y, c, d)$ (in the natural basis): a scaling in x by a/M_x, in y by b/M_y, and a translation by (c, d).

Note that this rasterisation, unlike that for the translation group, depends on the model M: larger models cause the scale dimensions of transformation space to be sliced more finely.

Affine transformation The group of affine transformations can be parameterised by six parameters. These might be a rotation, a shear, two scaling and two translation parameters, or three rotation and three translation parameters describing the motion of a rigid body in three dimensions. However, such parameterisations are difficult to adapt to the transformation uniformity condition. Instead, I parameterise this group by six parameters, $(t_{00}, t_{01}, t_{10}, t_{11}, t_x, t_y)$, defining the mapping

$$(x, y) \rightarrow (t_{00}x + t_{01}y + t_x, t_{10}x + t_{11}y + t_y)$$

which is left-multiplication of the vector $[x\ y]'$ by the matrix

$$T = \begin{bmatrix} t_{00} & t_{01} \\ t_{10} & t_{11} \end{bmatrix}.$$

followed by translation by (t_x, t_y). I rasterise this parameterisation using six basis vectors e_1 through e_6, defined by

$$e_1 = \left(\tfrac{1}{M_x}, 0, 0, 0, 0, 0 \right)$$

$$e_2 = \left(0, \tfrac{1}{M_y}, 0, 0, 0, 0\right)$$

$$e_3 = \left(0, 0, \tfrac{1}{M_x}, 0, 0, 0\right)$$

$$e_4 = \left(0, 0, 0, \tfrac{1}{M_y}, 0, 0\right)$$

$$e_5 = (0, 0, 0, 0, 1, 0)$$

$$e_6 = (0, 0, 0, 0, 0, 1)$$

where M_x and M_y are bounds on the model points, as above.

Given these definitions, e_1, e_2 and e_5 are x-linked; e_3, e_4 and e_6 are y-linked. The transformation uniformity condition holds, in the same manner as above: adding any x-linked basis vector to a transformation adds some value between 0 and 1 to the x coordinate of any transformed model point, without affecting the y coordinate; the y-linked basis vectors behave analogously. With this rasterisation, the raster basis transformation $[a, b, c, d, e, f]$ is the same as the natural basis transformation $(a/M_x, b/M_y, c/M_x, d/M_y, e, f)$.

I now introduce some notation for dealing with both the rasterised and continuous versions of transformations. The basic notation is that angle brackets, $\langle \cdot \rangle$, represent a rounding function. Also, square brackets are used to distinguish between the continuous and discrete versions of functions: the function notated with square brackets has some implicit rounding property, which is not present in the original version.

Suppose that g is a transformation, and $m \in M$ is a point of the model. Then $\langle g(m) \rangle$ denotes the result of applying g to m and rounding this to the nearest point on the image grid, by rounding in each dimension. I also write this as $g[m]$, making the rounding after the application of g implicit. $g[M]$ denotes the result of rounding each point of $g(M)$. Note that this is a multiset: several distinct points in M can transform to the same point in $g[M]$, and (for counting purposes) should be kept distinct. The Hausdorff distance requires no modifications to be extended to multisets.

Recall that $D_G(g)$ is defined as $H(g(M), I)$: the Hausdorff distance between the image I and the transformed model $g(M)$. $D_G[g]$ is then defined as $H(g[M], I)$: the distance between the image I and the rounded transformed model $g[M]$. $d_G[g]$ is similarly defined as $h(g[M], I)$, and $d'_G[g]$ as $h(I, g[M])$. In general, I actually use the partial versions of these functions (i.e., the partial Hausdorff distance from Sect. 2.4). $d_G[g]$ is thus computed by taking each point of M, transforming it by g, rounding the result, and determining the distance to the closest point of I. The f_Fth quantile of these distance values (one value for each point of M) is then the value of $d_G[g]$. Similarly, $d'_G[g]$ is computed by determining the distance from each point of I lying under the transformed model box (see Sect. 2.5) to the closest point of $g[M]$; the f_Rth quantile value of these distances is then $d'_G[g]$.

4.2 Computing the Minimum Hausdorff Distance

As I showed in Sect. 2.4, to make the Hausdorff distance useful in practice, it must be modified so when it is being evaluated, a certain fraction of the model and image (the worst-fitting portions) can be ignored as outliers, due to noise, occlusion, or other causes. The parameters involved, the forward fraction f_F and the reverse fraction f_R, determine what fraction of the model and image respectively should be used when the Hausdorff distance is computed (i.e., $1 - f_F$ is the fraction of the model points to be considered outliers; f_F is therefore the fraction of inliers). As I noted in Chap. 2, the forward and reverse Hausdorff distances as a function of transformation, $d_G(g)$ and $d'_G(g)$, are considered to be implicitly parameterised by f_F and f_R; the reverse distance is also considered to be the box-reverse distance from Sect. 2.5.

Once the space of transformations has been discretised, the task is that of determining the grid transformation g that minimises the Hausdorff distance between the image I and the (rounded) transformed model $g[M]$. In many cases, however, a better task might be to find not just the best (minimising) transformation, but instead find all transformations that bring the image and transformed model close to one another. More precisely, find all transformations g that satisfy the following two criteria:

Forward criterion The partial forward distance, $d_G[g]$ (recall that this is implicitly parameterised by f_F) must be no more than the **forward threshold** τ_F. As in Subsect. 2.4.1, f_F is referred to as the forward fraction.

Reverse criterion The partial box-reverse distance, $d'_G[g]$, (implicitly parameterised by f_R) must be no more than the **reverse threshold** τ_R. f_R is referred to as the reverse fraction.

f_F, f_R, τ_F and τ_R are set by the user to control which transformations are reported. A transformation satisfying both the forward and reverse criteria is called a **match**.

These criteria can also be viewed in a different way. Let g be some transformation. The forward distance $d_G[g]$ is below τ_F exactly when at least $\lceil f_F \#(M) \rceil$ of the transformed and rounded model points lie within τ_F of some image point. This leads to a new function, $f_G[g]$, defined by

$$f_G[g] = \frac{\#\left(\{m \in M \mid \Delta(g[m]) \le \tau_F\}\right)}{\#(M)}. \tag{4.1}$$

This function, which is implicitly parameterised by τ_F, is the *fraction* of all the model points that, when transformed by g and rounded, lie within τ_F of some image point. $f'_G[g]$ can be defined similarly: it is the fraction of the image points which lie within τ_R of some model points, out of the image points lying underneath the transformed model box (i.e., out of the image points which contribute to the box-reverse distance).

Given these definitions, it is possible to reformulate the forward and reverse criteria in terms of f_G and f'_G:

Forward criterion $f_G[g]$ must be at least f_F.
Reverse criterion $f'_G[g]$ must be at least f_R.

These new formulations are exactly equivalent to the original ones: from the definition of the partial Hausdorff distance, $d_G[g] \le \tau_F$ exactly when $f_G[g] \ge f_F$, and similarly for d'_G and f'_G. It is easier to make some observations when they are phrased in terms of f_G and f'_G rather than d_G and d'_G.

One such observation is that the function f_G is similar to the binary operation of dilate-and-correlate: suppose for the moment that the model is allowed to translate only (i.e., G is the group of translations Tr). Dilate the image by replacing each point with a circle of radius τ_F, translate the model by some g, and count how many model points land inside the dilated image. Considered as a function of g, this is exactly the same as correlating the model and the dilated image (treated as binary arrays). It is also equal to $\#(M)f_G[g]$. In this case, therefore, $f_G[g]$ is a scaled version of this dilate-and-correlate function. The forward criterion can then be looked on as a generalisation of binary correlation from Subsect. 1.2.7: if τ_F is zero, then f_G is a scaled version of the binary correlation function; the forward criterion therefore specifies exactly those places where the binary correlation of the image and model point sets exceeds some threshold. The correlation function, however, has no equivalent to the reverse distance or reverse criterion.

If G is not the group of translations, then this is no longer dilate-and-correlate, but instead is a generalisation of the same concept.

4.2.1 Bounding the Search

The transformation groups I am considering are all unbounded: there are an infinite number of transformations lying on the grid. It is possible to determine bounds on the possible location of matches in transformation space, so that any transformation lying outside these bounds cannot be of interest; this reduces the problem to that of examining a finite number of transformations. Here I present an example of such bounds for the translation-only transformation space Tr.

Let $I_x = \max_{i \in I} i_x$ and $I_y = \max_{i \in I} i_y$. Points in the image are then bounded by $0 \le i_x \le I_x$ and $0 \le i_y \le I_y$ for any $i = (i_x, i_y) \in I$. Let M_x and M_y be the upper bounds on the model points' coordinates, as before. Now, any translation (t_x, t_y) where either $t_x < -M_x - \tau_F$ or $t_x > I_x + \tau_F$, and either $t_y < -M_y - \tau_F$ or $t_y > I_y + \tau_F$ cannot possibly be a match: any such translation places every translated model point further than τ_F from any image point, so the forward criterion cannot be satisfied. Thus, only translations where $-M_x - \tau_F \le t_x \le I_x + \tau_F$ and $-M_y - \tau_F \le t_y \le I_y + \tau_F$ must be considered.

These bounds can actually be tightened further by examining the model. Consider expanding the image rectangle by τ_F on every side, giving the **expanded image rectangle** $[-\tau_F, I_x + \tau_F] \times [-\tau_F, I_y + \tau_F]$. Now, any translation where the fraction of model points lying outside the expanded image rectangle is more than $1 - f_F$ can be ruled out. This can be determined by simply counting the number of model points in each row or column, and tightening the translation bounds appropriately.

In the more general case, any transformation that transforms a large number of model points to locations outside the expanded image rectangle can be ruled out, because it cannot satisfy the forward criterion. Since the transformed model points are rounded after being transformed, two distinct transformations that generate the same set of rounded model points can be considered to be the same, and so only one of them needs to be considered. Put together, these statements imply that any transformation grid can be reduced to a finite grid, because there are only a finite number of possible transformed model point locations inside the expanded image rectangle. This observation is not very practical, though, as the number of transformations is still large.

In the case of the three transformation groups under consideration, and in most other cases, tighter bounds can be determined by using the transformation uniformity condition. The key point here is the monotonic aspect of the transformation uniformity condition: increasing the parameters of a transformation cannot decrease the coordinates of the transformed model points. Increasing some x-linked parameter causes all the transformed points' x coordinates to increase; in most cases, eventually sufficiently many points in the transformed model leave the expanded image rectangle, and so any transformation with a larger value of that parameter can be ruled out. Similarly, as the parameters are decreased, no transformed model point's coordinates can increase, so eventually enough points leave the expanded image rectangle, and so a lower bound on the transformation parameters can be determined.

4.2.2 Locating Matches

Finding all matches is now simple: enumerate all the transformations on the grid of transformations, lying within the bounds computed as described in the previous subsection. Determine, for each one, if it satisfies the forward and reverse criteria. Report all those which do.

This process has at its heart the **evaluation** of transformations: it computes for each transformation g the forward and reverse distances $d_G[g]$ and $d'_G[g]$, (i.e., $h^{f_F}(g[M], I)$ and $h^{f_R}_{\text{box}}(I, g[M])$), using the partial and box-reverse variants. It can also simultaneously compute $f_G[g]$ and $f'_G[g]$; I will show in Chap. 5 how these can be useful when considering how to accelerate this search process. Each of these transformation evaluations involves computing, for each point of $g[M]$, the closest point in I, and vice versa. In the following section, I describe the distance transform, which allows these distances to be pre-computed.

4.3   The Distance Transform

Computing $h(g[M], I)$ for some transformation g involves finding the distance from each point of $g[M]$ to the nearest point of I; finding all those transformations satisfying the forward and reverse criteria involves many such distance determinations. Since all the points of $g[M]$ lie on the image grid, this computation can be made significantly more efficient by pre-computing an array of these distance values: compute an array Δ such that $\Delta[x, y]$ (for integer x, y) is the distance from the point (x, y) to the closest point of I. This array is called the **distance transform** or **Voronoi surface** (by analogy to the Voronoi diagram) of I; it is the rasterised version of the continuous nearest neighbour function defined in (2.11).

A more formal definition of this is

$$\Delta[x, y] = \min_{i \in I} \|(x, y) - i\| . \tag{4.2}$$

$\Delta[x, y]$ is zero exactly when $(x, y) \in I$. The graph of the function $\Delta[x, y]$, considered as a three-dimensional surface, looks something like an egg carton: consider a collection of cones, of slope one, extending upwards from the plane. Each cone has its point at a

Fig. 4.1. The distance transform, or Voronoi surface, of a point set.

point of I. $\Delta[x, y]$ is the lower envelope of these cones. The shape of the cones depends on the norm in the plane: for L_2, they are true cones; for L_1 or L_∞ they are cones with square cross-sections. Figure 4.1 shows such a surface, generated for the L_2 norm. This figure shows the three-dimensional graph of $\Delta[x, y]$, viewed from below; each cone is coloured differently, to make the lines where they intersect more evident. The point set I which generated this surface is shown in Fig. 4.2.

The curves along which these cones meet are the ridge lines of the distance transform function. These ridge lines correspond (in the exact case) to the Voronoi edges of I, dividing the plane into Voronoi cells (see [PS1] for more details on these); this is the origin of the term Voronoi surface. Points lying along these ridge lines are equidistant from two of the points of I.

$\Delta[x, y]$ is a discrete version of the continuous $\Delta(\cdot)$ function defined in (2.11). Ideally, it should simply be a grid-sampled version of that continuous function: for every grid point $c = (x, y)$, $\Delta[x, y] = \Delta(c)$. In some cases, however, it is more practical to use an approximation to this exact sampling.

In this section, I primarily discuss the computation of the distance transform of the image I, which is used in the computing the forward Hausdorff distance. The reverse Hausdorff distance from the image I to the transformed model $g[M]$ is computed using the distance transform of $g[M]$, which can be computed using the same methods. Note that this distance transform may have to be recomputed for each different transformation g, while the distance transform of the image does not. However, in the case when G is

Fig. 4.2. The point set I generating Fig. 4.1.

the group of translations, the transformed model's distance transform does not change shape as the transformation varies, but instead keeps the same shape and undergoes shifts only. This means that the same distance transform array can be used for any transformed model, as long as the coordinates are adjusted appropriately before the array is accessed. Other transformation groups that include a translational subgroup (such as Sc and Aff) can also benefit from this: two transformations which differ only in their translational components can use the same distance transform array for the transformed model.

In practice, $\Delta[x, y]$ is represented as an array, and so the question of how large this array should be arises. Since the search only needs to find transformations satisfying the forward criterion, distances of greater than τ_F can be treated simply as "large". This means that it is always sufficient to compute a $\Delta[x, y]$ as large as the expanded image rectangle from Subsect. 4.2.2: it should be as large as the image I, plus borders of τ_F pixels on every side.

There are several different approaches to computing the distance transform $\Delta[x, y]$ of the image I. The class of **chamfer methods**, described in [Bo1, Da1, LL1], compute only an approximation to $\Delta[x, y]$ for the L_2 norm, though for the L_1 and L_∞ norms they compute $\Delta[x, y]$ exactly. The L_2 norm can be approximated to within 2% with one method [Bo1], and to within 0.09 pixels with another method [Da1, LL1]; other methods with different accuracies are also known. However, there is a tradeoff involved: the faster methods are less accurate, and the more accurate methods are slower. These chamfer distance transform methods are described in Sect. A.1. In any case, one requirement, imposed by implementation restrictions, is that the values in the distance transform array must be integers, and so any floating point values computed must be scaled (for example, by a factor of 100, to represent them to within 0.005), and rounded.

If even small errors in the distances (before scaling and rounding) are unacceptable, there are several methods which compute the exact (to within the minimum error allowed by the representation) L_2 distance transform. Two such methods are described in [Pa1] and [Ka1]. The method described in [Pa1] has the disadvantage that its running time, on a $m \times n$ distance transform array, is $O(m^2 n)$ in the worst case, while that in [Ka1] is $O(mn)$, which is optimal. However, in most cases, the method in [Pa1] runs in $O(mn)$ time. In any case, the actual running times are longer than the approximate methods above. I describe the method of [Ka1] in Sect. A.2; a very similar method is also described in [BGKW1].

If graphics hardware designed for three-dimensional rendering is available, it is possible to use it to compute the distance transform array. This relies on the characterisation of the distance transform as the lower envelope of a number of cones in three dimensions; this is described in more detail in Sect. A.3. In fact, a slight modification of exactly this distance transform calculation was used to produce Fig. 4.1.

4.4 Bounds on Rasterisation Error

Rasterising transformation space, as described in Sect. 4.1, involves replacing the continuous space of transformations with a discrete one. This process, while necessary, nonetheless introduces error into the computation of the transformation minimising the Hausdorff distance, as almost all transformations are no longer considered. Using the distance transform described in Sect. 4.3 also introduces error, since the transformed model points must be rounded to the nearest image grid location as part of the transformation evaluation process. This section quantifies how large the effects of these errors can be. I assume that the distance transform $\Delta[x, y]$ is exact (i.e., it is not, for example, one of the approximate L_2 distance transforms. This ensures that $\Delta[x, y]$ is just a grid-sampled version of the exact distance transform, $\Delta(\cdot)$.

The following lemma shows that a small perturbation of the points in one set has only a small effect on the (continuous, unrounded) Hausdorff distance.

Lemma 4.1. *Suppose that* $h(M, I) = d$. *Let* M' *be obtained by perturbing each point of* M *by some displacement of magnitude at most* δ. *Then the value of* $h(M', I)$ *can be bounded by*

$$d - \delta \leq h(M', I) \leq d + \delta.$$

This also holds for the partial Hausdorff distance $h^{f_F}(M, I)$, *no matter what value of* f_F *is used.*

Proof. Since $h(M, I)$ is just a special case of $h^{f_F}(M, I)$, consider only h^{f_F}.

Let m be a point of M and m' be the corresponding point of M'. Then $\|m - m'\| \leq \delta$. Suppose that m's nearest neighbour in I is i. Then $\Delta(m) = \|m - i\|$ by definition. Now,

$$\begin{aligned}
\Delta(m') &\leq \|m' - i\| \\
&\leq \|m - i\| + \|m - i'\| \\
&\leq \Delta(m) + \delta
\end{aligned}$$

by the definition of Δ and the triangle inequality. A symmetric argument shows that $\Delta(m) \leq \Delta(m') - \delta$ and so $\Delta(m')$ is bounded by $\Delta(m) \pm \delta$.

$h^{f_F}(M, I)$ is computed by taking $\#(M)$ values of Δ, one from the location of each point of M, and computing the f_Fth quantile of these values. Let $K = \lceil f_F \#(M) \rceil$. Then K of these values of Δ must be no greater than d. $h^{f_F}(M', I)$ is also computed from $\#(M)$ values of Δ, one from the location of each point of M'. Each of these values is within δ of the corresponding value used to compute $h^{f_F}(M, I)$. Thus, in the computation of $h^{f_F}(M', I)$, there must be K values no greater than $d + \delta$, and so the f_Fth quantile (i.e., $h^{f_F}(M', I)$) must be no greater than $d + \delta$. There are also $\#(M) - K + 1$ values of Δ in this computation that are greater than or equal to $d - \delta$; the f_Fth quantile value therefore cannot be lower than $d - \delta$. Thus, $h^{f_F}(M', I)$ is bounded by $h^{f_F}(M, I) \pm \delta$. $\square$

Lemma 4.1 also applies to the reverse distance, $h^{f_R}(I, M)$, and the undirected Hausdorff distance $H^{f_F f_R}(M, I)$, as long as the box-reverse distance is not used. In practice, however, the box-reverse distance is almost invariably used. In this case, even a slight perturbation of the points of I can lead to a large change in $h^{f_R}_{\text{box}}(I, M)$, since points of I might move into or out of the box lying under M, greatly changing the Hausdorff distance.

I can now show a bound on the maximum error in the minimum Hausdorff distance caused by rasterising transformation space and rounding transformed points.

Theorem 4.2. *Let g^* be a transformation of M which minimises $d_G(\cdot)$. Let $\hat{g}^*$ be a transformation of M, lying on the grid imposed on the space of transformations, which minimises $d_G[\cdot]$. Then*

$$d_G[\hat{g}^*] \leq d_G(g^*) + \|(n_x/2, n_y/2)\| + \|(1/2, 1/2)\|,$$

where $\| \cdot \|$ is the norm used in (x, y) space.

Proof. For any transformation g, $d_G[g]$ and $d_G(g)$ differ by no more than $\|(1/2, 1/2)\|$. In other words, rounding the points of M after they have been transformed by g makes only a small difference to d_G. This follows from an application of Lemma 4.1: rounding each point of $g(M)$ can move it by at most half a unit in each dimension. Its total movement, measured by the (x, y) space norm, is therefore at most $\|(1/2, 1/2)\|$.

Now, let $\langle g \rangle$ be the result of rounding g to the nearest point which lies on the grid of transformations, by rounding it in each of the transformation parameter dimensions. Then each coordinate of $\langle g \rangle$ differs from the corresponding coordinate of g by at most $1/2$. Let m be a point of M. Then the x coordinates of $\langle g \rangle(m)$ and $g(m)$ differ by at most $n_x/2$, since a change of $1/2$ in one of the x-linked coordinates of transformation space produces a motion of at most $1/2$ in x for any transformed point of M. Similarly, the y coordinates of $\langle g \rangle(m)$ and $g(m)$ differ by at most $n_y/2$. By Lemma 4.1, $d_G(g)$ and $d_G(\langle g \rangle)$ differ by at most $\|(n_x/2, n_y/2)\|$.

Combining these two observations, we see that $d_G(g)$ and $d_G[\langle g \rangle]$ differ by at most $\|(n_x/2, n_y/2)\| + \|(1/2, 1/2)\|$. This is the maximum total effect of rounding both the transformation and the transformed points. Thus, for any transformation g, $d_G[\langle g \rangle] \leq d_G(g) + \|(n_x/2, n_y/2)\| + \|(1/2, 1/2)\|$. Since $\langle g^* \rangle$ lies on the grid of transformations, and since $\hat{g}^*$ minimises $d_G[\cdot]$ for all transformations lying on the grid, we must have $d_G[\hat{g}^*] \leq d_G(g^*) + \|(n_x/2, n_y/2)\| + \|(1/2, 1/2)\|$, as required.

Further, note that if the space of transformations is such that any point of M transformed by any transformation lying on the grid always has integral coordinates, then the bound is $d_G[\hat{g}^*] \leq d_G(g^*) + \|(n_x/2, n_y/2)\|$, since the second term due to rounding the transformed points is no longer applicable, and so $d_G[\cdot]$ is simply a discrete sampling of $d_G(\cdot)$. This is the case when G is the group of translations. □

Table 4.1 shows the results of applying Theorem 4.2 to the three rasterisations presented in Sect. 4.1. Here, I am assuming that the norm used in (x, y) space is the L_2 norm. Note that the bound for the translation group is lower than the simple bound from Theorem 4.2, since no rounding of transformed points is necessary. These bounds are for the worst-case error; in practice, I have found that these bounds are never approached. Typical errors in practice are at most about half the worst-case errors.

4.5 Summary

In this chapter, I addressed the problems of exact computation of the minimum Hausdorff distance by imposing a discrete grid on the continuous space of transformations. I introduced the transformation uniformity condition to determine how this grid should be

Table 4.1. Bounds on error due to rasterisation and rounding.

Transformation group	n_x	n_y	Maximum error (pixels)
Translation	1	1	$\frac{1}{2}\sqrt{2}$
Translation and scale	2	2	$\frac{3}{2}\sqrt{2}$
Affine transformation	3	3	$2\sqrt{2}$

designed. I then showed how the grid may be bounded, so that no transformation lying outside the bounds can be of interest.

I also developed bounds on the maximum error introduced by the rasterisation of transformation space. The transformation uniformity condition limits the error to a small number of pixels.

Some of this work has been previously published in [HR1, HR2, HKR1, HKR2, HKR3].

Chapter 5

Efficient Computation

The exhaustive search of transformation space described in Sect. 4.2 locates all transformations satisfying the forward and reverse criteria (i.e., all matches of the transformed model to the image). However, it does this extremely inefficiently, especially when there are many transformations to be considered, as it is simply a brute-force search of the transformation grid within certain bounds. This is especially bad when the transformation space has high dimension.

This chapter presents several approaches to increasing the efficiency of this search. These approaches are all based around the principle that nothing should be missed: if a match exists, it must be found. Thus, the search algorithm must manage to eliminate most of the transformations from consideration, and process those that remain efficiently, while ensuring that a good transformation can never be accidentally eliminated; all the techniques it uses must be **guaranteed**. It must also never report anything as a match unless it actually is one, but this is not difficult to achieve.

Many of these techniques work solely with the forward distance and the forward criterion; they do not consider the reverse distance. This is because the forward distance is more constrained than the reverse distance. In particular, Lemma 4.1 applies to the forward distance, partial or not, but does not apply to the box-reverse distance. This makes it more difficult to limit the value of the reverse distance for a transformation, given its value at a nearby transformation.

In practice, I have found the strategy of searching (efficiently) for all transformations that satisfy the forward criterion then rejecting those transformations that do not satisfy the reverse criterion to be successful. Most of the total time is spent in the first, efficient search, phase; the second, verification, phase is almost never a bottleneck.

5.1 Early Rejection

In some cases, it is possible to deduce partway through the computation of $d_G[g]$ that it is greater than τ_F (i.e., that the forward criterion is not satisfied); the overall search process can be speeded up by recognising these situations and not completing the computation of $d_G[g]$. Recall that, for the complete (not partial) Hausdorff distance, $d_G[g]$ is computed by maximizing all the values of $\Delta[g[m]]$ for $m \in M$. That is, each point of M probes a location in the distance transform of I (at its rounded transformed location), and $d_G[g]$ is the maximum of all of these probe values. If a single probe value is over the forward threshold τ_F, then $d_G[g]$ must be over τ_F, and g cannot satisfy the forward criterion; none of the remaining probes need to be performed.

An analogous result holds for the partial distance. Let $K = \lceil f_F \#(M) \rceil$. The value of $d_G[g]$ is the K-th ranked value of $\Delta[g[m]]$, taken over all $m \in M$: probe Δ in $\#(M)$ places, record the results, and pick the K-th ranked value as the value of $d_G[g]$. As this

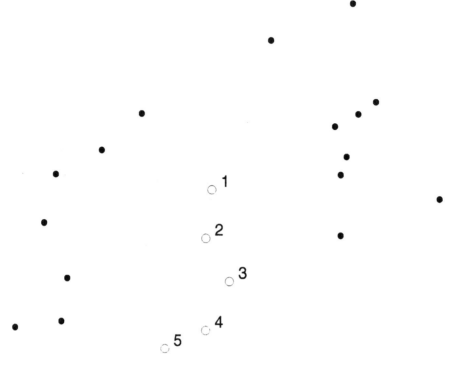

Fig. 5.1. An example of early termination.

is done, a count can be kept of the number of these values from Δ that exceed τ_F. If this count ever exceeds $\#(M) - K$, then the K-th ranked value must be greater than τ_F, and so $d_G[g] > \tau_F$, so no more locations need to be probed for this transformation: no matter what values these probes yielded, the forward criterion could not be satisfied. This method works best for large values of f_F, as the evaluation can then be terminated with a smaller count value; if $f_F = 1$, then, as in the previous case, even a single probe value over τ_F is sufficient to terminate the evaluation.

An example of this is shown in Fig. 5.1. The solid circles represent the points of the image, and the empty circles represent the points of the transformed model. Suppose that $f_F = 0.8$, τ_F is small, and the model points are scanned in the order shown. In this case, $\#(M) = 5$ and $K = 4$. The first model point is used to probe the distance transform of the image; this probe yields a large value (well above τ_F), so the counter is incremented to 1. The second model point is then used to probe Δ; this probe value is also more than τ_F, so the counter is incremented to 2. At this point, there is no need to continue the evaluation of this transformation, as it cannot satisfy the forward criterion.

The probe values accumulated thus far can be used to determine a conservative (low) estimate for $d_G[g]$ at this location, by assuming that the unprobed values are all 0 and calculating the K-th ranked value of this set of values. In the example above, this produces the minimum of the two probes that were actually made; this can be used to eliminate nearby values of (x, y) from consideration, as is described below in Sect. 5.2.

This technique can also be used when the reverse distance is being evaluated, even when the box-reverse distance is used.

5.2 Ruling out Spheres

Define a norm on the (continuous) space of transformations by

$$\|g\| = \left\| \left(\|g_x\|_1 \cdot \|g_y\|_1 \right) \right\|$$
$$= \left\| \left(\sum_{i=1}^{n_x} |g_{x.i}|, \sum_{i=1}^{n_y} |g_{y.i}| \right) \right\| \tag{5.1}$$

where the norm on the right-hand side of the equation is the norm defined on the regular (x, y) space, and $\|\cdot\|_1$ represents the usual multi-dimensional L_1 norm. Note that the parameters $g_{x.i}$ and $g_{y.i}$ are relative to the rasterised basis. If the (x, y) norm is any L_p norm, this new norm can be shown to have all the required norm properties. The following result now holds for the exact (not rasterised) Hausdorff distance:

Theorem 5.1. $|d_G(g) - d_G(\hat{g})| \leq \|g - \hat{g}\|.$

Proof. Let $m = (m_x, m_y)$ be a point of the model M. Then $\hat{g}(m)$ is no more than $\|g - \hat{g}\|$ away from $g(m)$: the x coordinate of $\hat{g}(m)$ can be no more different than $\|g_x - \hat{g}_x\|_1$ from the x coordinate of $g(m)$, since each difference of 1 in one of the x-linked dimensions makes at most a difference of 1 in the x coordinate of the transformed point. Similarly the y coordinates of $\hat{g}(m)$ and $g(m)$ differ by at most $\|g_y - \hat{g}_y\|_1$, and thus

$$\|\hat{g}(m) - g(m)\| \leq \left\| \left(\|g_x - \hat{g}_x\|_1 \cdot \|g_y - \hat{g}_y\|_1 \right) \right\|$$
$$= \|g - \hat{g}\| .$$

Applying Lemma 4.1 then gives the desired result. □

Note that this result holds for the exact directed Hausdorff distance, rather than the rasterised Hausdorff distance. However, it can be extended to the rasterised Hausdorff distance:

Theorem 5.2. *If g and $\hat{g}$ lie on the grid of transformations, then $|d_G[g] - d_G[\hat{g}]| \leq \|g - \hat{g}\|$.*

Proof. A useful property of the rounding function is that, if k is an integer, then $\langle x + k \rangle = \langle x \rangle + k$, no matter how x is rounded (as long as exact halves are consistently rounded either up or down). Also, if $a \leq k$, then $\langle x + a \rangle \leq \langle x \rangle + k$.

The central point of Theorem 5.1 is that for any model point m, $g(m)$ and $\hat{g}(m)$ can be no further than $\|g - \hat{g}\|$ apart. This also applies to $g[m]$ and $\hat{g}[m]$, the rounded results of applying g and $\hat{g}$ to m: the x coordinates of $g(m)$ and $\hat{g}(m)$ differ by no more than $\|g_x - \hat{g}_x\|_1$, and since $\|g_x - \hat{g}_x\|_1$ is integral, the x coordinates of $g[m]$ and $\hat{g}[m]$ differ by no more than $\|g_x - \hat{g}_x\|_1$. A similar result bounds the y coordinates of $g(b)$ and $\hat{g}(b)$; thus, the rounding of the transformed model points is not an issue, and $|d_G[g] - d_G[\hat{g}]| \leq \|g - \hat{g}\|$. □

These results are can be thought of as a sphere in transformation space projecting into a circle in (x, y) space: as a transformation is varied within a sphere (relative to the norm on transformation space just defined), the locus of each transformed point is bounded by a circle whose radius is equal to the radius of the sphere.

This property does not necessarily hold for the box-reverse Hausdorff distance d'_G. The box-reverse distance is computed using only the portion of the image under the model, as described in Sect. 2.5, and so there might be a location where, for example, translating the model by one pixel shifts some image points into or out of the window, which can change the value of d'_G by a large amount. This also implies that the property does not necessarily hold for the undirected Hausdorff distance D_G.

Now, suppose that we are searching for all transformations g of the model where $d_G[g] \leq \tau_F$, using a forward fraction of f_F (i.e., all transformations satisfying the forward criterion). Suppose that, as the search algorithm scans transformation space, it evaluates d_G for some g, and finds that $d_G[g] > \tau_F$. Then it can immediately deduce that $d_G[\hat{g}] > \tau_F$ for all $\hat{g}$ that are near g (closer than $d_G[g] - \tau_F$ to g). These transformations therefore need not be scanned at all, as they cannot possibly satisfy the forward criterion; all the transformations lying in a (hyper-)sphere in transformation space can be ruled out, after evaluating only one transformation. The search algorithm can therefore safely ignore all the transformations within this sphere, without having any chance of missing a transformation satisfying the forward criterion.

Figure 5.2 shows an example of this. The model and image are as in Fig. 5.1. Suppose that we are working over the group of translations, and the position of the model represents the current translation under evaluation. The cross-hair is the origin of the model: the location of its top left corner. Evaluating this translation results in the shaded circle being ruled out: no translation that places the model's origin anywhere in that circle can possibly satisfy the forward criterion. This shows how evaluating a single transformation can rule out quite a large number of transformations. This example was produced using $\tau_F = 0$. A larger value of τ_F results in a smaller circle being ruled out; the circle's radius is reduced by one unit for every unit that τ_F is increased.

In practice, the search algorithm needs to keep track of those grid locations that have been ruled out. For transformation spaces with few dimensions (for example, the group of translations), this can be done easily, by simply marking a two-dimensional array; for higher-dimensional transformation spaces, the overhead (both in memory and time spent marking) of this array may be prohibitive: it may not even be possible to mark off all of the transformations lying on the grid in any reasonable amount of time. Section 5.4 discusses a technique that requires less bookkeeping.

The order in which the grid of transformations is scanned is also significant. Suppose, for the moment, that the search algorithm is operating over a two-dimensional grid, and is scanning the grid in reading order (left-to-right along each row, then along the next row, and so on). It evaluates a certain transformation, and determines that its d_G value allows it to rule out a circle of a certain radius; it marks all the transformations within that circle as ruled out. It then scans forward along the current row, until it encounters a transformation that has not been ruled out, and then evaluates that one. It is likely that this transformation lies on the border of the circle that was just ruled out. This transformation probably causes another circle to be ruled out; however, close to half of this

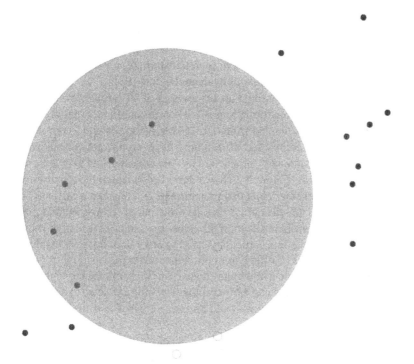

Fig. 5.2. An example of ruling out a circle.

0	8	2	10
4	12	6	14
1	9	3	11
5	13	7	15

Fig. 5.3. A possible scanning order to improve the performance of ruling out circles.

circle overlaps the previous circle, so the search algorithm is, in effect, ruling out some transformations twice. If the second transformation lies in clear space, with no ruled-out transformations near it, then ruling out a circle of the same size around it is more productive. This argues against using simple reading-order scanning, and for evaluating transformations in some other order, where each transformation being evaluated is as far as possible from all the transformations evaluated before it.

One possible scanning order is based on the bit-reversal of the bit-interleaved coordinates. Suppose that the grid of transformations is 4×4 with coordinates running from 0 to 3 in each dimension. Then a number from 0 to 15 is transformed into a coordinate pair by separating it into its even bits and its odd bits; the even bits are concatenated in reverse order to give one coordinate, and the odd bits are concatenated in reverse order to give the other coordinate. Figure 5.3 shows the order in which the transformations are considered by this scheme. Note that transformations considered early on are spaced somewhat far apart, so that the circles that they rule out overlap as little as possible, while transformations considered later on fill in the gaps, and so are likely to have been ruled out themselves. While this particular scanning order does not give maximal spacing between transformations, it offers an improvement over more straightforward scanning orders, and is fairly simple to compute. It also can be generalised to higher dimensional transformation spaces: instead of every other bit being extracted to determine each of the transformation parameters, every nth bit is used, where n is the number of transformation parameters.

In [Pa1] and [PFT1], a technique similar to ruling out circles is described, for chamfer matching under translation and rotation. A technique for determining the order in which transformations should be evaluated, similar to the one above, is also described.

5.3 Skipping Forward

This section describes a technique that relies on the order in which the grid of transformations is scanned. Suppose that the transformations are scanned in some raster order, with the lowest level being the $g_{x.1}$ dimension (i.e., an entire row is scanned in the $g_{x.1}$ direction, then some other coordinate is changed and another row is scanned), and this dimension is scanned in the direction of increasing $g_{x.1}$. This corresponds to reading-order scanning in the simple case of a two-dimensional transformation space.

Recall that increasing $g_{x.1}$ by 1 results in the transformed model points moving by at most 1 in the increasing x direction. Using this property, it is possible to rule out

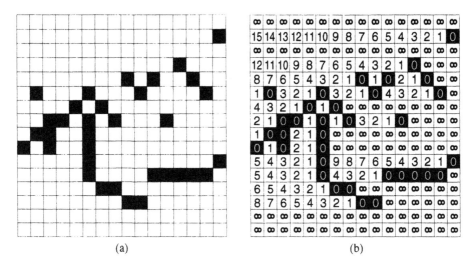

(a)   (b)

Fig. 5.4. An array and its $+x$ distance transform.

entire stretches of a row: for a transformation $g = [g_{x.1}, \ldots, g_{x.n_x}, g_{y.1}, \ldots, g_{y.n_y}]$, it is possible to determine a value $\gamma_{x.1}$ such that all transformations from g to $[g_{x.1} + \gamma_{x.1} - 1, g_{x.2}, \ldots]$ (inclusive) can immediately be ruled uninteresting (i.e., known not to satisfy the forward criterion). To do this, I use a variant of the distance transform of the image I.

Let $\Delta^{+x}[x, y]$ be the distance in the increasing x direction to the nearest location where $\Delta[x, y] \leq \tau_F$ and ∞ if there is no such location. Formally,

$$\Delta^{+x}[x, y] = \min_{\substack{\delta \geq 0 \\ \Delta[x + \delta, y] \leq \tau_F}} \delta. \tag{5.2}$$

Note that $\Delta^{+x}[x, y] \geq \Delta[x, y] - \tau_F$ and $\Delta^{+x}[x, y] = 0$ exactly when $\Delta[x, y] \leq \tau_F$. Computing $\Delta^{+x}[x, y]$ is straightforward once $\Delta[x, y]$ is known: simply scan right-to-left along each row of $\Delta[x, y]$, keeping track of the distance to the nearest location to the right of the current position whose value is under τ_F.

Consider the binary array obtained by thresholding $\Delta[x, y]$ above τ_F and inverting the result; this array is 1 wherever $\Delta[x, y] \leq \tau_F$, and 0 whenever $\Delta[x, y] > \tau_F$. $\Delta^{+x}[x, y]$ can then be thought of as a directional distance transform of this binary array: each pixel of $\Delta^{+x}[x, y]$ contains the distance in the increasing x direction to the nearest 1 pixel of this binary array; this is be called the $+x$ **distance transform** or **rightwards distance transform** of the binary array. Figure 5.4 shows such an array and its $+x$ distance transform.

$\Delta^{+x}[x, y]$ can be used to determine the closest location, in the increasing $g_{x.1}$ direction, where d_G might be no greater than τ_F, and thus there is some chance that the forward criterion is satisfied. This location can be determined by simply probing $\Delta^{+x}[x, y]$ instead of $\Delta[x, y]$ using the points of $g[m]$, and taking the f_Fth quantile. Call the value this produces $\gamma_{x.1}$. If $\gamma_{x.1}$ is 0, then $d_G[g] \leq \tau_F$, since at least f_F of the probe values returned 0, and so if $\Delta[x, y]$ had been probed, this many probes would have returned no more than τ_F. Thus, g satisfies the forward criterion, and repeating the process using $\Delta[x,y]$ determines $d_G[g]$'s exact value. If $\gamma_{x.1}$ is greater than zero, then not only is $d_G[g] > \tau_F$, but so are $d_G[g_{x.1} + 1, g_{x.2} \ldots], \ldots, d_G[g_{x.1} + \gamma_{x.1} - 1, g_{x.2} \ldots]$. Thus, once $\gamma_{x.1}$ is known, the search algorithm can increment $g_{x.1}$ by $\gamma_{x.1}$, rather than just by one, without missing any possibly interesting transformations.

The main advantage of this technique is its simplicity: the search algorithm merely probes a different distance transform array when evaluating a transformation, and gets back not only information about whether or not this transformation is interesting, but whether or not the next few transformations to be considered are interesting. The precomputation required (the computation of Δ^{+x}) is simple, and requires little space.

5.4 Cell Decomposition

Consider a rectilinear region in the (continuous) transformation space: let

$$R = [l_{x.1}, h_{x.1}] \times [l_{x.2}, h_{x.2}] \times \cdots \times [l_{x.n_x}, h_{x.n_x}] \times [l_{y.1}, h_{y.1}] \times \cdots \times [l_{y.n_y}, h_{y.n_y}], \tag{5.3}$$

and let

$$g_c = [(l_{x.1} + h_{x.1})/2, \ldots, (l_{x.n_x} + h_{x.n_x})/2, (l_{y.1} + h_{y.1})/2, \ldots, (l_{y.n_y} + h_{y.n_y})/2]$$

be the centre of R. Let δ be

$$\delta = \left\| \left(\frac{h_{x.1} - l_{x.1}}{2}, \ldots, \frac{h_{x.n_x} - l_{x.n_x}}{2}, \frac{h_{y.1} - l_{y.1}}{2}, \ldots, \frac{h_{y.n_y} - l_{y.n_y}}{2} \right) \right\|$$

where $\| \cdot \|$ represents the transformation space norm defined in (5.1). δ is the distance from the centre of R to its corners. Now, it is possible to evaluate $d_G(g_c)$ and determine from this single value whether it is possible that R contains some transformation satisfying the forward criterion: if $d_G(g_c)$ is greater than $\tau_F + \delta$ then every transformation in R has a d_G value that exceeds τ_F. This is a straightforward consequence of Theorem 5.1.

This can be extended to apply to the rasterised forward Hausdorff distance. In this case, the sides of R (the $l_{x.i}$ values etc.) are integers. It may not be possible to set g_c to the exact centre of R, since it may not lie on the grid, but g_c can be set to the closest grid transformation to the centre. Because of this, the distances from g_c to the corners of R are not equal; δ should be set to the largest of these distances. Then if $d_G[g_c]$ is greater than $\tau_F + \delta$, every transformation in R has a d_G value that exceeds τ_F, by Theorem 5.2. A single evaluation of d_G can therefore rule out an entire region of transformation space. More precisely,

$$d_G[g_c] > \tau_F + \left\| \left(\sum_{i=1}^{n_x} \lceil (h_{x.i} - l_{x.i})/2 \rceil, \sum_{i=1}^{n_y} \lceil (h_{y.i} - l_{y.i})/2 \rceil \right) \right\| \tag{5.4}$$

implies that R can contain no grid transformation satisfying the forward criterion.

Rectilinear regions of transformation space such as R will be referred to as **cells**. This leads to a multi-resolution method for searching the space of transformations:

1. Initialise a list of *possibly interesting* cells to a list of cells that are known to contain all transformations of interest. This is usually done by tiling the transformation space with cells of a certain size, so that all transformations within the bounds computed according to Sect. 4.2 are covered.
2. Scan over the current list of cells. For each cell, determine the value of d_G at its centrepoint (or the closest grid location to its centrepoint) g_c, and determine, using (5.4), if it is possible that the cell contains a transformation g satisfying the forward criterion. If so, mark this cell as *interesting*.
3. Once the entire list has been scanned, make up a new list of smaller cells (all the same size) that completely cover those cells found to be interesting. Cells found to be uninteresting need not be considered any further. Repeat steps 2 and 3 with this new list of (smaller) possibly interesting cells. Terminate when the current cell size becomes small enough (this is made more formal below).

Initially, the cells are very large and almost every cell is labeled as interesting, since the interest threshold is dependent on the cell size (i.e., δ is very large for these cells). However, those cells that actually do not contain any interesting regions are eliminated: they are subdivided and the subdivisions are found not to be interesting. The final result is a list of regions that represent transformations of the model that bring it into very close correspondence with (a section of) the image.

This algorithm is essentially an evaluate-subdivide cycle. Each cell is evaluated, and accepted (labeled interesting) or rejected (labeled uninteresting). Interesting cells are subdivided and their children in turn evaluated. Figure 5.5 shows this evaluate-subdivide process. All the cells of a certain size (i.e., all the cells in one level in this process) are evaluated, then all the cells at the next level generated by subdividing the interesting ones, and so on. The algorithm is basically searching transformation space using increasing levels of resolution, from coarse to fine.

The subdivision step takes all those cells that were labeled interesting and determines a set of smaller (finer resolution) cells that completely cover them. These finer-resolution cells are obtained by taking the coarser-resolution cell and dividing it in each dimension by a fixed constant r (I have been using $r = 2$); one coarser-resolution cell is therefore divided into $r^{n_x + n_y}$ finer-resolution cells. Any dimension that would be smaller than a single grid step is held at one grid step. This refinement should have the following properties:

– The finer-resolution cells should all be the same size.
– A single finer-resolution cell should be completely contained inside a single coarser-resolution cell; it should not overlap multiple coarser-resolution cells.
– The finer-resolution cells should not overlap each other.
– The finer-resolution cells should be as square as possible: their side lengths should be roughly equal in all dimensions.

Having all the cells (at a certain level in the search) be the same size makes evaluating a list of them more regular. The second and third properties make sure that a region of transformation space is not scanned twice. The fourth property is for efficiency: the number of grid transformations covered by a cell depends on its volume, whereas the threshold used to eliminate the cell depends on its diagonal length. The maximum ratio

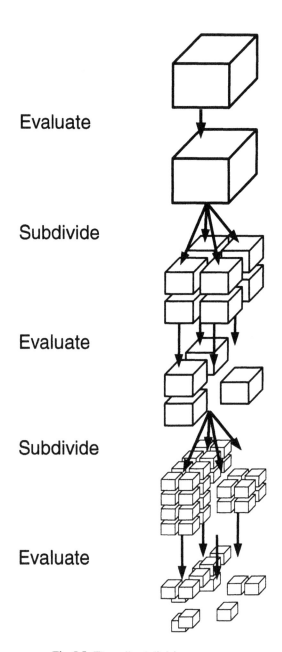

Fig. 5.5. The cell subdivision process.

of volume to diagonal length is achieved when the cell has side lengths equal in all dimensions. Cells of this shape allow the largest possible volume to be eliminated, for a given threshold.

The simplest way to ensure that these properties always hold is to set the cell sizes so that the lengths of the cell edges, in each dimension, are always a power of r, and are equal to each other. This is done by choosing the sizes of the coarsest-resolution cells appropriately.

If the cells at the current level are a single grid step wide in each dimension (i.e., each cell includes only one transformation), then no further refinement is possible. At this point, the list of interesting cells from the current level contains all those grid transformations g for which $d_G[g] \leq \tau$. The search algorithm then considers each of these individually. For each one, it computes the distance transform of the transformed model, and uses this to compute the box-reverse distance $d'_G[g]$. It rejects all those transformations for which this is greater than τ_R. Thus, it is left with a list of all the transformations that meet both the forward and reverse criteria.

5.5 Refinements of the Cell Decomposition Method

While the approach described in Sect. 5.4 searches the transformation space quite efficiently, there are still a number of aspects in which it can be improved. This section describes modifications of the basic cell decomposition method which offer increased efficiency.

5.5.1 Variable Thresholds

One observation which can be used to improve the efficiency of the search is that, although changing an x-linked coordinate of a transformation by one moves every point in the transformed model by at most one pixel in x, some points may consistently move less than this. Consider, for the moment, the transformation group Sc of translations and independent (x, y) scaling. Suppose that $m = (m_x, m_y) \in M$ is a model point, and that $m_x = 0$. Changing the x scale parameter of a transformation g does not affect $g[m]$ at all. In general, model points with smaller x coordinates are less affected by changes in the x scale parameter than model points with larger x coordinates. The same holds for y coordinates and the y scale parameter. Similar situations (in fact, several such situations) exist in the rasterisations affine transformation group Aff. In general, for most transformation groups, the change in a point's transformed coordinates depends on the position of that point within the model's bounds.

This observation can be used to improve the skipping forward technique described in Sect. 5.3. That technique was derived based on worst-case assumptions about how points moved as $g_{x.1}$ increased: that as $g_{x.1}$ increases by one, each transformed model point's x coordinate increases by one. Since not all the transformed points move as quickly as is possible in the worst case, it may be possible to skip farther forward. The idea behind the skipping forward technique is that given the results of evaluating a transformation g, it is possible to compute a conservative estimate of how much $g_{x.1}$ must be increased from its current value before $\Delta[g[b]]$ can reach τ_F, and use this to determine a skip distance. Clearly, the larger the estimate, the better, as long as it never exceeds the true distance to the next transformation satisfying the forward criterion. Suppose that increasing $g_{x.1}$ increases each model point m's transformed x coordinate proportionally to that point's x coordinate (i.e., m_x). Then, rather than simply probing $\Delta^{+x}[g[m]]$ for each $m \in M$ and taking the f_Fth quantile of these values, instead take the f_Fth quantile of the values

$$\max\left(\Delta^{+x}[g[m]], \frac{M_x}{m_x}\Delta^{+x}[g[m]] - 1\right)$$

and use that as the skip distance. This is always at least as large as the worst-case skip distance. The derivation of this formula is simple: for each $m \in M$, g can be changed by at least $\Delta^{+x}[g[m]]$ in the increasing $g_{x.1}$ direction before $\Delta[g[m]]$ can reach τ_F. In the exact case (ignoring rounding), g could be increased by $(M_x/m_x)\Delta^{+x}[g[m]]$, but given the possible rounding of the transformed model points, one should be subtracted from this, as the current pixel could have been rounded down, while an adjusted pixel might be rounded up, bringing it closer to the location where $\Delta[g[m]] \leq \tau_F$.

The cell-decomposition method can also be improved in a similar manner. Recall that a cell R is considered interesting if the fraction of model points, transformed by the centre transformation g_c, whose probe values from Δ exceed the threshold specified in (5.4) is less than f_F. Suppose that for some model point $m \in M$, $\Delta[g_c[m]] = v > \tau_F$. Then, from Theorem 5.2, all grid transformations g such that $\|g - g_c\| < v - \tau_F$ must have $\Delta[g[m]] > \tau_F$; in other words, any transformations in a sphere in transformation space transform m to a point where $\Delta > \tau_F$. The threshold from (5.4) places a limit on v such that if v exceeds this threshold, then the sphere encloses the entire cell R. If too many points of M generate spheres enclosing all of R, then R should be rejected, as no transformation inside it can bring enough points of M close enough to points of I.

This does not take into account the observation about the variable effect of transformation changes on transformed point positions. Taking this into account essentially expands the sphere to a larger ellipsoid. Thus, it may be possible to lower the threshold somewhat for this point: it may be possible to determine a threshold $\hat{\tau}$ such that if $\Delta[g_c[m]] > \hat{\tau}$, then $\Delta[g[m]] > \tau_F$ for all $g \in R$, and $\hat{\tau}$ is smaller than the threshold in (5.4): the ellipsoid where $\Delta[g[m]]$ must be greater than τ_F contains all of R. Every point $m \in M$ thus has a different threshold $\hat{\tau}$, but these can be pre-computed, as they do not depend on the location of the cell being probed, but only on its dimensions. If enough of the values of $\Delta[g_c[m]]$ exceed their respective thresholds, then the cell can be classified as uninteresting.

5.5.2 Early Acceptance

Consider the consequences of an error in the classification of a cell as interesting or uninteresting. If the search algorithm mistakenly classifies a cell as uninteresting, the entire volume covered by that cell is eliminated from any further consideration. This causes the search to miss any transformations in that cell that actually satisfy the forward and reverse criteria. This error therefore affects the outcome of the search, and cannot be allowed.

On the other hand, if the search algorithm mistakenly classifies a cell as interesting, when it actually is not, then the only consequence of this error is that a few more finer-resolution cells have been added to the list of possibly interesting cells at the next level. These cells are eventually evaluated and eliminated themselves; the search does not turn up any false positives, unless this mistake is made at the finest resolution.

Thus, if the search algorithm mistakenly classify a cell (not at the finest resolution) as interesting when it is not, this error has no significant consequence, and the search still succeeds, though it has done extra work; the search does not report any transformations that do not satisfy the forward and reverse criteria, and does not miss any that do. This property enables the use of a heuristic method to make the decision as to whether a cell is interesting or not, as long as the heuristic makes only false positive errors, and no false negative errors, and as long as it makes no errors when evaluating cells at the finest resolution. The overall time spent by the search may be reduced if this heuristic is less expensive to compute than a full evaluation of a cell.

The heuristic that I am using randomly selects some fraction s, $0 < s < 1$, of the points of M. It probes the distance transform of I at the transformed locations of these selected points. It then computes the fraction of points in this subset whose probe values are less than or equal to the threshold as specified in (5.4). If this fraction is at least f_F, then based on this partial evaluation, the cell looks promising, and so the search algorithm immediately says that this cell is interesting, and does not perform any further probes. If, on the other hand, the fraction is less than f_F, then the cell does not look promising (many of these probe values were large), but the algorithm does not immediately reject the cell, as this sampling of probe values might be misleading; it goes on to perform the rest of the probes and makes its decision based on the full set. In fact, it may not have to probe at the transformed locations of all of the points of M: as in Sect. 5.1, it can terminate the scan (and rule the cell uninteresting) if enough of the probes exceed the threshold.

Of course, it does not use this heuristic at the finest resolution. At this resolution it needs to actually compute d_G for all the transformations that are still possibly valid, since this (along with d'_G) determines which transformations are actually valid.

This heuristic has the advantage that it is trivial to compute: simply perform the normal probing process, in a random order, and check partway through whether or not this cell should be accepted without further computation. Other heuristics may be used; as long as they save enough time during the cell evaluations to make up for extra time spent correcting the errors, they decrease the overall time spent searching. The break-even point depends largely on the transformation group: using this technique makes evaluating each cell take less time, but at the cost of unnecessarily evaluating a number of finer-resolution cells whenever it makes an error. As the dimensionality of the transformation group increases, the number of finer-resolution cells examined unnecessarily increases exponentially, and so this technique is less likely to break even. For transformation groups with few dimensions (such as Tr and Sc), it is certainly worth using.

This technique is interesting because it represents an introduction of randomness and possible error in a process which is not allowed to produce erroneous results. The key point is that the errors made are self-correcting, and errors that are not self-correcting are still prohibited.

5.5.3 The Box Distance Transform

In Sect. 5.2, I noted that the projection of a sphere in transformation space was a circle in (x, y) space. Another observation is that that the projection of a box in transformation space is a box in (x, y) space. Let R be a box in transformation space as in (5.3). be a model point. Call the top left transformation (the transformation in R whose parameters all have their lowest values) g_l and the bottom right transformation (whose parameters all have their highest values) g_h. The coordinates of these two parameters are

$$g_l = [l_{x.1}, \ldots, l_{x.n_x}, l_{y.1}, \ldots, l_{y.n_y}], g_h = [h_{x.1}, \ldots, h_{x.n_x}, h_{y.1}, \ldots, h_{y.n_y}].$$

Let $t \in R$ be a transformation, and $m \in M$ a model point. Then $t(m)$ must lie within a box in the image whose top left corner is $t^l(m)$ and whose bottom right corner is $t^h(M)$ (where the origin of the image is considered to be its top left corner). Increasing any coordinate of a transformation cannot decrease the coordinates of any transformed model point, so the minimum and maximum values for the coordinates of the transformed point are achieved when the transformation coordinates achieve their maximum or minimum values. Figure 5.6 illustrates this effect.

The key to the cell subdivision method is step 2, where the search algorithm evaluates each cell and eliminates those that cannot possibly contain a transformation that satisfies the forward criterion, without inadvertently eliminating any cells containing such a transformation. It decides whether to subdivide a cell by computing a bound on the maximum possible value attained by $f_G[g]$ for any g in the current cell R, and rejecting the cell if this bound is below f_F. This is equivalent to rejecting the cell by proving that it cannot possibly contain any transformation satisfying the forward criterion.

Currently, step 2 determines a bound on the minimum possible value attained by $d_G[g]$ for any g in the current cell R, and rejects the cell if this value is above τ_F. As described in Sect. 5.4, this is done by evaluating $d_G[g_c]$ for the transformation g_c at the centre of R, and determining if the (hyper-)sphere ruled out by this value encloses all of R. This is inefficient because the smallest sphere enclosing R also encloses many transformations that are not contained in R. This means that it might not be possible to rule out this entire sphere, as one of these extra transformations may have a d_G value not exceeding τ_F, whereas if only the transformations inside R were considered, it would still be possible to rule out R.

Let $w = \sum_{i=1}^{n_x} (h_{x.i} - l_{x.i})$ and $h = \sum_{i=1}^{n_y} (h_{y.i} - l_{y.i})$. Now define

$$\Delta'_{wh}[x, y] = \min_{\substack{0 \le x' \le w \\ 0 \le y' \le h}} \Delta[x + x', y + y']. \tag{5.5}$$

Any portions of $\Delta[x, y]$ outside the boundary of the array it is stored in can be treated as being infinite, as the array has been created large enough that those portions are irrelevant to the search. Δ'_{wh} is called the **box distance transform** of the image I, using a box of size w by h. Note that the values in Δ'_{wh} do not depend on the location of R, but only on its size. Also, note that when R contains only a single transformation (i.e., $h_{x.i} = l_{x.i}$ and $h_{y.i} = l_{y.i}$) then $\Delta'[x, y] = \Delta[x, y]$: the box distance transform is equal to the regular distance transform when only a single transformation is being considered. Given the array Δ, Δ'_{wh} can be computed in $O(\log(w) + \log(h))$ passes through Δ, using prefix techniques; this is described more fully in Sect. A.4.

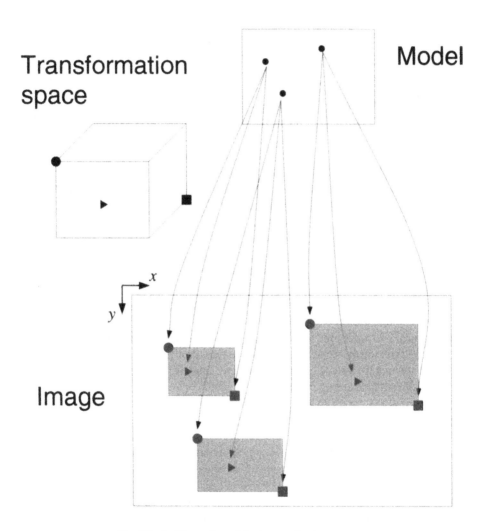

Fig. 5.6. An illustration of the box projection property.

Let $\mu = g_l[m]$ for some $m \in M$, and g_l as above. Now, $\Delta'_{wh}[\mu]$ is the minimum value achieved by $\Delta[g[m]]$ for any $g \in R$, since as g varies within the cell R, $g[m]$ varies within a box w by h, whose top left corner is at μ.

In order to evaluate a cell, and determine if it is interesting or not, the search algorithm performs the following steps:

- Compute Δ'_{wh} according to the size of the cell
- Transform each model point $m \in M$ by the top left transformation g_l
- Probe Δ'_{wh} at the (rounded) locations of the transformed points
- Count the number of these values that are τ_F or below
- If the fraction of such small values is at least f_F, then label the cell as interesting
- If this value is below f_F, then no transformation can bring enough model points close enough to some image point for the forward criterion to be satisfied, so reject the cell.

This can never reject any cell that contains a grid transformation g satisfying the forward criterion: any such transformation must map at least $\lceil f_F \# (M) \rceil$ points of M onto locations where $\Delta[g[m]] \leq \tau_F$, and so for each of those points, $\Delta'_{wh}[g_l[m]]$ can be no more than τ_F.

Since all the cells of any given level of the multi-resolution search are the same size, each level can use a single set of w and h values to compute a Δ'_{wh} that is used for the entire level. Each level of the search, evaluating cells of a certain size, must compute a different Δ'_{wh} array. The overhead of this method over the basic ruling-out-sphere-based cell decomposition method is fairly low (computing a few box distance transforms), and it should rule out more cells, making the search more efficient.

In practice, arrays are used to hold the various box distance transforms derived from Δ; these can be made the same size as Δ, as they are probed in the same locations. The only way in which the values of Δ'_{wh} are used is comparing them against τ_F, so Δ'_{wh} can be pre-thresholded at τ_F. This new boolean array is much smaller (only one bit per pixel is required to store it), so less memory is required; this reduction in memory usage also generally results in a slight speed improvement.

Using the box distance transform enables searching even transformation spaces that do not satisfy the transformation uniformity condition. For such transformation groups, ruling out spheres does not work, since there is not necessarily any simple bound on the change in a transformed model point's location caused by a small change in the transformation parameters. Also, it may not be possible to divide the transformation parameters into x-linked and y-linked parameters, and so a box in transformation space might not project to a box in the image. Nonetheless, it is possible to compute a worst-case bounding box for the projection of a cell of a certain size and use that to compute the box distance transform for each level of the search. The box distance transforms can then be used exactly as before: each point probes (via the box distance transform) all the locations in the image that it could be transformed to by some transformation in the current cell, and so the decision to reject the cell or not is guaranteed not to miss any interesting transformations. An adaptation of the zoning technique, described in the next subsection, can also be used to reduce the size of the worst-case box.

5.5.4 Zoning

It is possible to combine the box distance transform techniques from Subsect. 5.5.3 with the variable threshold techniques from Subsect. 5.5.1: the box in (x, y) space over which the transformed location of some point of M can move as the transformation is varied within a cell is not the same for all points of M; some have more restricted movement than others. This means that the probes into Δ'_{wh} have lower values than they might ideally have (because the boxes over which the minimisation is done are too large), making it harder to rule cells out.

In Subsect. 5.5.1, a similar observation was used to determine a different threshold for each point of M. A different box distance transform could be computed for each point of M, using the correct w and h (computed using that point's particular x and y coordinates) in (5.5), and have each transformed point probe the corresponding Δ'_{wh}. This would ensure that the correct-sized box was always used. However, in practice, this approach is infeasible, as it requires far too much storage: one copy of a boolean array the size of the distance transform Δ for each point of M, for each level of the multi-resolution search. A compromise solution is to divide the model M into several zones typically by dividing it into equal-sized rectangles and labeling all the points inside each rectangle as members of a single zone. Each zone then determines, based on the current cell size and the coordinates of the model points within that zone, a value for w and h and thus a Δ'_{wh} array. When cells are evaluated, each transformed model point probes the box distance transform that was constructed for its zone, and for the current level of the search, and determines if the probed value is greater than τ_F or not. In the upper limiting case, each point of M is in its own zone, and in the lower limiting case, all of M is in a single zone. These correspond respectively to the suggestion above, and to the approach in Subsect. 5.5.3. Efficiency increases as the number of zones increases, but memory requirements do as well. As before, each box distance transform can be replaced with a binary array by thresholding it at τ_F. This decreases the memory requirements, and so more zones can be used for the same amount of memory.

5.6 Directed Search Methods

The search method described in Sect. 4.2 attempts to find all transformations which satisfy both the forward and reverse criteria. This task is that of "find all matches". In some cases, however, this is not what the application performing the search actually requires: it might be satisfied with any match, or want only the best match. For the moment, consider only the forward criterion. Three typical requirements then might be:

1. Determine if there are any transformations that satisfy the forward criterion, and return one if so ("find any match").
2. Find the largest value of f_F for which there is some transformation that satisfies the forward criterion, and return such a match ("find the best match, ranked by f_G").
3. Find the smallest value of τ_F for which there is some transformation that satisfies the forward criterion, and return such a match ("find the best match, ranked by d_G").

These searches can be performed more efficiently than the full search, especially when the cell decomposition method is used. They can also be performed using a single modified search framework.

5.6.1 Find Any Match

Recall that the cell decomposition search method takes a list of cells, subdivides each, and determines whether or not each of the subdivided cells is interesting (might contain a match); the list of interesting cells is then used for the next level of subdivision. This method corresponds to a breadth-first search of the tree of cells. If the search task is to find only a *single* transformation that satisfies the forward criterion, then the search can be terminated once such a transformation is found. However, this eliminates only a small portion of the tree search: the search algorithm might be able to avoid scanning some of the finest-resolution cells, but by then the rest of the work has already been done. Searching the cells in another order than breadth-first can decrease the time to find such a match, by reaching some promising finest-resolution cells more quickly. One way of doing this is by performing a best-first search: instead of expanding all the cells in the current list, expand only the *best* ones, according to some measure that attempts to quantify which cells are most likely to contain a match. This is a standard beam search, which may lead to a match quickly, if the measure being used to rank the cells at all levels is accurate enough. However, it might not do so, in which case the search must backtrack. If there are no matches, the entire tree must be searched, but if a match does exist it should be found more quickly than by breadth-first search. Once a match is found, of course, the search can be immediately terminated; any as-yet-unevaluated cells need never be evaluated.

The beam width used (the number of cells on the current list which are expanded at one time) affects the performance of the search. Setting the beam width too high creates a breadth-first search, as before; setting it very low makes this procedure a ranked depth-first search, which may not perform well, as the coarse-resolution cells containing matches may not be ranked quite as highly as some other coarse-resolution cells that do not contain matches. In practice, the search algorithm adjust the beam width dynamically: the beam width starts out quite small, but is increased if the search finds itself exhausting its lists and backtracking too much; this reduces the overhead due to recursion and backtracking.

Note that any heuristic works for ranking the cells in the current to-be-expanded list, without affecting the correctness of the search, but only its speed. If this heuristic can be computed cheaply, or as a side-effect of other computation, then the overhead of the ranking step is minimised.

The decision as to whether or not a cell should be rejected is generally made based on counting the results of probes generated by the transformed model points: either enough probes into Δ have values below the threshold from (5.4), or (if the box distance transform is being used), enough probes into the appropriate Δ'_{wh} have values not exceeding τ_F. Thus, one measure which can be used for this ranking is simply the fraction of the probe values that were below the appropriate threshold. This is generated as a consequence of the evaluation of the cell in any case, so using it to rank the cells involves no extra cost other than that of actually sorting the list of cells. Cells that contain matches are more likely to have high values of this fraction than cells which do not. This heuristic has the advantage that it is free.

5.6.2 Find the Best Match

One possible search task might be to find the maximum possible value of f_F for which some transformation meets the forward criterion, along with such a transformation (this is equivalent to finding the transformation g maximising $f_G[g]$). This task can be addressed using the same form of search as in the previous subsection: try to find a transformation satisfying the forward criterion as early in the search as possible. However, when such a transformation is found, evaluate $f_G[g]$ rather than terminate the search, and strengthen the forward criterion based on this value of $f_G[g]$.

Recall that $f_G[g]$ is defined as

$$f_G[g] = \frac{\#\left(\{m \in M \mid \Delta[g[m]] \leq \tau_F\}\right)}{\#(M)}.$$

For any g found as a result of the search, this value is always at least f_F, since g satisfies the forward criterion. g would also have satisfied the forward criterion if f_F had any larger value up to and including $f_G[g]$. This means that, once g has been found, f_F can be increased by setting it to $f_G[g]$; even with this strengthening of the forward criterion, the search will still be able to find a transformation satisfying the forward criterion (since g satisfies this modified criterion). Further, no transformation g' for which $f_G[g'] < f_G[g]$ will be found after f_F has been increased: the strength of the forward criterion has been increased so that such transformations no longer satisfy it.

The best-first search from the previous section can therefore be modified in the following manner: instead of terminating the search whenever a transformation satisfying the forward criterion is found, increase f_F whenever one is found, and continue with the search. This strengthening of the forward criterion causes the search to terminate more quickly, because more cells are considered uninteresting, and so the search space is exhausted more quickly than with the original value of f_F; the search algorithm prunes out cells that cannot contain anything better than what it has already found. At the end of the search, the algorithm has found the transformation g^* that has the maximum value of $f_G[\cdot]$; the final value of f_F is equal to $f_G(g^*)$, as it was raised to that value when g^* was found. Only g^* (and other transformations having the same $f_G[\cdot]$ value) need to be reported.

This modified search is similar, in concept, to the "alpha" part of standard alpha-beta pruning: there is no need to expand part of the search tree if there is no possibility that it contains some transformation which is better than the current best; this type of search is often called "branch-and-bound".

This parameter update technique can also be used to search for the minimum possible value of τ_F for which some transformation meets the forward criterion. In this case, f_F is held constant, and whenever a transformation g satisfying the current forward criterion is found, τ_F is lowered to $d_G[g]$, strengthening the current forward criterion.

These optimising search methods are essentially searching for one of the method's parameters (f_F or τ_F) in parallel with the usual search for matches. This reduces the number of parameters that need to be specified for the search process.

5.6.3 Incorporating the Reverse Criterion

In describing these directed search techniques, I have so far been concerned only with the forward criterion. The reverse criterion can be incorporated in one of several manners. If only a single transformation satisfying both the forward and reverse criteria is required, as in Subsect. 5.6.1, then simply evaluate every transformation that satisfies the forward criterion to see if it also satisfies the reverse criterion; when some transformation satisfies both, then the search can be terminated.

The search modifications described in Subsects. 5.6.2 can also have the reverse criterion incorporated in this manner: any transformation satisfying the current forward criterion must also pass the reverse criterion before f_F or τ_F can be updated. However, it might be desirable to have f_R (or τ_R) track f_F (or τ_F) as it is increased (lowered). This means that as the forward criterion is strengthened, the reverse criterion is also strengthened. If the initial forward and reverse criteria were both relatively weak (in order to ensure that at least one match was found), it might not make sense to report matches that satisfy a strong forward criterion, but only a weak reverse criterion.

I first consider the case of searching for the highest possible f_F. I introduce two new parameters, $p^\times$ and p^+, and tie f_R to f_F by ensuring that, at all times,

$$f_R = p^\times f_F + p^+ . \tag{5.6}$$

When the search algorithm is evaluating a transformation g, it therefore computes $f_G[g]$ and $f'_G[g]$. If $f_G[g] \geq f_F$ and $f'_G[g] \geq f_R$, using the current values of f_F and f_R, then this transformation satisfies the current forward and reverse criteria, and may be used to strengthen these criteria. The algorithm therefore updates f_F and f_R by setting

$$f_F = \min\left(f_G[g], \frac{f'_G[g] - p^+}{p^\times} \right)$$
$$f_R = \min\left(f'_G[g], p^\times f_G[g] + p^+ \right) .$$

This ensures that g still satisfies the forward and reverse criteria with the new f_F and f_R, and that the constraint in (5.6) continues to hold.

A similar technique can be applied to finding the best τ_F; in this case τ_F and τ_R must satisfy

$$\tau_R = p^\times \tau_F + p^+ \tag{5.7}$$

and the rules for updating τ_F and τ_R are similarly modified to

$$\tau_F = \max\left(d_G(g), \frac{d'_G(g) - p^+}{p^\times} \right)$$
$$\tau_R = \max\left(d'_G(g), p^\times d_G(g) + p^+ \right) .$$

Incorporating the reverse criterion into the directed search method in this manner eliminates the need to specify a value for f_R (or τ_R); the search-for-best methods themselves remove the need to specify f_F (or, respectively, τ_F). However, this happens at the expense of having to specify two new parameters, $p^\times$ and p^+. In general, though, these new parameters are less variable than the old parameters: while the quality of the best match is variable, the relationship between the forward and reverse components of a single match is less so.

Note that this still uses the reverse criterion only at the lowest level of the search, as it was before; if the reverse distance is the limiting factor, then the directed search might not be as efficient as it could be, because the cell ranking is generally based only on the forward distance. However, the cell ranking heuristic could be modified to incorporate some estimate of the reverse distance.

5.7 Parallelising

In this section, I discuss the possibility of parallelising the search strategies described in the preceding sections. The brute-force search discussed in Sect. 4.2 is clearly massively parallel: every transformation lying on the grid of transformations is evaluated, and the ones that satisfy the forward and reverse criteria are reported. However, unless an enormous number of processors are available, this is still far too slow to be practical. While the efficient searching techniques may lose some of this inherent parallelism, an implementation using them and exploiting the remaining parallelism is nonetheless much faster in practice than a parallel implementation of the straightforward search.

I concentrate primarily on parallelising the cell decomposition search technique developed in Sect. 5.4. Recall that this worked by dividing transformation space into a list of cells, evaluating each cell, subdividing all the cells which passed the evaluation, evaluating each cell in this new list, and so on. One way to parallelise this is to subdivide the initial list of cells into groups, assign one group to each processor, and have the searches proceed independently. This approach suffers from load-balancing problems: some areas of the transformation space are easier to search than others (this, after all, is the whole premise of the cell-subdivision technique), and so some processors complete their search before others, possibly much before. Since it is not possible to *a priori* determine which areas of search space are easier or harder to search, static load-balancing does not work. However, dynamic load-balancing is not too difficult: whenever a processor completes its portion of the search, it sends out a broadcast to other processors, and collects some as-yet-unevaluated cells from each (or from the one with the most work remaining). It can then proceed with evaluating these cells. The overhead of this communication is relatively low, unless there are a very large number of processors, as the time taken to subdivide and search a list of cells is much greater than the time taken to send the list over an inter-processor channel. I have implemented this method on an eight-processor shared memory machine.

The directed search techniques from Sect. 5.6 can incorporated into this framework. Each processor independently searches the region of transformation space that it has been assigned, evaluating and ranking cells. Suppose that only one transformation satisfying the forward and reverse criteria is desired, as in Subsect. 5.6.1. Once any processor finds such a transformation, it broadcasts that fact; the other processors can then terminate their search. Several processors may find transformations at roughly the same time, so the process overseeing the entire computation must be prepared to ignore all but one.

The adaptive parameter update strategies of Subsects. 5.6.2 can also be included in a similar fashion: a processor finding a transformation and subsequently updating its parameters broadcasts these updated parameters; processors receiving such a broadcast update their own parameters. Some care must be taken that, if multiple such broadcasts occur simultaneously, only the best parameters are used.

A simpler method takes advantage of the parallelism in evaluating the lists of cells: these computations are independent, and so can be done in parallel. Thus, the main flow of the search can proceed as usual, except that it uses multiple processors to perform the cell evaluations. This exploits less of the available parallelism, but is simpler to implement, and requires no asynchronous inter-processor communication.

5.8 Interactions and Combinations

I have thus far described a number of techniques which improve the run-time performance of the search process. However, it is not feasible to incorporate all of these techniques into a single search algorithm, as some of them interact negatively. On the other hand, some of these techniques can be combined with good results. In this section, I describe these interactions.

- Early rejection interacts poorly with both the ruling out spheres technique and the skipping forward technique. These latter two techniques rely on the evaluation of a transformation to determine how many other transformations can be ruled out: the worse the evaluation of the initial transformation, the better, in some sense, as then a larger sphere can be ruled out, or a larger stretch skipped. However, early rejection causes the initial transformation to be rejected as soon as its value is known to be above threshold; the size of the sphere ruled out (or the distance skipped) based on this partial evaluation is likely to be small.

  If these techniques are to be used in combination, one possible solution for this problem is to modify early rejection so that it rejects a transformation not when its value is known to be above threshold, but when it is known that the radius of the sphere to be ruled out (or the distance to be skipped) is at least a certain value.
- The ruling out spheres technique and the skipping forward technique can be combined. This combination does have some drawbacks, though: every transformation must essentially be evaluated twice, once to determine how large a sphere to rule out, and once to determine how far to skip forward, as one value is based on probing Δ and one on probing Δ^{+x}. Also, the skipping forward technique requires that transformation space be scanned in a row-wise fashion, so all transformations along a single row must be considered in sequence (although the order in which rows are considered may be arbitrary); as noted in Sect. 5.2, such scanning is not optimal for ruling out spheres, as the spheres overlap excessively. However, in many cases, the distance skipped forward is greater than the radius of the sphere ruled out, as the factor limiting the size of the sphere may not be in the direction along the current row. This leads to slightly greater efficiency than a straightforward row scan, as it does not always evaluate something just on the edge of the most recently ruled out sphere.
- Early rejection can be used together with cell decomposition to good effect: each cell evaluation results in a binary accept/reject decision, rather than a qualitative result (how large a sphere can be ruled out, or how far to skip forward). The early

rejection counting technique fits well into this framework: as the search algorithm probes the image's distance transform or box distance transform, it counts the number of probes exceeding the current threshold. If too many exceed this threshold, then the cell can be rejected immediately, without performing any further probes.

- Skipping forward and cell decomposition may also be combined: instead of dealing with a single cell at a time, gather together a group of cells which lie adjacent to each other along a single dimension (say, an x-linked dimension) in transformation space, scan these cells in order, and use the evaluation results of one to skip over some of the ones following it.

The cell decomposition method works by probing the image's distance transform and comparing the probe results with a threshold based on τ_F and the size of the current cell, or probing the box distance transform (based on the size of the current cell) and comparing the results of that probe with τ_F. In either case, the distance transform can be replaced with a binary array containing the pre-computed results of these comparisons; the number of large (over threshold) probe values are counted, and if too many are too big, then the cell is rejected. Since this is a binary array, distance transform techniques can be applied to it. In particular, consider computing the $+x$ distance transform of this array, and probing that instead of the array itself: when evaluating a cell, instead of simply counting the number of large-valued probes, examine the $+x$ distance transform distance values and compute their f_Fth quantile. If this value is greater than zero, then the cell should be rejected since the locations where the $+x$ distance transform is zero are exactly the locations where the original binary array was below threshold. If this value is greater than zero, then it indicates a distance by which the cell could be shifted along any x-linked dimension and still be ruled out. If this value is greater than the distance between this cell's centre and the centre of the next adjacent cell in the row, then that following cell can be ruled out; it may also be possible to rule out others along the row.

This technique is less useful at coarser cell resolutions, as the distances between cell centres is greater and so a larger skip value is required before any additional cells can be ruled out. Also, the overhead required to order the cells into rows may be prohibitive when the transformation space has high dimension.

- It is also possible to combine the ruling out spheres and basic cell decomposition techniques. Recall that a cell is rejected if the transformation at its centre has a sufficiently large d_G value that a sphere enclosing the entire cell can be ruled out. If this sphere is sufficiently large that it also encloses other cells at the current level, these too can be ruled out. The overhead for determining this may be too great in practice, especially for transformation spaces with high dimension.

This can still be done even when the box distance transform is used, by computing the distance transform of the (binary) thresholded box distance transform and probing this array rather than the thresholded box distance transform, similarly to the way in which the $+x$ distance transform was used above. This array is probed, and the f_Fth quantile value of these probes is taken. If this value is zero, then the cell should be accepted. If it is nonzero, then the cell should be rejected; the value then represents the radius of a sphere in transformation space through which the top left corner of the cell can be shifted while still being ruled out. If this sphere is large enough that it encloses the top left corners of other cells, then these too can be ruled out. Again, the overhead of performing this check is probably too high for practical use.

- Early acceptance and early rejection may be combined, as they do not conflict with each other; both are based on counting binary values based on probe results. If it is possible to reject a cell without performing all of the probes, then it is unlikely that the cell will be accepted based on an initial sequence of the probes.
- The box distance transform can be used in conjunction with early acceptance and early rejection; again, both of those techniques rely simply on counting binary values, and this same count is used to make the accept/reject decision for the cell.
- Variable thresholds and zoning can generally be combined with other techniques which are compatible with the cell decomposition method. However, since several thresholds or distance transforms are used, combining these techniques with ruling out spheres or skipping forward is quite complex.
- The directed search methods interact somewhat with early acceptance: if the cell ranking heuristic is based on some value computed during the accept/reject decision process, then the fact that this process was not completed must be taken into account in the heuristic. If the heuristic described above, ranking by the fraction of probes which were below the current threshold, is used, then cells which are accepted early do not have an accurate figure for this fraction, making the ranking process less accurate.
- While I have only described parallelising the cell decomposition method, the overall search is highly parallel and so it is probable that other methods could be parallelised as well.

5.9 Summary

In this chapter, I have developed several different methods which greatly increase the efficiency of the search for matches between the model and the image. These are based on the structure of the Hausdorff distance and the manner in which I rasterised transformation space, and exploit the regularities in this structure. All of the methods have the property that no valid match is missed, and no invalid match is reported.

Some of this work has been previously published in [HR1, HR2, HKR1, HKR2, HKR3, Ru6].

Chapter 6

Implementations and Examples

In this chapter, I present several of the implementations of the minimum Hausdorff distance image search method that I have developed. I also demonstrate the performance of the Hausdorff distance in several examples.

I have developed three (related) implementations: one dealing with searching for all translations of the model that make the Hausdorff distance small, one dealing with searching for translations and (x, y) scales, and one dealing with searching for affine transformations. All of these implementations use the L_2 plane norm.

These implementations all currently use the approximate L_2 chamfer distance transforms from Sect. A.1, even though they are not exact, and so the bounds derived in Theorem 5.2 do not hold. However, computing the chamfer distance transform is several times faster than computing any of the exact distance transforms; in many cases (especially when searching under translation), the time spent computing the distance transform is a significant fraction of the total run time. Also, I have not noticed any errors caused by this use of an approximate distance transform. When the box distance transform is used, in fact, it is possible to show that no errors are made, since Theorem 5.2 is not necessary to show that this method works.

6.1 Translation

The first, and simplest, implementation is the one that searches for all translations satisfying the forward and reverse criteria. The implementation that I have developed uses the cell decomposition method from Sect. 5.4, in combination with the box distance transform, early rejection, and early acceptance (using a sampling fraction $s = 0.2$). This implementation also provides the directed search modes (search for one, search for best fraction, search for best distance) from Sect. 5.6. The implementation is written in C. All translations where the translated model box overlaps the image at all are considered; this range could be reduced somewhat by considering the model, as in Sect. 4.2, but in practice these outermost translations are eliminated very quickly.

This range can be reduced or increased by the user, if desired: the user can supply **borders** for the image. Four borders can be specified, one for each of the four edges of the image. All translations where the translated model fits *entirely* within these borders are considered; translations outside this range are not considered. Positive border values correspond to increasing the size of the image, and increasing the range of translations to be searched. Negative border values can also be supplied. In this case, the effect is to reduce the effective size of the image: the outermost parts have effectively been trimmed off. This can be useful when the user wants to search only a part of the image for the model, not the entire image; in the next chapter, I will demonstrate how this can be used

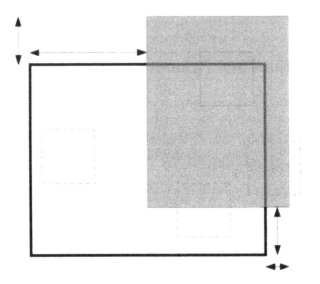

Fig. 6.1. Using borders to restrict the search range.

effectively when the user has some idea of where in the image the model is likely to be found.

Figure 6.1 illustrates this idea. In this figure, the image is shown outlined in bold. The top border is 25% of the image height, the left border is -50% of the image width, the bottom border is -25% of the image height, and the right border is 10% of the image width. The shaded area is the area that is searched: only translations that bring the entire model into this area are considered. Several translations of the model are shown; only the one with a solid outline is actually considered, with this setting of the borders.

This implementation makes extensive use of caching, as do the other implementations described in the following sections. Whenever something is computed (for example, a distance transform), and it is possible that it might need to be re-used later, it is stored in a cache. To avoid excessive memory use, the total size of each cache is limited, so some previous cached value may be replaced. In practice, values are almost always available for re-use when they are needed.

I now consider some examples in order to illustrate the performance of the Hausdorff distance methods developed above, using this implementation. The first test image is shown in Fig. 6.2. The original grey-level camera image is shown in Fig. 6.2(a), and the binary edge image produced by applying an edge operator (similar to [Ca1]) is shown in Fig. 6.2(b). This size of this binary edge image is 360×240 pixels.

The model to be compared with the first test image is shown in Fig. 6.3. The outline around the figure delineates the boundary of the bitmap representing the model. The model is 115×199 pixels. Comparing this model against this image with $\tau_F = \tau_R = 2$ pixels, $f_F = 0.8$ and $f_R = 0.5$ takes approximately 0.9 CPU seconds on a Sun SPARCServer-1000E, including all I/O overhead, and all the precomputation required for the box distance transforms. This produced two matches, at $(87, 35)$ and $(87, 36)$.

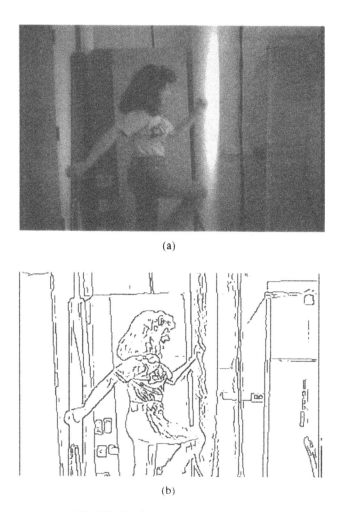

(a)

(b)

Fig. 6.2. The first translation test image.

Figure 6.4 shows the match at $(87, 36)$ overlaid on the image. The efficient search examined 3208 cells; there were over 200,000 possible translations of the model placing it so that it overlapped the image, so over 98% of those translations were eliminated without being explicitly considered.

I also ran the algorithm on the image and model shown in Figs. 6.5 and 6.6, using $\tau_F = \tau_R = \sqrt{2}$, $f_F = 0.66$ and $f_R = 0.35$. The image is 256×233 and the model is 60×50. Four matches were found, at $(99, 128)$, $(100, 128)$, $(99, 129)$ and $(100, 129)$. Figure 6.7 shows the match at $(99, 129)$ overlaid on the image. The computation took approximately 0.9 seconds.

My third test case consists of the image and model shown in Figs. 6.8 and 6.9, using $\tau_F = \tau_R = 2\sqrt{2}$, $f_F = 1$ and $f_R = 0.5$. The image is 360×240 and the model is 38×60. The model was digitized from a different can, held at approximately the same orientation and same distance from the camera. Four matches were found, at $(199, 95)$,

Fig. 6.3. The first translation object model.

Fig. 6.4. The first test image overlaid with the best match.

(a)   (b)

Fig. 6.5. The second translation test image.

Fig. 6.6. The second translation object model.

Fig. 6.7. The second translation test image overlaid with the best match.

$(199, 98)$, $(200, 98)$ and $(199, 99)$. Figure 6.10 shows the match at $(199, 98)$ overlaid on the image. The computation took approximately one fifth of a second.

If several models are to be compared against the same image, then the distance transform of the image and the derived box distance transforms need only be computed once. My implementation takes about a quarter of a second to compute the distance transform of a 256×256; once this has been computed, the searches can take as little as one fortieth of a second per model (in the Coke-can example just presented). The time taken depends on the τ_F, τ_R, f_F and f_R values used; larger τ_F and smaller f_F values increase the time taken. A more cluttered image also increases the time required.

In order to compare the directed Hausdorff distance with binary correlation, I computed the correlation of the stump model in Fig. 6.6 with the second test image. I defined a match for the correlation case to be a translation where the correlation function was at a local peak. For this image, binary correlation performed poorly. There were seventeen incorrect matches that had a higher correlation value than the correct match and a number that had an equal correlation value; the correct match had a value of only 77% of the largest peak. None of the incorrect matches was close (spatially) to the correct match; Fig. 6.11 shows these incorrect matches, and the correct match, overlaid on the input edge image.

The examples in these images support my theoretical claim that the partial Hausdorff distance works well on images where the locations of image pixels have been perturbed. Moreover, these same images cannot be handled well by binary correlation.

6.2 Translation and Scale

The implementation that searches the group Sc for translations and scales of the model satisfying the forward and reverse criteria is quite similar to the translation-only imple-

(a)

(b)

Fig. 6.8. The third translation test image.

Fig. 6.9. The third translation object model.

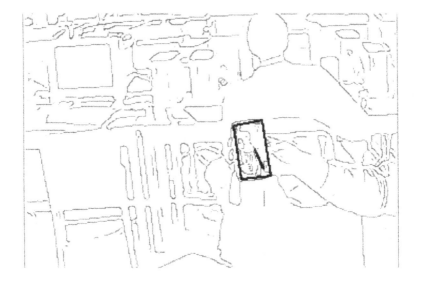

Fig. 6.10. The third translation test image overlaid with the best match.

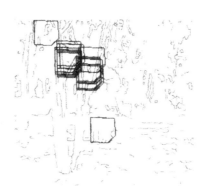

Fig. 6.11. Incorrect matches (and one correct match) from binary correlation.

mentation, using the same set of techniques. There is also a parallel variant, running on an eight-processor shared-memory machine, similar to the parallelisation mentioned in Sect. 5.7, where the processors independently work on sections of transformation space, and communicate for dynamic load-balancing and parameter update. There is some additional inter-processor communication for synchronisation, primarily when the search's caches are updated, as the caches are shared so some locking must be done whenever a cache is updated.

As was noted in Sect. 4.3, computing the reverse distance for some transformation (s_x, s_y, t_x, t_y) (representing a scaling of the model by a factor of s_x in x and s_y in y, followed by a translation by (t_x, t_y)) requires the distance transform of the transformed model $g[M]$. Now, if two transformations differ only in their t_x and t_y values (i.e., if they specify the same scaling of the model, but different translations), then their distance transforms are translations of each other; thus, the distance transform need only be computed once. When the search for transformations satisfying the forward criterion is complete, the method must check each of those transformations to see if they also satisfy the reverse criterion. If these transformations are binned so that all the transformations sharing the same s_x and s_y values are evaluated together, then the transformed model's distance transform can be computed as few times as possible, and no memory is needed to cache old model distance transforms, since they are not re-used once that bin has been processed.

As in the previous section, borders can be used to restrict the range of transformations being searched: only transformations where the entire transformed model box fits inside the borders are considered; all others are eliminated.

It is also necessary to restrict the ranges of the scale parameters directly. Recall that the box-reverse distance is computed using only the part of the image which lies under the translated and scaled model box. Now, suppose that the model x and y scales are allowed to become very small, so that the scaled model box is only a single pixel across. If it is translated so that it lies on top of an image point, then the forward distance is zero (as every transformed model point lies on that image point), and the reverse distance is also zero (as that image point, being the only image point under the transformed model box, is on top of every transformed model point); this is therefore a perfect match. This match is correct, in some sense: the search has essentially discovered that any point looks just like the model object, if the model object is very, very far away. Nonetheless, this is not likely to be the correct location of the object.

To eliminate this problem, the user can specify values $s_x^{\min}$ and $s_y^{\min}$, which are the minimum x scale and y scale values to be considered. Also, when s_x is much greater than s_y, or vice versa, the transformed model has a grossly distorted (**skewed**) aspect ratio. The user can control this effect by specifying an additional search parameter, $\alpha_{\max}$; any transformation for which $s_x/s_y > \alpha_{\max}$ or $s_y/s_x > \alpha_{\max}$ is ruled to be outside the range of transformations under consideration.

Usually, the model represents the model object at full scale: searching for an instance of the object that is larger (in the image) than model is an unlikely scenario. The user can therefore specify two more parameters, $s_x^{\max}$ and $s_y^{\max}$, which are usually both set to 1; these are the largest x and y scales that are considered. However, the search implementation is capable of handling any values for these parameters.

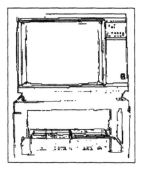

Fig. 6.12. The first scale test model.

I now consider some examples in order to illustrate the performance of this implementation. The single-processor timings given are user-mode CPU times for one processor of an eight-processor SPARCServer-1000E; the parallel timings are total wall-clock times for the same machine, but using all eight processors in parallel.

The first test model is shown in Fig. 6.12. This binary image is 190×220 pixels, and was produced by applying an edge-detection operator to a grey-level camera image. I compared this model against three test images. Each image is a half-size NTSC video frame (320×240 pixels). For each test image, I show the grey-level image, its edges, and the edges overlaid with the scaled and translated model.

For the first two test images, I used $\tau_F = \tau_R = 2\sqrt{2}$ pixels, $f_F = 0.95$, $f_R = 0.75$, $s_x^{\min} = s_y^{\min} = 0.4$ and $\alpha_{\max} = 1.02$. In the third test image, however, the model object is partially out of view. In order to allow it to be matched, I reduced f_F to 0.85, allowing up to 15% of the model points to match nothing in the image. I also used $\tau_F = \tau_R = 2\sqrt{2}$, $f_R = .65$, $s_x^{\min} = s_y^{\min} = 0.7$ and $\alpha_{\max} = 1.02$. In all of these cases, I wanted to find only the best match; the directed search for best fraction mode was used. Running times for these three examples are shown in Table 6.1. For each of the three tests, I show the single and multi-processor CPU times and wall-clock (elapsed) times. It is difficult to compare the simple-processor and multi-processor times directly, as they may have evaluated different numbers of cells due to a different search order; one run might have led to the best match more quickly than the other. In my experience, the overhead of multi-processing leads to an increase in CPU time of between 5 and 20 percent for an equivalent search; the decreased overall run times make up for this increase. In this example, the multi-processor search was approximately three times faster than the single-processor search for all three parts. While this may not be as large a speedup as might be desired from an eight-processor machine, it should be remembered that this parallelisation is a relatively simple one, and a number of phases of the algorithm are still executed serially, limiting the opportunity for parallelism; furthermore, these are fairly short runs, increasing the effect of startup overhead.

Each example generated multiple matches; in each case, these formed a single connected component in the transformation space (i.e., were essentially the same transformation). For each test image, I therefore picked the best match as a representative; this is shown overlaid on the image.

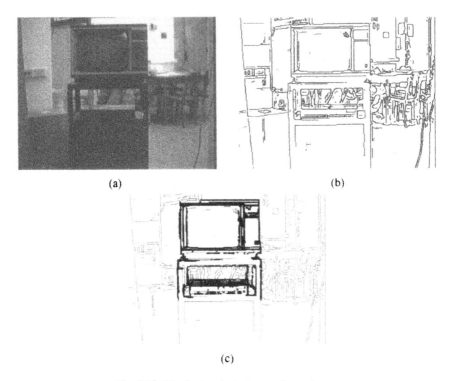

(a)   (b)

(c)

Fig. 6.13. The first scale test example, part one.

Table 6.1. Running times for locating the first scale test model.

| | Single processor | | Multi-processor | |
Test	CPU	Wall	CPU	Wall
1	19.5	19.9	25.9	6.2
2	7.3	7.5	8.5	2.2
3	15.1	15.4	13.4	4.6

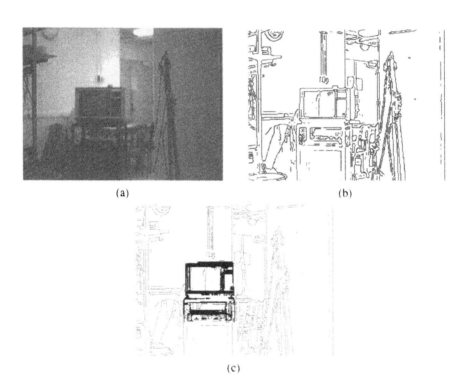

(a)

(b)

(c)

Fig. 6.14. The first scale test example, part two.

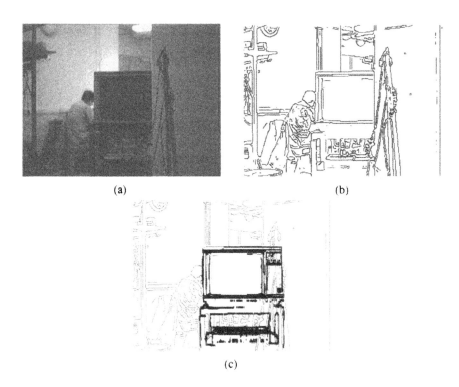

(a)

(b)

(c)

Fig. 6.15. The first scale test example, part three.

Fig. 6.16. Incorrect matching due to not using the reverse distance.

Fig. 6.17. The second scale test model.

One point to be noted: if the reverse distance had not been applied to the first test image, then an incorrect match would have been found. Figure 6.16 shows this error: the transformation which gives the best forward distance is nowhere near the correct transformation, but instead places the model in a region where the image is very cluttered. This shows the necessity of having something similar to the reverse distance, to detect such false matches.

My second example involves finding circles in an engineering drawing of a part to be machined; this might be done in order to automatically determine where holes should be drilled. The model is shown in Fig. 6.17. It is 175×175 pixels, and contains a circle of radius 75 pixels.

Since engineering drawings typically contain text, arrows, and overlapping parts, the reverse distance is not a reliable indication of the quality of the match: if the model matches some circle which happens to be crossed by a line, then the reverse distance will be increased, even though the match might otherwise be good; in this domain, the model must be considered to be, in a sense, completely transparent, which is not often an issue in the domain of physical objects. Cluttered regions, such as the one which caused problems above, are also not generally present. For this reason, I have used only the forward distance as an indicator of match quality. The results of these tests are shown in Figs. 6.18 and 6.19. The figures show the original bitmaps of the two test images, the locations and sizes at which the circles were found, then the original bitmaps overlaid by the scaled and translated model. The bitmaps are from a blueprint which was photo-reduced and scanned at 150dpi. Note that some of the circles have been broken up, and there is some background noise due to the speckling of the original blueprint.

Table 6.2. Running times for locating the second scale test model.

Test	Single processor		Multi-processor	
	CPU	Wall	CPU	Wall
1	11.6	12.8	16.1	5.3
2	6.9	7.1	9.3	2.3

The first example shows several circles of different sizes. Using $\tau_F = 1$, $f_F = 0.9$, $s_x^{\min} = s_y^{\min} = 0.2$ and $\alpha^{\max} = 1.01$, my method correctly located all the circles. The matches which my method detected formed multiple connected components in transformation space, one component for each circle in the image. The figures display the best match for each component.

The second example illustrates how the search method can find circles drawn with dashed lines, using the same (solid) circle model. With $\tau_F = \tau_R = 1$, $f_F = 0.82$, $s_x^{\min} = s_y^{\min} = 0.14$ and $\alpha^{\max} = 1.01$, again all the circles were correctly located. Due to the low resolution of the scan, the concentric dashed circles were too close to be reliably separated. The running times for these tests are shown in Table 6.2; in this case the speedups on an eight-processor machine are up to about 3.1.

I now use these examples to quantify the effects of some of the algorithmic techniques presented in Chap. 5.

For the first scale example, there are approximately 1.2×10^9 transformations where the scale and translational parameters lie within the bounds described in Subsect. 4.2.1. Of these, approximately 2.4×10^8 transform the model so that it lies within the image bitmap. The additional aspect ratio skew restriction leaves about 1.0×10^7 transformations still to be considered. The number of cells actually evaluated by the search was approximately 5.7×10^4 — about 99.5% of the remaining transformations were eliminated by the hierarchical search, without being explicitly considered. If no zoning had been used (if the model was considered to be a single zone), then 7.3×10^4 cells would have been evaluated, a 50% increase. The search took about 26 CPU seconds; if early rejection had not been used, the search would have evaluated exactly the same number of cells, but would have taken approximately twice as long.

Table 6.3 gives similar numbers for the other examples. In each of the examples, the restriction that the transformed model must lie inside the image has eliminated a substantial fraction of the transformations; the aspect ratio skew restriction has eliminated a large number of transformations. This is not surprising, as the aspect ratio skew is constrained to be close to one, effectively reducing the number of degrees of freedom by one. The efficient search then only examines a small fraction of these remaining transformations. Using 4×4 zoning is clearly effective, as shown in the next column, reducing the number of transformations examined substantially for a moderate cost in memory and some additional computational overhead. Increasing the number of zones above 4×4 reduces the number of transformations examined somewhat, but generally not enough to balance out the increased overhead and memory use. Finally, the last two columns summarise the CPU and wall-clock times required for these searches.

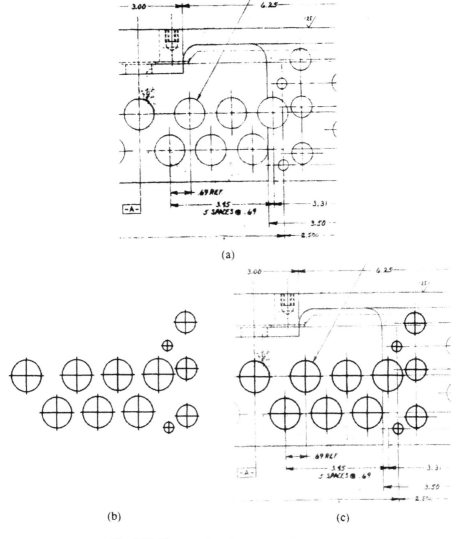

Fig. 6.18. The second scale test example, part one.

Table 6.3. The effects of the efficient search techniques on the scale tests.

Example	Transformations			Cells evaluated		Time (sec)	
	Within bounds	Inside borders	Satisfying restrictions	With 4 × 4 zoning	Without zoning	CPU	Wall
First test, part one	1.2×10^9	2.4×10^8	1.0×10^7	5.7×10^4	7.3×10^4	25.9	6.2
First test, part two	1.2×10^9	2.4×10^8	1.0×10^7	3.1×10^4	4.2×10^4	8.5	2.2
First test, part three	2.9×10^8	3.2×10^7	3.5×10^6	4.5×10^4	4.6×10^4	13.4	4.6
Second test, part one	1.0×10^{10}	7.3×10^9	1.1×10^8	1.1×10^5	1.8×10^5	16.1	5.3
Second test, part two	2.7×10^9	1.4×10^9	1.6×10^7	9.0×10^4	1.4×10^5	9.3	2.3

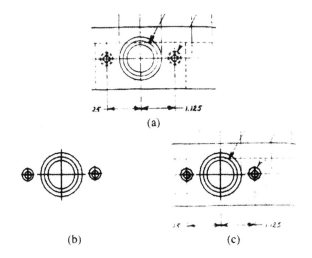

Fig. 6.19. The second scale test example, part two.

6.3 Affine

The most complex implementation, corresponding to the most complex group, is the implementation that searches the group *Aff* of affine transformations. It uses the cell decomposition method, using the box distance transform and zoning variants. It does early rejection, but does not do early acceptance: the higher branching factor in the subdivision means that correcting errors is more expensive (correcting each error involves evaluating more subcells), and so is not worthwhile. A parallel implementation, similar to the implementation described in the previous section, has also been done.

The model is divided up into 16 zones, by quartering it in both x and y. This may not divide up the model points well: some zones may contain many more points than others. It may well be worthwhile to modify the division procedure so that it attempts to balance out the number of points in each zone, but I have not done this.

This implementation, like the previous implementations, allows the user to specify borders, restricting the portion of the image that is actually searched. As in the previous section, it is useful to restrict the parameters in such a way that degenerate or near-degenerate poses (where the transformed model has shrunk to a point or a line) are eliminated.

Recall that a transformation g in *Aff* can be represented by a matrix T and a translation $t = (t_x, t_y)$; g performs the mapping

$$(x, y) \rightarrow (t_{00}x + t_{01}y + t_x, t_{10}x + t_{11}y + t_y)$$

when T is the matrix

$$T = \begin{bmatrix} t_{00} & t_{01} \\ t_{10} & t_{11} \end{bmatrix}.$$

One way to restrict the transformations being searched might be to supply parameters $t_{00}^{\min}$, $t_{00}^{\max}$ and so on, but this does not directly address the problem of the model collapsing to a line or a point. A more direct way is to consider the determinant of T,

$d = t_{00}t_{11} - t_{01}t_{10}$. This value is the relative area of the transformed model: how much larger or smaller it is than the original model. Degenerate transformations can then be eliminated by insisting that every transformation under consideration must have $d^{\max} \geq d \geq d^{\min}$, for some parameters $d^{\max}$ and $d^{\min}$; this eliminates transformations that make the model too large or too small. In any case, d should be positive: transformations whose relative area d is negative represent reflections of the model.

Consider the effect of the transformation g on a unit square. It performs the following mappings:

$$(0,0) \rightarrow (t_x, t_y)$$
$$(1,0) \rightarrow (a_{00} + t_x, a_{10} + t_y)$$
$$(0,1) \rightarrow (a_{01} + t_x, a_{11} + t_y)$$
$$(1,1) \rightarrow (a_{00} + a_{01} + t_x, a_{10} + a_{11} + t_y).$$

In other words, this unit square has been transformed into an arbitrary parallelogram. The range of valid transformations can be further restricted by considering the parallelograms that they produce. For example, if the side lengths are too different, then the aspect ratio of the transformed model is too skewed, so the transformation should be excluded. The user can therefore specify the maximum allowed aspect ratio skew $\alpha^{\max}$, and thereby reject any transformations where

$$\max \left(\frac{\sqrt{a_{00}^2 + a_{10}^2}}{\sqrt{a_{01}^2 + a_{11}^2}}, \frac{\sqrt{a_{01}^2 + a_{11}^2}}{\sqrt{a_{00}^2 + a_{10}^2}} \right) > \alpha^{\max}.$$

A third possible transformation restriction relies on the observation that the dot product of the sides of this parallelogram (normalised for the scaling of the edges) determines how greatly shearing the transformation t is: when it is small, the parallelogram is still roughly a (possibly rotated) square. As I will show below, restricting this shear value can be useful. Thus, another predicate that causes transformations to be rejected is

$$\frac{|a_{00}a_{01} + a_{10}a_{11}|}{\sqrt{a_{00}^2 + a_{10}^2}\sqrt{a_{01}^2 + a_{11}^2}} > s^{\max}.$$

As each cell is evaluated during the search, it is also checked to make sure that it contains some valid transformation; if every transformation inside the cell is eliminated by one or another of these restrictions, then the cell is rejected.

Once these parameters are in place, it is possible to restrict the range of transformations in interesting ways. For example, if $s^{\max} = 0$ and $\alpha^{\max} = 1$, then the only valid transformations consist of a uniform scale of the model, followed by a rotation and a translation. This transformation group is the target of several other visual recognition methods. Further restricting transformations by setting $d^{\min} = d^{\max} = 1$, means that only members of the group *Rig* of two-dimensional rigid motions (translations and rotations) are valid.

In practice, setting these parameters to exactly these limiting values causes problems: the restricted transformations subgroups are lower-dimensional manifolds in the continuous space of affine transformations. However, the search considers only a grid

Fig. 6.20. The model for the first affine example.

in this space; few locations on this grid lie exactly on the manifold. It is therefore a good idea to set these parameters to values that are slightly above or below the exact limiting values; this allows a certain amount of error, and thus allows grid transformations lying close to (but not on) the manifold of interest to be considered.

Figure 6.20 shows a model, extracted from an image of a planar object. Figure 6.21 shows a grey-level image, the edges extracted from that image, and the model located in that image. The image is 640×480 pixels. The directed search for best distance mode was used; the parameters were $\tau_F = \sqrt{5}$, $f_F = 1$, $\tau_R = 2$, $f_R = 0.6$, $d^{\min} = 0.5$, $d^{\max} = 1$, $\alpha^{\max} = 2$, $s^{\max} = 0.1$. The wall-clock time taken to locate the model was 0:02:22 (hours:minutes:seconds). The speedup (CPU time divided by wall-clock time) was 6.67.

This time is low enough for some practical applications, but probably not any interactive applications. It should be noted, however, that this image is larger than any of the images used in previous tests, and also that the number of points in the image and model are many times larger than can be handled by other methods which search under affine transformation: 17009 points and 1473 points, respectively.

Figure 6.22 shows the results of locating the same model in a second image. In this case, since there are two instances of the model present in the image, the directed search modes could not be used, as they might only have found one of the instances. The parameters used were $\tau_F = \tau_R = \sqrt{5}$, $f_F = 1$, $f_R = 0.8$, $d^{\min} = 0.3$, $d^{\max} = 1$, $\alpha^{\max} = 2$, $s^{\max} = 0.4$. The total time taken was 0:09:19 and the speedup was 5.91. One of the reasons for the time being longer than the previous test is the fact that the directed search modes could not be used; these would have increased the efficiency of the search.

The next example, shown in Fig. 6.23 shows how a partially occluded model can be located. The parameters used were $\tau_F = \tau_R = 1$, $f_F = 0.8$, $f_R = 0.6$, $\alpha^{\min} = 0.7$, $\alpha^{\max} = 1$, $\alpha^{\max} = 1.5$, $d^{\max} = 0.6$; the directed search for best fraction was also used, with parameters $p^{\times} = 0.75$, $p^{+} = 0$. In other words, as better and better matches were found, and the forward fraction f_F was increased as a consequence, f_R was also increased so $\tau_R = 0.75\tau_F$ at all times during the search. The wall-clock time was 0:29:33, and the speedup was 7.89, indicating that there is more parallelism present than is being exploited, and that close-to-linear speedups can be expected from adding more processors. Since the model is nearly rotationally symmetric, the search had to try many slight variations on the two wrong rotations, to see if they could be made to fit better than the right rotation, approximately tripling the time required.

I have also used this implementation on feature sets which are similar to those used by many other image search methods, illustrating its performance when the number of points in the image and model is small. Figure 6.24(a) shows the model object, and Fig. 6.24(b) shows the model point set. This consists of a number of corners which

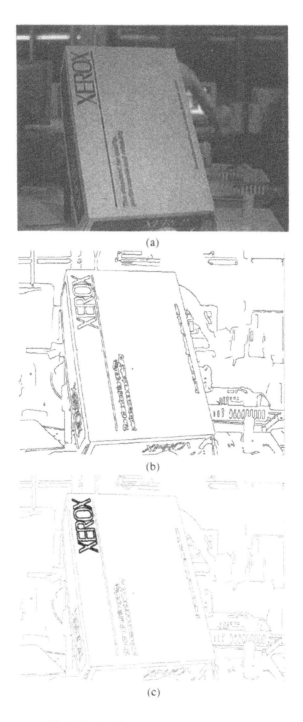

(a)

(b)

(c)

Fig. 6.21. The first affine example, part one.

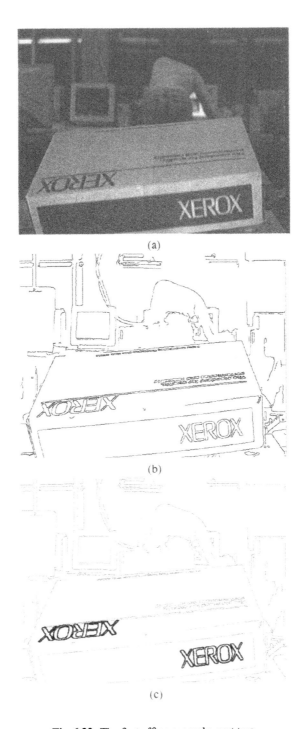

(a)

(b)

(c)

Fig. 6.22. The first affine example, part two.

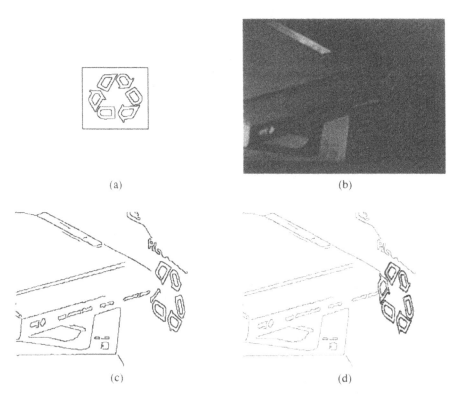

(a)

(b)

(c)

(d)

Fig. 6.23. The second affine test: locating a partially occluded object. (a) The model. (b) The image in which the model is to be located. The image is 320×240 pixels. (c) The edges extracted from the image. (d) The located model overlaid on the image edges.

were extracted, by hand, from the grey-level image; Fig. 6.24(c) shows them overlaid (as white circles) on the original image.

I then located that model object in three other images. The parameters used for all of these tests were $\tau_F = \tau_R = 2\sqrt{2}, f_F = 1, f_R = 0.8, d^{\min} = 0.2, d^{\max} = 1, \alpha^{\max} = 3,$ and $s^{\max} = 0.6$. Also, the directed search for best distance mode was used, with the reverse threshold tracking the forward threshold, with parameters $p^{\times} = 1, p^{+} = 0$. In other words, as better and better matches were found, and the forward threshold τ_F was decreased as a consequence, τ_R was decreased to match, so $\tau_F = \tau_R$ at all times during the search.

Figure 6.25(a) shows the input grey-level image for the first part of the test. Figure 6.25(b) shows the image point set. The computation took 3.8 seconds wall-clock time, and 6.4 seconds CPU time. A number of transformations, all of the same quality, were found. Figure 6.25(c) shows one of them (as black circles) overlaid on the image point set. Figure 6.25(d) shows the transformed model point set overlaid (as white circles) on the original image. Similarly, Figs. 6.26 and 6.27 show the images and test results for the second and third parts of this test. The time taken for the second part was 4.1 seconds wall-clock time, 6.7 seconds CPU time. The third part took 3.6 seconds wall-clock time and 7.9 seconds CPU time. All three images are 360×240 pixels.

I have also used the system to perform whole-frame registration. Figure 6.28 shows this application. The input is two grey-level images, taken by the same camera a second or so apart. There is significant depth in the scene, the camera has moved between the frames, and there is a large object that has moved in the world between the two frames. A large number of edge points in each image have no corresponding point in the other image; the moving object also occludes a significant (and different) part of each image. The task is to find the affine transformation that best aligns the two frames. The image point set consists of the edges from the first frame; the model point set is formed by decimating (by 95%) the edges from the second frame.

The first step is to find the pure translation of the model that brings it into best alignment with the first image. This is done using a special-case translation-only search engine (designed using the same set of principles as the more general search engine). This first step uses parameters $\tau_F = \sqrt{2}, f_F = 0.5,$ and the directed search for best fraction. It searches a translational range of ± 50 pixels in x and y. The translation it finds, $t = (-41, 5)$, is shown in Fig. 6.28(e). The forward fraction $f[t]$ is about 0.65. In other words, when the model point set is translated by $(-41, 5)$, about 65% of its points land within $\sqrt{2}$ pixels of some point of the first image. The alignment is good in some places, but poor in others. This translational alignment takes 2.3 seconds.

Once this translation has been found, the next step is to search for a slight affine distortion of it, in order to improve the match quality. Only a small range of transformations is searched: the translational range is ± 5 pixels about $(-41, 5)$; the other parameters are bounded by

$$\begin{bmatrix} 1 \pm 0.03 & \pm 0.03 \\ \pm 0.03 & 1 \pm 0.03 \end{bmatrix}.$$

The range of transformations is further restricted by $d^{\min} = 0.95, d^{\max} = 1.05, \alpha^{\max} = 1.02, s^{\max} = 0.02$. Thus, only a small range of the affine transformation space around the identity transformation is searched. I use $\tau_F = \sqrt{2}$, as before. I also use the directed

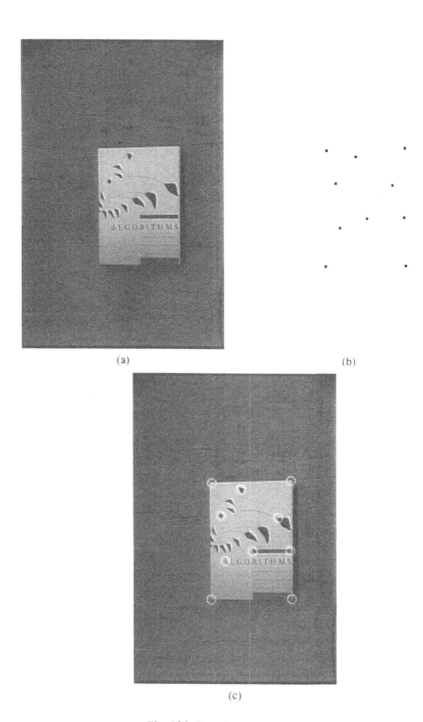

(a)

(b)

(c)

Fig. 6.24. The third affine test model.

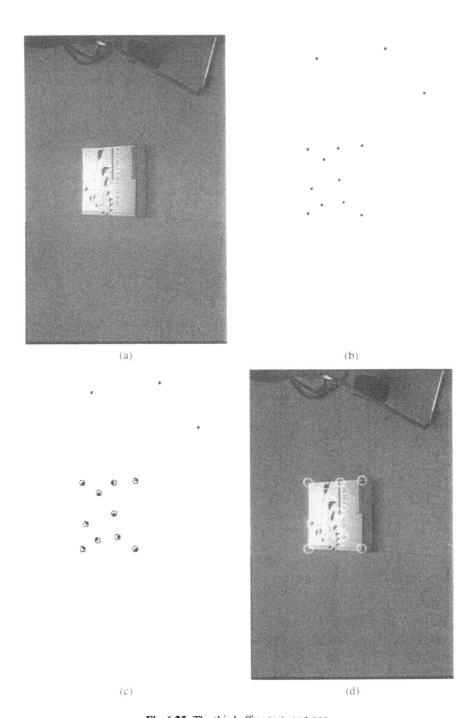

Fig. 6.25. The third affine test, part one.

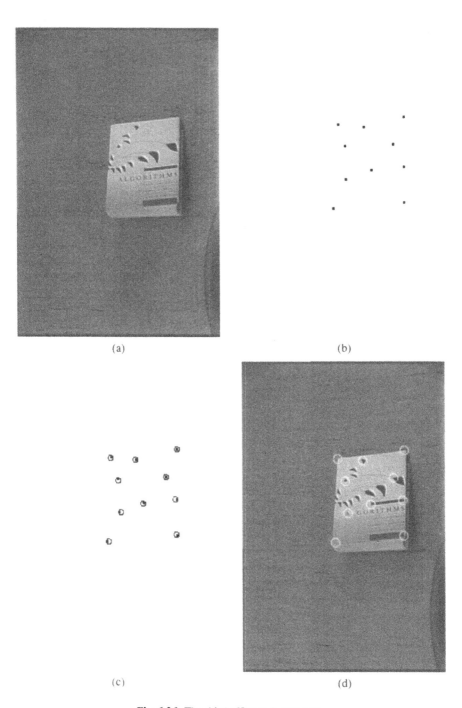

(a)

(b)

(c)

(d)

Fig. 6.26. The third affine test, part two.

126

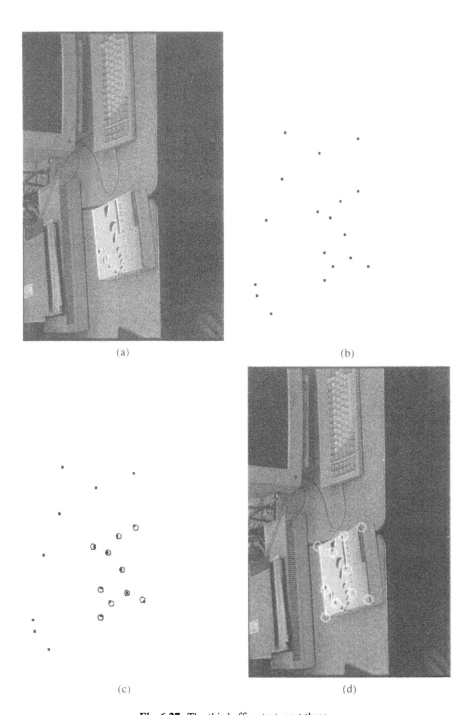

(a)

(b)

(c)

(d)

Fig. 6.27. The third affine test, part three.

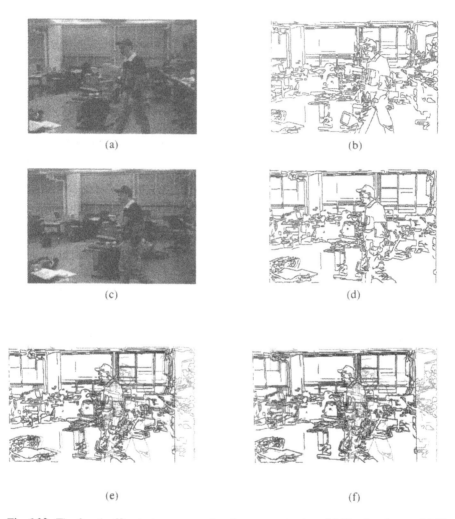

(a)

(b)

(c)

(d)

(e)

(f)

Fig. 6.28. The fourth affine test: compensating for camera motion. (a) The first frame. (b) The edges extracted from the first frame. (c) The second frame. (d) The edges extracted from the second frame. (e) The translation best aligning the two frames. (f) The affine transformation best aligning the two frames.

Fig. 6.29. The rigid motion test model.

search for best fraction as before, but with f_F initially set to 0.65 (since the translation found before is within the range being searched, and so the best transformation must be at least as good as it). This search took 32 seconds wall-clock, 220 seconds CPU time.

The final step is to ensure that this transformation is also a good match for the entire second edge image (not just the decimated subset used thus far). This is done by searching a very small region of transformation space around it (one grid step in each direction) and picking the best transformation; this takes only a second or two. The results of this search are shown in Fig. 6.28(f). The overall quality is significantly improved from the initial (purely translational) transformation. $f[t]$ for this transformation is 0.693 ($f[t]$ for the decimated model only is 0.725). The reverse fraction $f'[t]$ is 0.743.

Above, I claimed that by setting some of the range restriction parameters appropriately, the search could be restricted to the subgroup *Rig* of rigid motions. Figure 6.30 presents an example of such a restricted search. I restricted the search by setting $d^{\min} = 0.98$, $d^{\max} = 1.02$, $\alpha^{\max} = 1.02$ and $s^{\max} = 0.02$ (these parameters should not be set to their exact limiting values because of the rasterisation of transformation space). I also set $\tau_F = \sqrt{5}$ and $f_F = 0.9$. The reverse distance was not used because of the markings on the faces of the blocks, which are not present in the model. Since the model is four-way rotationally symmetric, I also restricted the transformation range to include rotations between 0 and $\pi/2$ only. A number of matches were found; these were grouped into connected components and the best match from each component was reported. The time taken for this search was 2.6 seconds wall-clock, 7.8 seconds CPU time.

As I did in Sect. 6.2, I now quantify some of the effects of the various efficient search techniques.

For the first part of the first example, there are approximately 1.3×10^{15} affine transformations where the affine and translational parameters lie within the *a priori* bounds discussed in Subsect. 4.2.1. Of these, approximately 3.5×10^{14} transformations (1) transform the model so that it lies within the image bitmap, and (2) have a positive determinant (they do not correspond to a reflection of the model bitmap). The additional scale, skew and shear restrictions leave about 8.4×10^{12} transformations still to be considered; thus, these parameter restrictions have eliminated all but one-fortieth of the remaining transformations, including many degenerate or near-degenerate transformations. The number of cells actually evaluated by the search was approximately 2.6×10^7 — over 99.999% of the remaining transformations were eliminated by the hierarchical search, without being explicitly considered. If no zoning had been used (if the model was considered to be a single zone), then 7.8×10^7 cells would have been evaluated, a threefold increase.

Table 6.4 gives similar numbers for the other examples. In each of the examples, the restriction that the transformed model must lie inside the image has eliminated a substantial fraction of the transformations; the exception is the fourth test, where this restriction

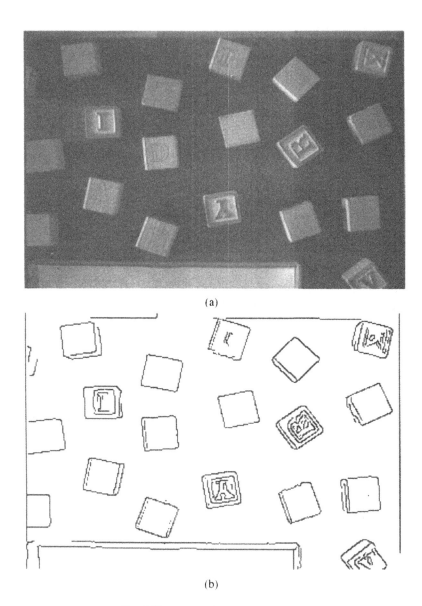

(a)

(b)

Fig. 6.30. The rigid motion test image.

Fig. 6.31. The rigid motion test results.

was not enforced, as a substantial fraction of the transformed model points had moved outside the bounds of the image. The restrictions on the overall transformation scale, skew and shear again reduced the number of transformations to be considered; in the rigid motion example, this reduction was especially pronounced, because of the restriction to essentially a three-dimensional subspace of the space of affine transformations. The efficient search then only examines a small fraction of these. This is more effective in the cases where the transformations were less restricted. It is especially effective in the third test, where the model and images were all sparse; in general, sparser images lead to more effective pruning, as the thresholded box distance transforms are correspondingly less dense. The last two columns summarise the CPU and wall-clock times required for these searches.

Both the second and fourth examples used the directed search for best fraction. If this had not been used, then the second example would have examined 2.8×10^8 transformations, approximately doubling its time, and the fourth example would have examined 3.2×10^6 transformations, again nearly double.

6.4 Summary

In this chapter, I have described the three implementations of the Hausdorff distance search method which I have developed. All of these implementations are built around the cell decomposition search technique. In the simpler search cases, some of the modifications to this technique are not worth adding, as they decrease the search time, but increase the pre-computation time required by more than the amount of time saved in the search.

Table 6.4. The effects of the efficient search techniques on the affine tests.

Example	Transformations			Cells evaluated		Time (sec)	
	Within bounds	Inside borders	Satisfying restrictions	With 4×4 zoning	Without zoning	CPU	Wall
First test, part 1	1.3×10^{15}	3.5×10^{14}	8.4×10^{12}	2.6×10^{7}	7.8×10^{7}	946.83	141.99
First test, part 2	1.3×10^{15}	3.5×10^{14}	4.9×10^{13}	1.0×10^{8}	3.9×10^{8}	3077.76	559.11
Second test	1.1×10^{14}	2.1×10^{13}	1.2×10^{12}	1.4×10^{8}	5.5×10^{8}	13984.79	1773.32
Third test, part 1	2.8×10^{14}	4.4×10^{13}	1.3×10^{13}	2.6×10^{5}	1.1×10^{6}	6.38	3.79
Third test, part 2	2.8×10^{14}	4.4×10^{13}	1.3×10^{13}	3.6×10^{5}	1.6×10^{6}	6.68	4.11
Third test, part 3	2.8×10^{14}	4.4×10^{13}	1.3×10^{13}	5.6×10^{5}	2.6×10^{6}	7.87	3.57
Fourth test	1.6×10^{7}	1.5×10^{7}	4.4×10^{6}	1.9×10^{6}	2.4×10^{6}	219.54	32.21
Rigid motion test	5.1×10^{11}	1.8×10^{11}	1.7×10^{6}	1.4×10^{5}	2.4×10^{5}	7.75	2.57

I have shown how parameters can be added to the search methods in order to restrict the search to reasonable transformations, and also to restrict it to interesting subgroups of the group *Aff* of affine transformations.

I have presented a number of examples of the operation of this method, showing that it is accurate, locating the object or object correctly in each case. In almost all cases, the search times were quite small; the exception was for searching under general affine transformations, when there were a large number (thousands) of points in the image and model. I believe that it is possible to develop further efficient search techniques that will reduce these times considerably.

Chapter 7

Applications

In the previous chapter, I showed how the minimum Hausdorff distance search works very well at finding an object in an image: it is accurate, robust in the presence of noise, and, except for searching for affine transformations, fast. In this chapter, I present some applications of the Hausdorff distance, showing how these robustness and speed properties are sufficient to build systems that interact with the world. These systems work reliably in the presence of noise and other complicating factors, at speeds which are fast enough to allow them to interact with a changing world.

7.1 Tracking

The work described in this section was done jointly by myself, Dan Huttenlocher, and Jae Noh; it has been previously described in [HNR1, HNR2].

In this section, we describe a model-based method for tracking nonrigid objects moving in a complex scene. The basic idea underlying the technique is to decompose the image of a solid object moving in space into two components: a two-dimensional motion and a two-dimensional shape change. Using the Hausdorff distance, the motion component can be efficiently factored out and the shape change can then be represented explicitly by a sequence of two-dimensional models, one corresponding to each image frame. The major assumption underlying the method is that the two-dimensional shape of an object changes slowly from one frame to the next. There is no assumption, however, that the two-dimensional image motion between successive frames is necessarily small.

7.1.1 Introduction

The problem of tracking moving objects has received a good deal of attention in the computer vision community over the last few years (e.g., [DG1, Ge1, KDTN1, Lo2, UM1, VGD1, WZ1]). Here, we focus on the problem of tracking nonrigid objects in complex scenes, including the case where there are other moving objects present. We use a model-based method in which two-dimensional models are extracted from the image data, and matched to successive frames of the image sequence. Because a model-based approach is able to exploit global attributes of the object being tracked, it can provide significant advantages over purely local methods for situations in which the environment is cluttered, there are multiple moving objects, or there may be a large motion of an object from one frame to the next. A number of other researchers have taken a model-based approach to motion tracking (e.g., [KDTN1, Lo2, UM1]). What characterises our approach is that there is no constraint on where in the image an object may have moved from one frame to the next, and there may be multiple moving objects in the scene. Moreover, the model of an object is acquired dynamically from the image sequence, rather than being provided *a priori*.

The central observation underlying this method is the fact that the two-dimensional image of an object moving in three-dimensional space can be decomposed into two parts

- a two-dimensional shape change, corresponding to a new aspect of the object becoming visible or an actual shape change of the object, and
- a two-dimensional motion (of some restricted kind) in the image, corresponding to the motion of the visible aspect of the object. The efficient translation-based Hausdorff distance search code described in Sect. 6.1 can be used to determine this motion.

The main condition imposed by our method is that the two-dimensional shape of an object not change greatly between two successive frames of an image sequence. In particular, there is no assumption that the two-dimensional motion from one frame to the next be small. This is a less restrictive assumption regarding the nature of the motion than is made by local differential methods. Such methods must assume that the entire change in the object from one image to the next is small (local), whereas we only assume that the *shape* change is small, and not the motion.

We represent an object as a sequence of binary images, one corresponding to each frame of the input image sequence (which also consists of a sequence of binary images). The model at time t is a subset of the image features at time t: each frame of the model specifies a set of points (nonzero pixels) in a given sub-region of the corresponding image frame. These pixels constitute the appearance, or shape, of the object being tracked at that time. Thus a model evolves from one time step to the next, capturing the changes in the image shape of an object as it moves. In the current implementation, the input binary images are intensity edges extracted from a sequence of grey-level images. However, any other means of deriving binary features from an image sequence could be used.

The basic tracking method operates by comparing the model at a given time, M_t, to the image at the next time step, I_{t+1}, in order to find the transformation specifying the best location of that model in that image (where the model and image are binary images derived by some feature extraction mechanism). Then a new model, M_{t+1}, is formed by selecting the subset of I_{t+1} that is near the transformed model M_t. This new model, M_{t+1}, represents the shape of the object at the next time step. The method of tracking an object is thus based entirely on comparing two-dimensional geometric structures, as represented by binary image models, between successive frames. There is no computation of local differential image quantities such as the optical flow or motion field. There are no a priori models of the object being tracked.

As an illustration of the method, Fig. 7.1 shows the images and the corresponding models for six frames from a 100 frame sequence. Each entry in the figure contains an image frame (360×240 pixels), the intensity edges found using a method similar to [Ca1], and the model extracted for that frame. The model at each time is a subset of the intensity edges for that frame. Each model is shown with a bounding box; note that the size of the models changes dynamically. The third frame in the figure illustrates a situation where the object was changing shape very rapidly from one frame to the next, so while the object is still being tracked successfully, the representation of its two-dimensional shape is relatively degraded. Despite the fact that the object changes two-dimensional shape substantially in successive frames, and even more so during the entire sequence, it is tracked successfully through all 100 frames. (Note that the models shown in the figures are the result of tracking the entire sequence of 100 frames.)

The current implementation of the method can process approximately six frames per second on a four-processor SPARCstation-10. This includes the initial edge detection process. The frames are half-resolution NTSC video images (360 × 240 pixels).

The major aspects of our approach are:

1. Decomposing the image of a moving 3D object into two parts: a 2D motion and a 2D shape change. The shape change is assumed to be relatively small from one frame to the next, but the motion can be arbitrarily large (i.e., there is no local search window in the image).
2. Capturing the 2D shape change between successive images with 2D geometric models that evolve across time. The models provide global geometric constraints for tracking an object.
3. Fast 2D model matching using the minimum Hausdorff distance under translation.

The remainder of this section is organised as follows. In Subsect. 7.1.2 we describe how to use the Hausdorff distance to do tracking. In Subsect. 7.1.3 we describe an implementation of the tracking method, and in Subsect. 7.1.4 we discuss extensions of the method to handle multiple moving objects and objects that can disappear from view.

7.1.2   Tracking Using the Hausdorff Distance

One of the interesting properties of the Hausdorff distance is the asymmetry inherent in the computation. The fact that every point of the model (or some fraction subset of the model) is near some point of the image says nothing about whether every point of the image (or some subset) is near some point of the model. In other words, the forward and reverse Hausdorff distances can attain very different values.

With the above-mentioned asymmetry of the Hausdorff distance in mind, let us now examine the tracking problem. The idea is to exploit the asymmetry in the distance to perform two different functions: (1) finding where the model at a given time, M_t, moved to in the image at the next time, I_{t+1}, and (2) computing the new model, M_{t+1}, from M_t and I_{t+1}. For the remainder of this section we will assume that the model M_t has m points (i.e., in the binary image representation of M_t there are m nonzero pixels).

Locating the Object in a New Image   The forward distance measures the degree to which some portion of the model resembles the image. The minimum value of this distance identifies the best position of M_t in I_{t+1}, under the action of some group G. Intuitively, the minimum forward distance identifies the best position, g^*, of M_t in the image I_{t+1}. Figure 7.2 illustrates the forward distance computation, where the transformation group G is the group of translations Tr. The figure shows a model, an image, and the translation of the model that minimises the partial directed Hausdorff distance when the forward fraction f_F is set to 0.8. The distance at this minimizing translation is $\sqrt{2}$, meaning that at least 80% of the model points lie within one pixel (diagonally) of some image point.

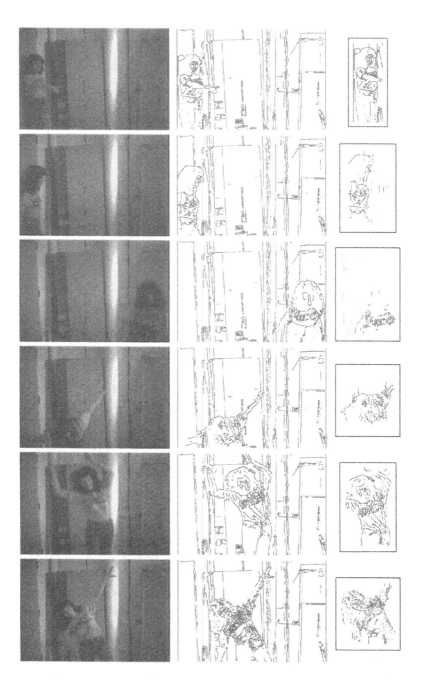

Fig. 7.1. Six selected frames (numbers 1, 20, 40, 60, 80 and 100) from a 100 frame motion sequence, and the corresponding models of the object being tracked. Each model is a subset of the edge pixels from that image frame.

136

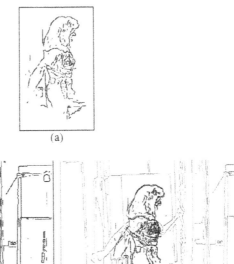

(a)

(b)   (c)

Fig. 7.2. Using the forward distance to locate a model in an image.

Updating the Object Model Having determined the best location g^* of the model M_t in the subsequent image frame I_{t+1}, it now remains to build M_{t+1} by determining which points of I_{t+1} are part of the new model. We are interested in finding some subset of the image I_{t+1} that agrees well with the transformed model $g^*(M_t)$. We do this by using the distance from each point of I_{t+1} to the nearest point of $g^*(M_t)$ as a criterion for selecting the subset of image points that belong to M_{t+1}. That is, we define

$$M_{t+1} = \{a \in I_{t+1} \mid \min_{b \in M_t} \|g^*(b) - a\| \le \delta\} \tag{7.1}$$

for some distance δ. In other words, M_{t+1} is all those points of I_{t+1} that are within distance δ of some point of $g^*(M_t)$. Note that this can be determined using the distance transform of the model M_t.

The choice of the distance δ controls the degree to which the method is able to track objects that change shape. For instance, if $\delta = 0$ then only those points of I_{t+1} that are directly superimposed on $g^*(M_t)$ will be included in M_{t+1}, and thus the method will track only motions in G and not shape changes. In practice, setting $\delta = 0$ causes the tracker to lose an object after several frames even if the object shape does not actually change, due to noise and uncertainty in the locations of features. The larger the value of δ, the more that the tracker is able to follow nonrigid motion, and to pick up new parts of an object that have come into view since the previous frame. The parameter δ should be thought of as reflecting how much of the change from one frame to the next will be incorporated into the model (versus being left in the background). Thus, as δ becomes larger the ability to track nonrigid motion increases, at the cost of also possibly tracking the background.

Often, in sequences showing people walking, the body and head change shape very little from one frame to the next, while the arms and legs move rapidly compared with the overall motion. The body and head are included in the models M_t since they tend not to change shape, while even if an arm, say, is in M_t, it may well not be included in M_{t+1} since it might have moved more than δ pixels. However, if an arm is not initially in M_t but is held stationary (or moves only slowly) relative to the body, it will gradually be re-acquired over the next few frames (at a rate of about δ pixels per frame). This phenomenon can be seen in the models shown in Fig. 7.1.

The models in Fig. 7.1 were generated by running the tracker with f_F set to be 0.8 for the forward match, and with a δ of 8 pixels for constructing the models. The group of transformations, G, was the translation group. These parameter values were used successfully in all the examples shown here, and in many other sequences which we have analyzed with this tracker. In the following section we describe the tracker in more detail. We then consider some other techniques that are used to enhance the basic method. At a high level, however, the method is simple:

– Use the minimum forward Hausdorff distance from the model to the image to find where the object has moved. This tracks the two-dimensional motion of the object.
– Use the distance from the image to the transformed model as a criterion to select a subset of the image points that form part of the next model. This tracks the two-dimensional shape change of the object.

7.1.3 An Implementation of the Tracker

Recall that the basic observation underlying the method is to decompose the image of an object moving in space into a two-dimensional motion and a two-dimensional shape change. In the current system, we use the group of translations as the group of allowable two-dimensional motions. That is, any change in the image of an object other than a translation is encoded as a change in the two-dimensional shape of that object (i.e., a change in the model from one frame to the next). Allowing only translational motion means that rotation or scaling in the image are treated as changes in shape. While it is possible to allow larger groups of image motions (e.g., rotation and scale in addition to translation) there is a significant computational cost to doing so.

Finding the Model's New Location Possible locations of the model M_t are identified in the image at the next time step, I_{t+1}, by finding the translation giving the minimum forward distance. However, rather than computing the single translation giving the minimum distance, we identify the set of translations of M_t, call it X, such that the partial directed Hausdorff distance is no larger than some value τ_F. This is the set of translations which satisfy the forward criterion. Intuitively, X is the set of possible locations of M_t in I_{t+1} — the translations for which the translated model matches a portion of the image well.

We find all the translations where the distance is small, rather than the single best translation, because there may be multiple translations that are essentially the same quality, in which case simply finding the best translation does not allow us to detect the presence of multiple matches.

Once the set of possible translations, X, has been computed, it is partitioned into equivalence classes based on connected components in the grid of translations. This is because one instance of the object in the image may result in a number of translations that are below the threshold τ_F, and these are likely to all be neighboring translations. Thus we break X into sets X_i of neighboring translations (i.e., connected components in the translation-space where the forward distance is below τ_F). Each of these sets of neighboring translations corresponds to a possible instance of the object, and is processed separately. We find the best translation in each X_i, and use that translation as the representative possible location of the model for the set X_i.

For each translation $x \in X_i$ we know the actual distance from the model to the image at this translation, $d_{Tr}(x)$. This distance can be used to rate the quality of the translations in X_i, those with lower distance being better. Moreover, for each translation $x \in X_i$ we know the actual number of model points that are within distance d of image points, given by $f_{Tr}(x)m$. Therefore, each position $x \in X_i$ of the model is scored by a pair $(d_{Tr}(x), f_{Tr}(x))$.

We thus define the best match in each set X_i as the translation that minimises d_{Tr}, which is only natural as we are seeking the minimum forward Hausdorff distance. If there are multiple translations with the same (minimal) value of d_{Tr} then we select the one with the largest forward fraction f_{Tr}. This match is the representative position of the model in the image for the equivalence class X_i. For the remainder of this subsection, we assume that there is just one equivalence class of translations, $X_1 = X$. In general this is the case, because multiple matches only occur when there are several objects of nearly the same two-dimensional shape in the image. In Subsect. 7.1.4 we handle the case of multiple matches, and of no match. The translation $x \in X_1$ with the best match score specifies the location of M_t in I_{t+1}. We call this translation x^*.

Updating the Model Having found the best translation, x^*, of M_t with respect to I_{t+1}, the new model M_{t+1} is constructed by selecting those points of I_{t+1} that are within distance δ of some point of $M_t \oplus x^*$, as described in (7.1). This is done by dilating M_t by a disk of radius δ, shifting this by x^*, and then computing the logical **and** of I_{t+1} with the dilated and translated model.

In order to allow for models that may be changing in size (e.g., objects that are getting closer or farther away, or changing shape by stretching), the size of the array in which M_{t+1} is stored is increased whenever there are a significant number of points near the boundary, and is decreased whenever there are relatively few points near the boundary. The height and width of the model array are adjusted separately.

The initial model, corresponding to the first frame of the image sequence, must be computed specially because there is no previous model. The user specifies a rectangle in the first frame that contains the initial model. The image is then processed to select a subset of the points in this rectangle. This is done by assuming that the camera does not move between the first two frames, and using this fact to filter the first image frame based on the second image frame (with the filtering operation described below in Sub-subsect. 7.1.4). Those points in the user-selected window that moved between the first and second frames are then used as the points of the initial model. Thus the only input from the user is a rectangle in the first frame of the image sequence that contains the moving object (and as little else as possible).

7.1.4 Extensions to the Basic Method

In this section we describe four extensions to the basic tracking method presented above. The first of these is a filtering process, in which the stationary parts of the image frame I_{t+1} are removed before the model M_t is matched to it. This improves the performance of the method in cluttered scenes. The second extension is searching for a lost object. When the tracker cannot find M_t in I_{t+1}, it tries matching previous models to the image. The third extension deals with situations where the image may contain multiple objects of similar shape. In this case, simple trajectory information is used to help disambiguate multiple possible matches. The fourth extension also uses this trajectory information to accelerate the matching process by directing the search for the new position of the model.

Filtering Stationary Background For cluttered scenes or highly textured images, the basic tracking method can be quite sensitive to the choice of the value of δ (recall that δ is the threshold for determining whether or not a point of I_{t+1} is made part of M_{t+1}). The problem is that if δ is too small then the method will not tolerate much change in shape from one frame to the next. On the other hand, if δ is even moderately large, the model will start to pick up clutter in the background as part of the object. One means of dealing with this problem is to eliminate certain forms of clutter from the image and from the model. In particular, things that did not change from one frame to the next are not worth tracking, and can be removed from I_{t+1}. When the object moves but the camera stays still, such a filtering process removes much of the background in an image. When the camera moves, in general nearly all of the image changes, so the filtering process does very little.

The filtering is implemented as follows. Any point of I_{t+1} that is directly superimposed on a point of I_t is removed from I_{t+1} as a pre-processing step (prior to matching M_t or constructing M_{t+1}). A shot-noise filter is then applied to remove small connected components (e.g., points in I_{t+1} that extend just beyond the structures of I_t). Note that if nothing moves from frame I_t to I_{t+1}, then the filtering removes the entire image. This is fine, however, because if nothing moved then no tracking is required; we simply let $M_{t+1} = M_t$. This is not the same as losing the object; in that case there is change in the image from one frame to the next but the model cannot be located.

Finding a Lost Object The tracking method as described thus far does not work when the object being tracked temporarily disappears from view or changes shape suddenly from one frame to the next. In such cases, no match is found of the model M_t to the image I_{t+1} at the distance τ_F. When this happens, we compare additional models to that image frame, I_{t+1}, in which the object no longer was found. These additional models are the models from certain previous frames, $M_{t_1}, M_{t_2}, \ldots$ ($1 \leq t_i \leq t$) which were chosen as canonical views of the object. We refer to this as "hunt down mode", because the past history of the system is used to hunt for the missing object.

In this mode, the canonical models are matched to the image, until either a good match is found, or the set of canonical models has been exhausted. The first canonical model that matches the image is then used to construct M_{t+1} in the normal manner. If none of the canonical models match I_{t+1} then the tracker has lost the object at that time. No model array M_{t+1} is constructed for such a frame. Rather than giving up when no match is found, the tracker continues trying to match M_t and the set of canonical models to each successive image frame until a matching image frame is found. This allows us to continue tracking the object if it returns to view, or moves so as to present a familiar aspect to the camera.

The set of canonical models, C, is constructed by selecting distinctive-looking models from certain frames of the image sequence. After each model M_{t+1} is created, it is compared with the current set of canonical models. If the model is sufficiently different from all the models in C, then it constitutes a new view of the object and is added to the set. This comparison is done using the *undirected* minimum Hausdorff distance. The process of comparing each model with the set C is relatively fast, because the different models are in general approximately the same size, and so there are not many translations to consider.

For the image sequences presented here, and a number of others we have looked at, there are generally around 10 or 12 canonical models formed for a given object (out of the 100 frames). It should be noted that the process of matching multiple models to I_{t+1} is not much slower than just using the single model M_t. This is because many of the computations performed when matching M_t to I_{t+1}, such as the computation of the distance transform of I_{t+1}, may be re-used when matching other models with I_{t+1}.

The sequence in Fig. 7.3 shows a person walking around as the camera pans (the camera was under manual control). The tracked object moves almost entirely out of the image, but is correctly re-acquired after a few frames, when a sufficiently large portion has reappeared. It is not necessary to wait for the object to reappear completely, as the partial directed Hausdorff distance can successfully locate an object when it is partially obscured.

Disambiguating Multiple Matches The tracking method as described thus far may not work for sequences containing multiple moving objects of approximately the same 2D shape. In such cases the model M_t may be incorrectly located in the image I_{t+1}. We now discuss some extensions to the tracker, in which simple trajectory information is used to help with this problem. (Note that this also addresses the case in which multiple matches of a model are found due to erroneous matching of the model to the background, but in practice we have not observed this to happen.)

The idea is to use trajectory information in order to identify frames where the object being tracked might be incorrect. For instance, frames in which the trajectory of the object being tracked has changed suddenly are candidates for places where the tracker might have made an error and started to track the wrong thing in the image. In such a case, the tracking program enters "suspicious mode" in which additional models are

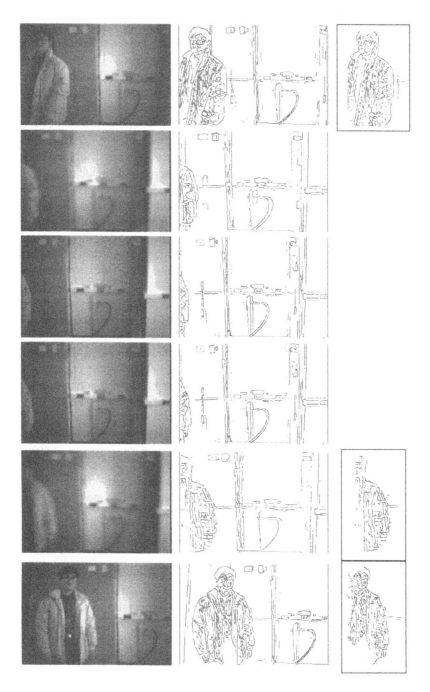

Fig. 7.3. Six selected frames (numbers 70, 72, 74, 76, 78 and 80) from a 100 frame motion sequence, and the corresponding model of the object being tracked. Note that no model was generated for frames 72, 74 or 76.

used in order to see if any of them match the image as well as M_t does. In effect, this checks whether M_t corresponds to some impostor in the image.

Currently we use very simple trajectory information, in order to detect situations in which the tracker may have started to follow the wrong object. The trajectory of the object is defined to be the translation from frame I_{t-1} to I_t. That is, the model M_{t-2} matched I_{t-1} at some translation x^*_{t-1} and the model M_{t-1} matched I_t at some translation x^*_t. The vector $v_t = x^*_t - x^*_{t-1}$ is defined to be the current trajectory of the object (i.e., simply its motion from the previous frame). The current motion of the object is then $v_{t+1} = x^*_{t+1} - x^*_t$, where x^*_{t+1} is the location of the match of M_t to I_{t+1}. When there is a significant change between v_t and v_{t+1}, the tracker enters suspicious mode.

When the tracker goes into suspicious mode, it compares the models from the previous several frames (currently the previous 5 models) with I_{t+1}, in addition to the normal comparison with M_t, since it believes that M_t might be an impostor. Given the matches of all these models, the tracker selects the match that has the closest trajectory to v_t. Once the tracker goes into suspicious mode, it stays that way for several frames (currently 5 frames or until one of the other models matches better than M_t, whichever comes first). This is because the object being tracked may be temporarily hidden from view, so the tracker gives it a few frames to re-appear.

Using suspicious mode, objects in image sequences such as the one shown in Fig. 7.4 can be correctly tracked. During the sequence in the figure, each object passed in front of the other several times, and so was obscured from view. The objects also changed their two-dimensional shape quite significantly. Nonetheless, each one was successfully tracked through the entire sequence, and the tracker did not misidentify one object as the other (although it did temporarily track the wrong person for a frame or two while the correct person was hidden from view). This sequence illustrates the potential power of model-based methods in which two-dimensional shape is used to track an object. Without such additional global constraints (or overly strong trajectory constraints), it is very difficult to track objects that pass behind other similar objects. It should be noted that the third and fourth columns of Fig. 7.4 show the result of two *independent* runs of the tracker using the same image sequence as input, and differing only in their initial models. In other words, the tracker did not know that there were two moving objects, and that it was supposed to avoid confusing them.

Accelerating the Search As stated before, this method does not restrict the allowable motion of the object between one frame and the next: it can move anywhere in the image, and will be found as long as its shape has not changed too much. However, most objects moving in the world follow smooth trajectories; they do not teleport randomly around. We can use this to accelerate the search for M_t in I_{t+1} by making the assumption that the trajectory of the object is likely to be constant, or close to constant. We therefore predict that the location of M_t in I_{t+1} will be $x^*_t + v_t$. This gives us an initial search location; we search for translations of M_t which lie in a 16×16 pixel square centered at this location. If no match is found in that square, then we expand the search to the entire image (i.e., remove any restrictions).

If a match is found in that square, then the search is not continued. It might seem that in this case, the method might lose track of the object, by choosing a similar-looking im-

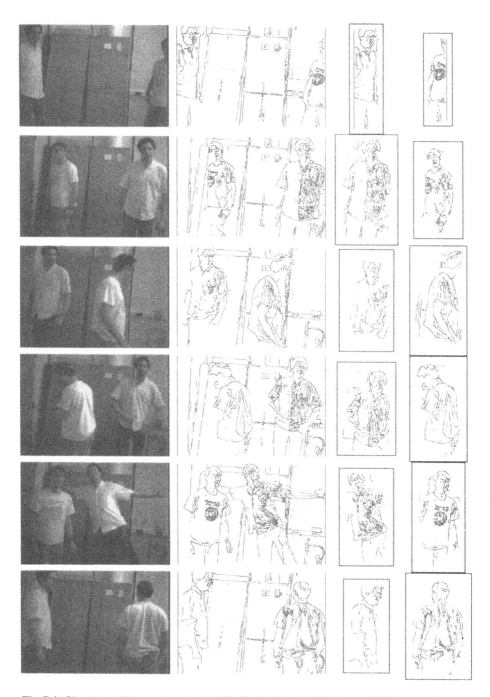

Fig. 7.4. Six selected frames (numbers 1, 20, 40, 60, 80 and 100) from a 100 frame motion sequence, and the corresponding models of the two objects being tracked.

144

postor, when the real object was not found, because its trajectory had changed. However, in this case, multiple matches of the model would have been found if the full search had been conducted, and as stated above, the one whose trajectory closest matched the previous trajectory would have been chosen; this is the one which the restricted search found. This restriction therefore does not change the answer produced, and is much faster in the case where the object's trajectory in the image is roughly constant.

7.1.5 Summary

The steps of the tracking method are thus as follows.

1. Filter the image edges of I_{t+1} to remove stationary background.
2. Find the best matching position of the model from previous time, M_t, with respect to the filtered image I_{t+1}, using the partial directed Hausdorff distance (where we have used $f_F = .8$ and $\tau_F = 10$ pixels).
   - Use trajectory information as described in Subsubsect. 7.1.4 to disambiguate multiple matches.
   - Use the set of of canonical models C to locate the object if no match of M_t to I_{t+1} is found.
   - Accelerate the search by using trajectory information to search first around the most likely location.
3. Construct the new model, M_{t+1}, by selecting those points of I_{t+1} that are within distance δ of points of the translated M_t (where we have used $\delta = 8$ pixels). Update the size of the model array if required. Compare M_{t+1} to the models in C and add it to C if it is different enough from all of the current members.

Although there are several parameters to the algorithm, we have used the same values for these parameters in successfully processing many image sequences, including those shown here.

In summary, the method consists solely of locating two-dimensional geometric models in two-dimensional edge images. There is no limitation on the search in the image — the model can translate anywhere from one frame to the next (though it is found faster if its motion is predictable). The nontranslational motion, however, must be small from one frame to the next, as this is considered to be a change in the two-dimensional shape of the object. The method can successfully track objects through image sequences in which they change overall shape substantially, they move large distances from one frame to the next, and they may be partially or fully occluded in several successive frames. It can also be computed quickly, processing about six half-resolution NTSC video images (360×240 pixels) per second. This shows how the efficient search techniques of Chap. 5 have yielded an application of the Hausdorff distance which operates at real-time speeds.

This method is able to work so quickly for three reasons.

1. The Hausdorff distance search engine that it uses is built using the efficient search techniques we have described.
2. It usually only has to search only a small portion of the transformation space, as it predicts the tracked object's location using a simple estimate of its velocity.

3. In a somewhat circular manner, it is able to work so quickly because it can work so quickly: if the images which it processes are close enough together in time, then the translational approximation to the motion of the object is quite good, and so only the group of translations needs to be searched; this means that the search takes little time, and so it is able to process another image very soon, so the images it processes are close together.

7.2 Navigation

This section describes a method for navigating a robot from an initial position to a specified landmark in its visual field, using a sequence of monocular images. The location of the landmark with respect to the robot is determined using the change in size and position of the landmark in the image as the robot moves. The landmark location is estimated after the first three images are taken, and this estimate is refined after each motion. One of the novel aspects of this method is that it uses no explicit three-dimensional information.

7.2.1 Introduction

The work described in this section was done jointly by myself, Dan Huttenlocher, and Michael Leventon; it has been previously described in [HLR1, HLR2].

In this section, we describe a method for using two-dimensional shape information to determine the location of a mobile robot with respect to some visual landmark in the world. The task is for the robot to navigate to a specified target or landmark in its visual field, possibly in the presence of obstacles. The landmark is initially specified either by marking some portion of an image (containing the landmark) or by providing a prior model. The location of the landmark with respect to the robot is recovered from the change in apparent size and position of the landmark in the image, as a function of the motion of the robot. The size and position of the landmark are determined by comparing two-dimensional shapes from successive images taken as the robot moves. The minimum Hausdorff distance under translation and scale is used to locate the landmark visually as the robot moves.

The key aspects of the method are,

1. The position of the landmark is expressed in terms of the robot-centered quantities range (distance) and bearing (orientation), rather than world coordinates.
2. The range and bearing are calculated using the change in size and location of the object in the image, as a function of the translation and rotation of the robot. The methods do not require prior camera calibration.
3. The identification of the landmark in the image data is performed by comparing two-dimensional shapes that can translate and scale, without the use of three-dimensional shape information. The range and bearing to the landmark are used to predict its size and location in the image as the robot moves, in order to speed up the processing.

Our approach differs from much of the previous work in visually guided robot navigation since it uses recognition of a specific object in the world instead of extracting some more global image properties; see, for example, the use of stereo in [GTS1]. While this only gives us essentially a single depth reading, it allows us to concentrate on the landmark, and so obtain a high degree of overall accuracy in motion, as we continually confirm that we are on track towards the specified target. One consequence of this is that the method can handle highly cluttered scenes. In contrast with work such as [ZF1], we do not construct any explicit three-dimensional models. Our work also complements the system described in [ZBT1] for finding distinctive landmarks along a route, by providing an effective means of navigating from one landmark to the next.

Our system is basically a camera mounted on a wheeled robot, TOMMY. TOMMY is shown in Fig. 7.5. A description of the design and implementation of the systems which make up TOMMY can be found in [RD1] and [Br2]. The robot is designed to move across a relatively flat surface. The camera is mounted at a fixed position on the robot, with its focal point at approximately the center of rotation of the robot, its optic axis approximately in the direction of forward motion of the robot, and its image plane approximately perpendicular to the ground plane. The camera may therefore move perpendicularly to its image plane, or rotate about its focal point.

The overall operation of the navigation method consists of the following steps: (1) grab an image of the current visual field of the robot, (2) use a two-dimensional model to localise the landmark in the current image (this shape comparison is currently done off-board on a Sun SPARCstation), (3) compute the range and bearing using the localised landmark and the robot motion since the previous image was taken, (4) construct a new two-dimensional model to use in localizing the landmark in the next image, and (5) command the robot to make the next motion (a forward motion or a rotation), whereupon return to step 1. Initially we will describe the method assuming that the robot stops moving during steps 1–4, but in practice these operations actually happen concurrently with the robot motion. We have experimented extensively with the navigation system, and it generally can successfully bring the robot into contact with a target that is approximately half a meter in each dimension.

The method described here shares some characteristics with the method in Sect. 7.1. In particular, it uses a very similar locate-update cycle. However, it differs in that the model scales as well as translates, and also in that the principal source of change in the model is the motion of the camera, rather than the motion and shape change of the tracked object. Shape change, as long as it is not too significant from one frame to the next, can also be handled by this navigation method.

7.2.2 Determining the Range to the Landmark

In this subsection we describe the method used to compute the range, r, to a landmark, and discuss the assumptions underlying the method. The only quantities that are measured are the change (increase) in the apparent size of the landmark in the image, s, and the distance that the robot moved, m. Consider a pinhole camera with focal length f, and a landmark of length L whose center lies D away from the optical axis, as illustrated in Fig. 7.6. The camera moves a distance m in the direction of the optic axis (thus towards the landmark, as the landmark is visible). Before the motion, the image of the

Fig. 7.5. The Cornell mobile robot TOMMY.

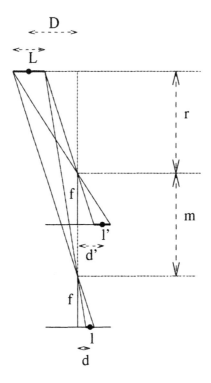

Fig. 7.6. Determining the range to the landmark.

---

landmark is of length l, and after the motion is of length l'. The offset of the center of the landmark from the center of the image is d in the first image and d' in the second. From the projection equations,

$$\frac{f}{d+l/2} = \frac{r+m}{D+L/2}$$

and

$$\frac{f}{d'+l'/2} = \frac{r}{D+L/2}$$

and thus $(r+m)(d+l/2) = r(d'+l'/2)$. Similarly $f/d = (r+m)/D$ and $f/d' = r/D$, and thus $(r+m)d = rd'$. From this we obtain $(r+m)l/2 = rl'/2$ and rewriting in terms of r yields

$$r = \frac{m}{\frac{l'}{l}-1} = \frac{m}{s-1} \tag{7.2}$$

where $l'/l = s$ is the change in size of the landmark in the image.

The quantity $r = m/(s-1)$ depends only on the size change s and the distance moved m, but not the camera parameters. Implicitly, however, the accuracy of the range measurement depends on the motion being nearly directly towards the landmark. This is because r only measures the actual range to the landmark when the motion is directly

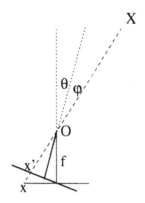

Fig. 7.7. Computing focal length.

---

towards the object (i.e., the quantity D is zero). There are two sources of inaccuracy when $D \neq 0$. The first is that r only measures the component of the range in the direction of the motion. The second source of inaccuracy when $D \neq 0$ comes from that fact that the derivation of $r = m(s - 1)$ assumes that the landmark is in a plane perpendicular to the direction of motion of the camera (see Fig. 7.6). When $D = 0$ (and the landmark is small or far away), the landmark projects directly onto the optical center, and this assumption is not necessary. When D is nonzero and the landmark is in a plane that is not perpendicular to the direction of motion (or is not planar), there is error in computing the range. These two sources of inaccuracy thus lead to a navigation strategy of heading directly towards the landmark, so that the resulting errors are small.

7.2.3 Centering the Landmark in the Image

The above method for computing the range to a landmark requires centering the landmark in the image, so that the robot can head directly towards the landmark in order to estimate the range. Centering the landmark in the image is straightforward given an estimate of the focal length of the camera. Since rotating the robot rotates the camera about its focal point, a rotation of the robot simply changes the x-coordinate of an object in the image. Thus if the landmark is centered at some image location $c = (c_x, c_y)$, a rotation by $\theta = \tan^{-1}(c_x/f)$ places the landmark at the image center ($x = 0$), where f is the focal length of the camera. We do not assume that f is known, but rather determine it from the motion of the landmark in the image as a function of the rotation of the camera. The initial estimate of f is obtained by rotating the camera a known amount, and is then refined during subsequent motion towards the landmark, until the robot is close enough that perspective effects and other sources of error become significant.

Figure 7.7 illustrates the manner in which we compute an approximation to f by rotating the camera some known amount about the focal point. Consider a point X in the world that projects to a point x in the image. If the camera is rotated about the focal point by some amount θ, then X will project to some new location x' in the resulting image. Let φ be the angle between the optic axis of the rotated camera and the line $\overline{XO}$

(where O is the focal point of the camera). Let $\psi = \theta + \varphi$ be the angle between the optic axis of the original camera and the line $\overline{XO}$.

We know that $\tan(\psi) = x/f$ and $\tan(\varphi) = x'/f$, and hence

$$\tan(\psi) - \tan(\varphi) = \frac{x - x'}{f}.$$

This can be used to approximate f by noting that since $\theta = \psi - \varphi$, when $\tan(\psi) - \tan(\varphi) \approx \tan(\psi - \varphi)$ then

$$f \approx \frac{x - x'}{\tan(\theta)}. \tag{7.3}$$

This approximation is close when $\cos(\psi - \varphi) \gg \sin(\psi)\sin(\varphi)$ which clearly holds when ψ and φ are both small, and which holds very well over the range of rotations that occur with our camera, which has a visual angle of $\pm 15°$.

7.2.4 Locating the Landmark in the Image

As the robot moves, the landmark changes size and position in the camera image. After every motion, the robot recomputes the range and bearing to the landmark so that it may adjust its course, in order to ensure that it continues to move directly towards the landmark.

The robot's time frame is divided into time steps; each time step corresponds to the robot completing a motion (either a forward translation or a rotation). At the beginning of time step t, the robot has a model of the landmark object M_t, an estimate r_t of the range to the landmark, and the position x_t of the landmark in the camera image (i.e., the bearing to the landmark). It performs some motion, then acquires a new frame from the camera and detects the intensity edges (using a detector similar to [Ca1]). This produces a binary edge image I_{t+1}, in which the robot must locate the landmark, using its previous model M_t.

Since the robot has moved, the landmark has also moved (translated) in the image. It has also enlarged, as the robot is getting closer to it. Also, if the robot rotates, or does not move directly towards the landmark, then the landmark may appear to shrink slightly in x. The expected change in shape and position of the landmark is therefore well-modeled by the group of translations and independent (x, y) scales. We use the parallel implementation described in Sect. 6.2 to locate the landmark visually in each frame. It determines the best transformation of the model as a quadruple (t_x, t_y, s_x, s_y), giving a translation and a scale of the model M_t which minimises the forward Hausdorff distance from the model to the image I_{t+1}.

The stages in the processing of I_{t+1} are as follows. First, the robot uses the information that it knew from the previous time step (the size and position of the landmark) together with its knowledge of the motion it performed to estimate a new size and position, and uses the Hausdorff distance implementation to search around that location for a section of I_{t+1} which closely resembles M_t. It searches for the scaling and translation of M_t which brings it into the best possible alignment with I_{t+1}. Next, the p_x component of this transformation is converted into the new bearing to the landmark and the scale value s_y is used to determine the new estimate of the range to the landmark, as described in (7.2); it has now computed r_{t+1} and x_{t+1}. The robot then builds a new model of the landmark, M_{t+1}, by simply cutting out a rectangular box around the location in I_{t+1} where M_t was found, determines what motion should be carried out next, and proceeds.

A possible source of inaccuracy in the computation of the range and bearing arises from the fact that the image of the landmark may change shape in ways other than translation and scaling, due to perspective effects and the fact that different parts of the object are visible in successive images. It is also possible for the landmark object itself to change shape in some nonrigid manner. The Hausdorff distance shape comparison method is less sensitive to errors in the locations of individual features than are methods based on correspondences between a small number of features (where errors in a few features may cause a significant error in the shape comparison). Using this method, we have found the effects of perspective and correspondence to be negligible until the camera is quite close to the object (within a meter or so using a camera with a 16 mm lens and an image width of about $\pm 15°$), as will be seen in the experimental results subsection below.

7.2.5 The Overall Navigation Method

Initially the robot grabs an image of the visual field which is presumed to contain the landmark. An initial model is given, which consists of a set of two-dimensional intensity edges (as discussed above this model can be extracted from an image of the scene, or can be obtained in some other manner such as from a modeling system). The navigation process is divided into an initialization stage and an approach stage. In the initialization stage a crude approximation to the range is obtained and the focal length of the camera is estimated. In the approach stage, the robot moves in a direction that is the current best estimate of the heading to the landmark, and updates the range and focal length values, as well as computing some other quantities discussed below. The approach stage is divided into steps, where at each step the robot grabs an image of the visual field and matches a model from the previous step to this image, in order to update the range and bearing estimates.

In the initialization stage, the robot makes two pre-programmed movements in order to calculate the range to the landmark and the focal length of the camera. Before the robot executes either of these movements, an image is grabbed and the initial landmark model is matched to this image, in order to determine the initial size. The robot then moves forward a known distance, currently 50cm, and grabs another image. The initial model is matched to this image; this yields the scale change s of the landmark over a 50cm motion, and thus the range to the landmark, using (7.2). A new model is generated by selecting the rectangular portion of the image where the landmark was found.

The robot then executes the second of the pre-programmed initialization movements, in order to estimate the focal length of the camera. The robot rotates a known amount, currently 8 degrees, in the direction that results in the landmark being closer to the center of the image frame, and grabs an image. After matching the new model to the image, the robot uses the amount of rotation and the landmark's change in x-position in the image to calculate an estimate of the camera's focal length, as described by (7.3). The robot then rotates to center the landmark in the frame.

At this point, the landmark is centered in the image frame, and the robot enters the approach phase in which it proceeds towards the object. Ideally, moving forward when the landmark is centered in the image frame should always keep the robot on a direct course, until the robot eventually makes contact with the landmark. However, factors such as the object not being completely centered and the robot not moving exactly as commanded may cause the landmark to drift off center in the frame. During the approach, the landmark may drift in the frame, signifying that the robot is slightly off target. Before each forward motion, the robot therefore calculates how much rotation is required to center the landmark in the frame, and performs this rotation simultaneously with the forward motion.

During each step of the approach process, the scale change between the current image and the previous image is computed. Rather than simply computing the range from this scale change, the scale changes for the last several images are combined in order to produce a more accurate estimate of the range. That is, the overall scale change across the sequence of images and the total motion during that sequence are used to compute the range from (7.2). All of the images taken since the last rotation of the robot are used in this computation.

Concurrent Moving and Matching In practice, the amount of time required to grab an image, extract its edges, and perform a matching step is usually about 3-4 seconds on a Sun 670. At the robot's usual translational velocity, this corresponds to about 20cm of forward motion. We can therefore improve the overall speed of the process by performing motion and matching in parallel: the robot grabs a frame, and begins searching for the landmark. It simultaneously begins moving forward. Usually, the search locates the landmark within a few seconds. The robot knows the range and bearing to the landmark that it had when it grabbed that frame. It can therefore predict the current range and bearing, and compute a rotation which keeps the landmark centered (and the robot on course). It can then update its model, execute this rotation (while continuing to move forward), grab another image, and begin another matching step.

In order to ensure that the robot does not go too far off course by continuing to move far away from the location where the last matched image was grabbed, we set a safe distance limit (currently 20cm) on the distance that it is allowed to travel while processing a match. In almost all cases, the robot completes the matching step before traveling this far; it therefore rarely has to stop moving.

Obstacle Avoidance The obstacle avoidance algorithm was added to handle the case when there are obstacles in the robot's path to the landmark. We assume that the obstacles do not interfere with the camera's line of sight to the landmark, but just impede the robot's path. We also assume that the surfaces of the obstacles are flat. A simple strategy, described in [JR1] is used to determine the surface orientation from the robot's bumpers, once it has made contact with an obstacle. The robot then moves along this surface until the obstacle is cleared (as indicated by sonar).

During this process, the robot maintains (using odometry) the angle and distance traveled since first contact with the obstacle. From these parameters and the previous range to the landmark, the robot calculates the expected range and bearing to the target, and rotates to that bearing. The robot then grabs an image, locates the landmark, recenters, and resumes the approach.

Partial Matching As the robot approaches the object, the landmark gets larger in the image frame, and at some range portions of the landmark may begin to fall outside the frame. When this happens, the model from a given step does not match the image at the next step (after a forward motion) very well, because large parts of the object are missing. At this point, the matching process is changed to allow for partial matches of the model by allowing the Hausdorff distance search method to locate poorer matches than were previously required (by decreasing f_F significantly).

The navigation system goes into the partial matching phase once the robot has gotten close enough to the object that part of it lies close to the boundary of the image frame (within 15 pixels of any border). In addition, the robot moves smaller intervals between successive images (the safe distance is reduced), since the shape change in the landmark is relatively great when the robot is close.

7.2.6   Some Experimental Results

Here we describe the results of some experiments we have performed using this technique. In each case, the robot was started some distance away from the landmark, with the landmark in view. The user then outlined a rectangular area which enclosed the landmark; this was used as the first model.

Figures 7.8 and 7.9 show an example of the robot navigating to its target LILY, one of the lab's other mobile robots. Only the top portion of the robot is initially visible, so this is used as the initial model. Note that the images are quite cluttered. Each line of the figure contains three images: the image acquired by the robot at that time step (I_t), the model from the previous time step overlaid on the image at the location where it was found (M_{t-1} overlaid on I_t), and the model extracted from the image (M_t).

Images 1, 2 and 3 show the initial calibration movements described in Subsect. 7.2.5. Image 1 is the image seen before any movement. It does not have a previous model, so no overlay is shown; the original image is shown instead. Image 2 is after a forward movement of 50cm to determine the initial range, and Image 3 is after the $8°$ rotation to determine the camera focal length. Image 4 is at a position intermediate between the initial position and the first obstacle. Image 5 is just before the robot makes contact with the first obstacle; Image 6 is just after it has cleared that obstacle. Images 7 and 8 bracket the avoidance of the second obstacle. Image 9 is intermediate between Image 8 and the location of the landmark. Image 10 was taken just before the robot made contact with the target. The total distance traveled was 9m; 43 images in total were processed. The time between images acquisitions in these examples was typically around 5 seconds, and the forward movement between acquisitions was usually slightly less than 20cm, so the robot was usually able to begin the next movement without actually coming to a stop. If the robot encountered an obstacle and had to navigate around it, this of course took more time.

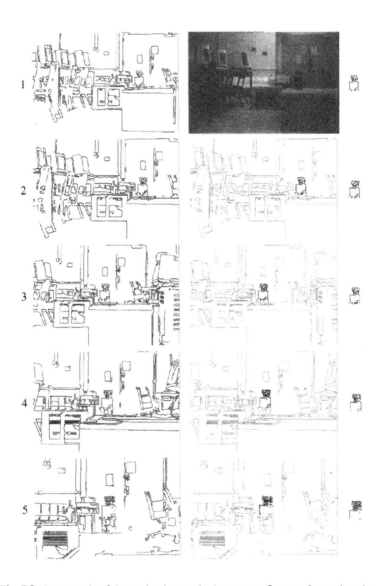

Fig. 7.8. An example of the navigation method, part one. See text for explanation.

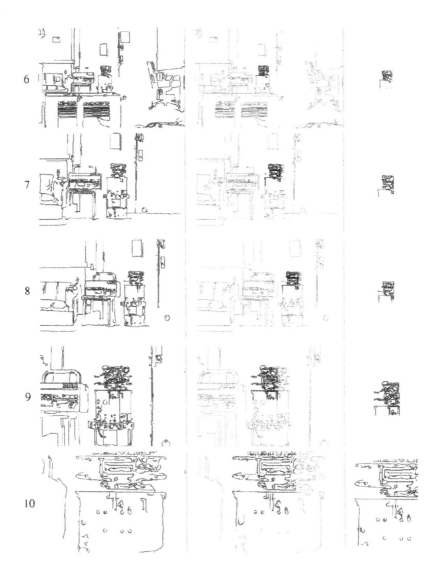

Fig. 7.9. An example of the navigation method, part two. See text for explanation.

7.2.7 Summary

We have presented a method for using visual information to navigate a mobile robot to a landmark in its visual field. The method operates by comparing two-dimensional edge images in order to recover the change in location and size of the landmark in the image as the robot moves. The change in image location is used to keep the landmark centered in the robot's visual field (and thereby keep the robot moving straight towards the landmark). The change in image scale is used to estimate the range to the landmark.

The method does not make use of world coordinates, or of any explicit three-dimensional information. The robot always maintains an estimate of the range and bearing to the landmark from the last place that a picture was taken, and updates that estimate after each successive image is obtained. The method has been used in our laboratory to control a mobile robot, and has been successful in a large number of instances. The matching technique is fast enough (on a SPARCstation) that it can run concurrently with the motion of the robot. Overall, the method is quite simple, not requiring complex representations of objects, or accurate calibration of the camera system.

7.3 Other Applications

The Hausdorff distance search methods and their implementations which we have developed have been used in a number of other applications. In [DJ1], they are used to match moving cars passing by two stationary cameras. In [FHS1], they are used to verify the results of colour-based recognition. In [HJ1], they are used in a preliminary matching phase of a motion segmentation algorithm. Finally, in [Br1], the Hausdorff distance search engine is used as the recognition component in a robot surveillance system.

Chapter 8

Conclusions

I have presented the Hausdorff distance, and how it can be used for visual recognition tasks. I have shown that the properties of the Hausdorff distance make it well-suited for use in model-based recognition: it encodes an intuitive notion of shape resemblance, and degrades gracefully in the presence of increasing positional noise. The Hausdorff distance is a metric; I have shown how, in some cases, the minimum Hausdorff distance under transformation is also a metric. Again, this corresponds well to an intuitive concept of shape resemblance.

The Hausdorff distance may be modified so that it is robust in the presence of outliers, occlusion, and images which contain multiple objects. This modified Hausdorff distance has some useful pseudo-metric properties. The most important of these is the triangle inequality; this means that if two models both match the same part of a given image then the models must be similar to one another.

The box-reverse distance is useful in reducing the problem of a model matching a cluttered, incorrect, portion of the image; none of the other feature-based visual recognition systems that I discussed had any similarly effective way of addressing this problem.

I have constructed some lower bounds which indicate that finding the exact transformation that minimises the Hausdorff distance may be too expensive to be practical. Because of this, I have suggested a rasterisation of transformation space. The fineness of this rasterisation is based on the fineness of the image and model rasterisation, and the rasterisation itself is constructed so that the transformation uniformity condition holds. This condition has allowed me to prove bounds on the error introduced by this rasterised approximation to the original continuous transformation space.

I have developed and presented techniques which allow the transformation grid to be searched efficiently, by eliminating the vast majority of the transformations on the grid without explicitly considering them, while still ensuring that the transformations which are the target of the search cannot be mistakenly overlooked. The principal search technique used is transformation space subdivision: recursive subdivision of regions in transformation space, until all transformations satisfying the forward and reverse criteria are found. I have also developed modifications to this search technique allow the best transformation to be found more efficiently.

I have discussed the implementations of the methods that I have developed, along with a number of examples showing the method in action. These examples demonstrate, on real images, the reliability and efficiency that I have claimed for my techniques and implementation. These implementations are also fast and reliable enough to be applied to practical problems such as motion tracking and mobile robot navigation.

In summary, I have shown that my visual recognition system, which uses the Hausdorff distance (computed using my efficient search techniques)

– Works on dense feature sets, such as intensity edges,

158

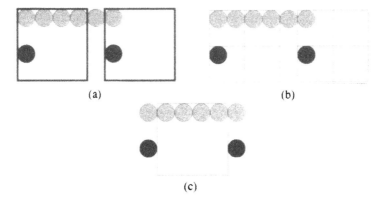

(a)   (b)

(c)

Fig. 8.1. Exploiting grouping.

- Works on many different types of models and images, containing occlusion and multiple objects,
- Works reliably when its input contains positional error and outliers, and
- Works quickly — quickly enough that it is useful in many practical applications.

8.1 Future Work

There are a number of ways in which the work presented here could be further developed. In this section, I briefly discuss some of these. Some of these are possibilities for new efficient search techniques, and some of them extend the domain of application of the Hausdorff distance.

8.1.1 Grouping

All the efficient search techniques that I have developed implicitly assume that the model points are widely separated, and so must be handled independently. However, in most cases, this is not true: the model points occur in groups. It should be possible to exploit this grouping, in some fashion, to increase the efficiency of the search. Figure 8.1 shows one way in which this might be done. It shows a line of six model points, in grey, and two image points, in black. The search task is to find translations where at least five of the model points lie directly on top of some image point, and the search is using the box distance transform. In this case, each translated model point probes a box in the image, reporting "yes" if there is an image point in that box, and "no" if there is not; at least five "yes" responses are necessary to proceed. Figure 8.1(a) shows the boxes which are probed by two of the model points. In this case, the pattern of responses from the six model points is "YNYYYY": five "yes" and one "no", so the method should examine the subdivisions of these boxes.

However, this is not the correct decision. Figure 8.1(b) shows some of the sub-boxes that are probed at the next finer level of the search: the leftmost point probes the four boxes shown near it, and the rightmost point probes the four boxes shown near it. Both probe their top left box, with the other model points behaving similarly, then all probe their top right box, and so on. The largest number of "yes" responses from this process is three.

It might seem that this is to be expected: not every cell in translation space that looks interesting at one level looks interesting when considered in more detail. However, the decision to reject the higher-level cell could have been made if the *pattern* of responses had been examined, rather than just the *count* of responses. Consider the single "no" response which was obtained. Figure 8.1(c) shows what this indicated: that the shaded box contained *no* image points. Given this information, it can be seen without any further information that the maximum number of "yes" responses that could be produced at the next finer level is four, not five: either the leftmost point must probe a box contained in this empty region, or the third point from the left must do so; while they both reach one of the image points in one of the four sub-cases, it is impossible for them to do so simultaneously. Thus, even though there were five "yes" responses, the single "no" response is guaranteed to grow, either to the left or the right, so no more than four "yes" responses can be obtained at any finer resolution.

This example illustrates one manner in which the grouping of model points might be exploited; further techniques, or a generalisation of this technique, may yield large improvements in search efficiency.

8.1.2 Gradient Descent

At the moment, the search for transformations which satisfy the forward and reverse criteria (matches) is, essentially exhaustive; all the efficient search techniques do is eliminate regions of the transformation space quickly. Because of this, they are all guaranteed: they cannot miss a match if one exists. However, losing this guarantee might be worthwhile if the reward is a huge increase in processing speed.

One possibility, which might give such a huge increase in processing speed, is that of gradient descent: seeding transformation space with a number of initial poses; each pose then modifies its parameters to reduce the Hausdorff distance between the transformed model and the image, until it reaches a local minimum.

As I showed in Chap. 3, there can be a very large number of such local minima; unless there were a similar number of seed poses (which would make the cost prohibitive), the global minimum would probably not be found. This problem might be reduced by the use of simulated annealing, or some similar technique; simulated annealing is intended to reduce the likelihood that a pose gets stuck in a local minimum by allowing it to increase its distance, with some probability; the hope is that this enables it to hop out of local minima.

The technique of Borgefors, in [Bo2], where the seed poses minimised their mismatch values in a multi-resolution image edge pyramid, would also be interesting to investigate.

One other possible approach is to reduce the number of local minima by smoothing out the function a little: instead of evaluating the Hausdorff distance at a certain transformation, evaluate it at every (grid) transformation within a small area, and then attempt to minimise this function. It should be smoother, and so have fewer, or shallower, local minima; this may aid the gradient descent process.

8.1.3 Analog

At the moment, the model and image point sets are binary arrays, where "1" values represent locations where features are present and "0" values represent locations where features are absent. However, many feature detectors actually produce features with associated strengths; these strengths are then thresholded to produce the binary arrays.

It would be interesting to investigate replacing the image binary array with an array where the values were numbers between 0 and 1, representing some form of feature strength or confidence (the model would remain a binary array). Extending the Hausdorff distance search methods to this type of image is possible, in an interesting way: define a new distance transform for this type of array. The forward distance is, in practice, computed by probing a distance transform array and computing some quantile of these probe values; matches are defined by their forward distance values being below the forward threshold τ_F. If the distance transform of the image binary array is replaced by some variant distance transform of an image feature confidence array, the forward distance remains well-defined. Such a variant distance transform should, ideally, be identical to the regular distance transform in the case when all the image confidences are 0 or 1; however, being one pixel away from a low-confidence feature should give a larger distance than being one pixel away from a high-confidence feature. This problem is an "apples and oranges" problem: how far away must I be from a 0.85-confidence feature, before I am an equivalent distance away to a distance of 5 pixels from a 0.3-confidence feature? I feel that some variant of the distance transform could be developed which works well in practice.

While the forward distance is well-defined, it is not clear how the efficient search techniques can be extended to this new problem. After all, many of them depend on Theorem 5.2, which depends on the distance transform having a maximum slope of one; this may not be true of the variant distance transform. However, the box distance transform search method does *not* depend on this property; it just computes the minimum distance transform values over a number of boxes. It should therefore be possible to simply replace the image distance transform with some variant distance transform, and use the cell subdivision technique, based around the box distance transform, and have the same search efficiency as with the regular, binary, images.

This works for the forward distance; applying this idea to the reverse distance is a bit less clear, but it should be possible to use the same principle which was used to generate the variant distance transform and apply it to determining the distance from a weak feature to a model feature (as opposed to the distance *from* a model feature *to* a weak feature, as in the distance transform).

8.1.4 Multichannel

At the moment, I have been using the Hausdorff distance only on features of a single type: it is possible for any model feature to correspond to any image feature. The feature detector, however, might produce features of different types: some features might be corners, some T-junctions, some edges, some coloured red, and so on; in this case, a corner should correspond only to a corner, and so on. The image and model, for this type of matching, consist of several distinct bands of features. It is easy to extend the forward

Hausdorff distance to this sort of banded model and image: instead of each transformed model feature probing the image distance transform, and some quantile being taken of these probe values, there could be a number of image distance transforms, one for each type of features; each model feature could probe the appropriate one. This ensures that stray T-junctions, for example, do not affect the distance to the nearest corner feature. Once all these probe values have been determined, they can be ranked and some quantile taken. Alternately, they could be ranked within each band, and the maximum of the resulting quantile values taken to determine the forward distance; this means that well-matching, but common, features such as edges could not swamp the bad news that almost no corners are well-matched.

The reverse distance can be computed in a similar manner, by probing several distance transforms of the model features (one distance transform for each band).

It might be possible to extend this idea to situations where the features are all of the same type, but have some associated information (such as edge direction); in this case, features should only be allowed to correspond if their, say, directions are within some tolerance of each other. This could be done by dividing up the circle of edge directions into a number of areas, and treating each area as a different band. In this case, a model feature might have to probe a number of different distance transforms, to ensure that it does not miss an image feature whose direction is similar to it, but which lies in an adjacent band.

8.1.5 Further Reading

This work was initially published as a series of conference and journal articles, technical reports, and as my Ph.D. dissertation [HKR1, HKR2, HKR3, HNR1, HNR2, HR1, HR2, HLR1, HLR2, Ru3, Ru2, Ru5, Ru4, Ru6, Ru1]. The dedicated reader might find it informative to peruse those earlier publications, to examine the growth and maturation of the ideas presented here.

Huttenlocher and Jaquith [HJ2] have examined the problem of false matches with the Hausdorff distance. Just about any model, and any transformation of the model, satisfies the forward criterion when the image contains a large number of features, densely packed, but in such cases the match probably does not mean anything. The work described in [HJ2] derives formulas that give the probability that a given match could have been caused by chance, with the given model and image.

Subsection 8.1.4 describes how the Hausdorff distance method might be applied to multichannel images, or images where there is additional information associated with each image and model feature, to be used to restrict matches. Olson and Huttenlocher [OH1] have developed a system along those lines that uses oriented points to restrict matching: for a model point to match an image point, the model point's orientation must, after transformation, be similar to the image point's orientation.

Huttenlocher, Lilien and Olson [HLO1] have used eigenspace methods to allow the computation of the forward fraction between a *number* of models and an image simultaneously. They represent the collection of models as a smaller number of eigenvectors: the eigenvectors are determined by a principal components analysis of the entire collection, and each model is then represented by the coefficients obtained by projecting it onto each eigenvector. They then search the image using using these eigenvectors, using similar search techniques to the cell decomposition technique described in Sect 5.4. It is possible to determine, to within a small error, how well a portion of the image would have matched a translated model (i.e., the forward fraction between the translated model and that portion of the image) by comparing that portion of the image with the eigenvectors, and then considering the coefficients associated with that model. Since the eigenvectors are shared by all the models, and there are many fewer eigenvectors than models, the entire collection can effectively be compared with a portion of the image in a much smaller amount of time than it would have taken to compare each model individually against that portion.

Appendix A

Computing Distance Transforms

A.1 Chamfer Methods

There are several standard approaches to the computation of the distance transform of the image I, $\Delta[x,y]$. One commonly used one is the chamfer method, as described in [Bo1]. Suppose, for the moment, that the norm defined on the plane is the L_1 norm. Let C be the mask

$$
\begin{array}{ccc}
 & 1 & \\
1 & 0 & 1 \\
 & 1 &
\end{array}
$$

with coordinates such that $C[0,0]$ refers to the zero value at the centre of C. I now show a parallel algorithm which computes $\Delta[x,y]$.

Algorithm A.1. *Compute the distance transform array $\Delta[x,y]$ giving, for each location (x,y) the L_1 distance to the closest point of I.*

1. Initialise $\Delta[x,y]$ to zero wherever $(x,y) \in I$. Initialise $\Delta[x,y]$ to infinity everywhere else (in practice, any sufficiently large number can be used).
2. Place the mask C at every pixel (x,y), and minimise the sums of each mask entry with the corresponding entries of $\Delta[x,y]$. That is, for each (x,y), in parallel,

$$
\Delta[x,y] \leftarrow \min\left(\begin{array}{ccc} & \Delta[x,y-1]+1. & \\ \Delta[x-1,y]+1. & \Delta[x,y], & \Delta[x+1,y]. \\ & \Delta[x,y+1]+1 & \end{array} \right).
$$

   (Any references outside the bounds of the $\Delta[x,y]$ array can be treated as having value infinity).
3. Repeat this update step until no entries in $\Delta[x,y]$ are changed. At this point, the algorithm has converged.

Initially, the entire array is set to infinity, except for the points which are in I, where it is zero. After one update step, the 4-connected neighbours of these points are set to 1; every subsequent step extends the influence of each point of I.

The same algorithm can be used for other norms, by varying the minimisation convolution mask C. For the L_∞ norm, C should be

$$
\begin{array}{ccc}
1 & 1 & 1 \\
1 & 0 & 1 \\
1 & 1 & 1
\end{array}
$$

reflecting the fact that a diagonal step is the same distance as a horizontal or vertical step. Step 2 then becomes

$$\Delta[x, y] \leftarrow \min \begin{pmatrix} \Delta[x-1, y-1]+1, \ \Delta[x, y-1]+1, \ \Delta[x+1, y-1]+1, \\ \Delta[x-1, y]+1, \qquad \Delta[x, y], \qquad \Delta[x+1, y], \\ \Delta[x-1, y+1]+1, \ \Delta[x, y+1]+1, \ \Delta[x+1, y+1]+1 \end{pmatrix}$$

A distance transform based on the L_2 distance cannot be computed exactly with this method. However, it is possible to approximate it to within 2% by using the mask

$$\begin{array}{ccccc} & 225 & & 225 & \\ 225 & 141 & 100 & 141 & 225 \\ & 100 & 0 & 100 & \\ 225 & 141 & 100 & 141 & 225 \\ & 225 & & 225 & \end{array}$$

which produces a distance transform where the distance values have been scaled by 100 to make them integers. It is possible to use other (possibly larger) masks, with comparable or better results; see [LL1] for a discussion of these masks.

The parallel algorithm converges after some number of update steps. The number of steps required depends on the size of the array $\Delta[x, y]$ being computed; it is at most the L_1 diameter of this array (its width plus its height). It is most suitable for systems where a single processor can be assigned to each pixel in $\Delta[x, y]$. On more conventional, serial, processors, a different algorithm should be used. The serial version of the algorithm operates in two passes, using the same mask array as the parallel method, split into two halves. The first pass iterates over the indices x, y of $\Delta[x, y]$ in increasing reading order (left to right, then top to bottom), using just the first half of the mask to do the minimization computation of Step 2 in the above algorithm. The first half of a mask C is those entries which precede the centre $[0, 0]$ point in reading order, plus the centre point. For example in the L_1 mask the first half is

$$\begin{array}{ccc} & 1 & \\ 1 & 0 & - \\ & - & \end{array}$$

and the minimisation update at each point in this pass is

$$\Delta[x, y] \leftarrow \min \begin{pmatrix} & \Delta[x, y-1]+1, \\ \Delta[x-1, y]+1, & \Delta[x, y] \end{pmatrix}.$$

It should be noted that this update is fundamentally different from that in Step 2 of Algorithm A.1: in that step, the current value of every $\Delta[x, y]$ is read, and then they are all simultaneously updated. On the other hand, this serial update is done a pixel at a time, so that the $\Delta[x, y]$ value written for one pixel might be used immediately to compute $\Delta[x+1, y]$.

On the second pass, the indices of $\Delta[x, y]$ are iterated over in reverse reading order and the minimization uses just the second half of the mask, that is, the centre point and all those entries which follow it in reading order:

$$\begin{matrix} & \overline{} & & \\ - & 0 & 1 & . \\ & 1 & & \end{matrix}$$

After these two passes have been completed, the array $\Delta[x, y]$ contains the same values that would have been computed by the parallel algorithm. The L_∞ and approximate L_2 masks can also be used. The output of either the sequential or the parallel method is a discrete distance function array.

The serial implementation of the chamfer method has the advantage that the time taken is linear in the number of pixels whose values need to be determined. For the L_1 and L_∞ norms, it computes exact distances. However, for the L_2 norm, it cannot compute the exact distance from a location to the closest point of I, but only an approximation. Some applications do not require that the distance values be exact, and in such cases this method is a good choice. In [Da1] and [LL1], methods for computing the L_2 distance transform similar in concept to the chamfer method are presented. Like the chamfer method, these methods consist of several passes in different directions, each pass applying some masked operation at every point in the distance transform array. However, they typically maintain more information for every point: not only the distance to the nearest point of I, but also the location of that nearest point. The update rules are more complex (and thus slower) because of this. These methods are able to produce more accurate results than the chamfer method: instead of the computed distances being within 2% of the true distances, the computed distances are within a small additive amount (less than 0.09 pixels) of the true distances, and most of the computed distances are exactly correct (up to floating point precision, or rounding error introduced in scaling the distances to produce integers).

A.2 Exact Methods

I now present a brief description of the method from [Ka1]. It works by dividing the points of the array $\Delta[x, y]$ into two classes: black points, which correspond to points (x, y) where $(x, y) \in I$, and white points, which are all the remaining points. The method then proceeds by the following steps.

Algorithm A.2. *Compute the distance transform array* $\Delta[x, y]$ *giving, for each location* (x, y) *the* L_2 *distance to the closest point of* I.

1. First, compute $\Delta^y[x, y]$. If (x, y) is a black point (i.e., $(x, y) \in I$), then $\Delta^y[x, y] = 0$. If (x, y) is a white point, then $\Delta^y[x, y]$ is the vertical distance from (x, y) to the closest black point in the same column. Formally,

$$\Delta^y[x, y] = \min_{\substack{\delta \\ (x, y+\delta) \in I}} |\delta| .$$

Note that this can be infinite, if there are no black points in the same column as (x, y). Δ^y is also called the y distance transform, or vertical distance transform of the image I. Figure A.1 shows an image and the corresponding $\Delta^y[x, y]$ array.

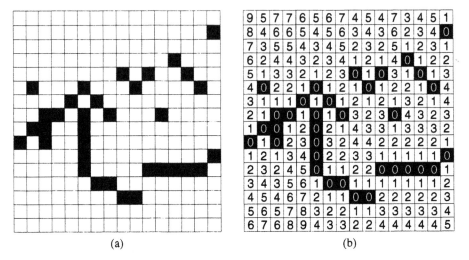

9	5	7	7	6	5	6	7	4	5	4	7	3	4	5	1
8	4	6	6	5	4	5	6	3	4	3	6	2	3	4	0
7	3	5	5	4	3	4	5	2	3	2	5	1	2	3	1
6	2	4	4	3	2	3	4	1	2	1	4	0	1	2	2
5	1	3	3	2	1	2	3	0	1	0	3	1	0	1	3
4	0	2	2	1	0	1	2	1	0	1	2	2	1	0	4
3	1	1	1	0	1	0	1	2	1	2	1	3	2	1	4
2	1	0	0	1	0	1	0	3	2	3	0	4	3	2	3
1	0	0	1	2	0	2	1	4	3	3	1	3	3	3	2
0	1	0	2	3	0	3	2	4	4	2	2	2	2	2	1
1	2	1	3	4	0	2	2	3	3	1	1	1	1	1	0
2	3	2	4	5	0	1	1	2	2	0	0	0	0	0	1
3	4	3	5	6	1	0	0	1	1	1	1	1	1	1	2
4	5	4	6	7	2	1	1	0	0	2	2	2	2	2	3
5	6	5	7	8	3	2	2	1	1	3	3	3	3	3	4
6	7	6	8	9	4	3	3	2	2	4	4	4	4	4	5

(a)   (b)

Fig. A.1. An image and its vertical distance transform.

2. Once $\Delta^y[x, y]$ has been computed, scan along each row, breaking the row up into intervals of consecutive white points. Each interval is then considered separately. The sign of the vertical distance from a black point to the interval does not matter; only its magnitude is significant. Thus, without loss of generality, let us assume that the closest black point vertically to any (x, y) is $(x, y + \Delta^y[x, y])$. Figure A.2(a) shows such an interval, taken from Fig. A.1; it shows the $\Delta^y[x, y]$ values along with the x coordinates. The black point lying to the left of the interval has been included; since the interval ends at the right edge of the image, there is no black point there.

3. Suppose that we are considering the interval $(x_l, y), \ldots, (x_r, y)$. Every point in this interval is a white point. We want to compute numbers $z_1, \ldots, z_{k+1}$ and $v_1, \ldots, v_k$ (for some k) such that if $z_i \leq x < z_{i+1}$, then the closest black point to (x, y) is $(v_i, y + \Delta^y[v_i, y])$. In other words, we want to divide up the interval into subintervals. The ith subinterval consists of the points whose x coordinates are z_i through $z_{i+1} - 1$, and the closest black point to each of the white points in this subinterval is the same. That closest point is given by $(v_i, y + \Delta^y[v_i, y])$: the closest black point in column y to (v_i, y). Note that this need not be the closest black point to (v_i, y): (v_i, y) need not be one of the points in subinterval i.

This is done by scanning the interval from left to right. Initially, k is set to 1, z_1 is set to x_l, z_2 is set to $x_r + 1$, and v_1 is set to $x_l - 1$, unless x_l is on the left-hand edge of the array, in which case v_1 is set to x_l. This initial setup puts the entire interval in one subinterval, with the closest black point set to $(x_l - 1, y)$, if this point exists, and the vertically closest point to (x_l, y) if it does not.

Each point in the interval is now considered in turn. Suppose that the point at (x_0, y) is being considered. If $\Delta^y[x, y]$ is infinite, then this point need be considered no further. Otherwise, let $P_N = (x_0, y + \Delta^y[x_0, y])$ be the closest point vertically to (x_0, y), and let $P_O = (v_k, y + \Delta^y[v_k, y])$ be the closest point vertically to (v_k, y), using the current value of v_k. A value s is computed. s divides the horizontal line

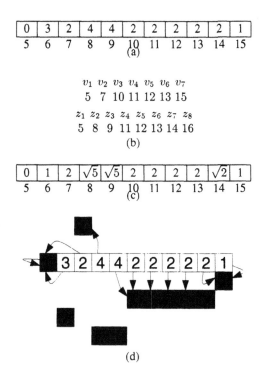

Fig. A.2. An example of processing an interval.

with height y into two regions. If $x < s$ then the closest black point to (x, y) is P_N; if $x \geq s$ then P_N is the closest. s is the location where the perpendicular bisector of the two black points P_O and P_N intersects the row containing the current interval, rounded up to the next integer. There are now three cases to be considered.

(a) If s is beyond the right hand edge of the current interval ($s > x_r$), nothing needs to be done: for no point in this interval is P_N closer than P_O. Note that at all times $z_k = x_r + 1$.

(b) If $s > z_{k-1}$, then the current rightmost subinterval should be subdivided. All points to the left of s remain associated with v_k, and all points to the right become associated with x_0 through the following steps, which create a new subinterval:

$$z_{k+1} \leftarrow z_k$$
$$z_k \leftarrow s$$
$$v_{k+1} \leftarrow x_0$$
$$k \leftarrow k + 1$$

(c) If $s \leq z_{k-1}$, then the current rightmost subinterval must be deleted: all points in it are closer to P_N than P_O, and so for no point in the entire interval is P_O the closest black point. This deletion is done by simply merging the rightmost subinterval with the next rightmost, decrementing k. Once this has been done, s should be recalculated (since P_O has changed), and this process continued until one of the previous two cases is encountered. It is possible that this step deletes all the subintervals; in this case, just create a single subinterval containing the entire interval, associated with x_0 (i.e., $v_1 \leftarrow x_0$).

4. If the rightmost point of the interval is not on the right-hand edge of the array, then the black point lying just to the right of the interval should also be considered, in the same manner.

5. After every point in the interval has been processed, what has been generated is a list of subintervals within the interval, where the closest black point for each subinterval is known. Figure A.2(b) shows z_i and v_i for the interval in Fig. A.2(a). The next step is to scan the interval again, assigning distances ($\Delta[x, y]$ values) for each point; Fig. A.2(c) shows the distances that are assigned for the example interval, and Fig. A.2(d) shows the interval together with its $\Delta^y[x, y]$ values, and the closest black point found for each point in the interval.

The interval scan in Step 3 can be thought of as computing a line cross-section of the Voronoi diagram of the black points by incrementally constructing it; the subintervals correspond to the portions of the line lying in different cells of the diagram. This also implies that each black point can be associated with only one subinterval: each black point generates only one Voronoi cell, and Voronoi cells are convex.

Each interval can be scanned in time proportional to the number of white points that it contains. While Step 3c takes more than a constant amount of time to complete, it is deleting subintervals created by Step 3b. Since there are at most a linear number of these ever created (at most one for every white point), the total amortised time is linear in the length of the interval. The entire process of computing $\Delta[x, y]$, therefore, takes time proportional to the size of the $\Delta[x, y]$ array. This is the same time, to within a constant factor, as that taken by the chamfer methods. However, the operations performed per pixel are more complex for these exact methods (multiplications and divisions may be necessary to compute s, not to mention the square roots needed to determine the actual distance given the location of the closest point of I), and so their running time may be significantly longer. If the time taken to compute the distance transform is large compared with the time taken for other parts of the image search, this may be a problem.

The article from which this presentation is drawn has only been published in Russian. A recent publication [BGKW1] in English describes a very similar exact distance transform algorithm, having the same running time, and may be more easily available.

A.3 z-Buffer Methods

A third way of generating the distance transform involves using special-purpose graphics hardware, and as such can be very fast. The form of $\Delta[x, y]$ is, as noted in Sect. 4.3, somewhat like an egg carton: the lower envelope of a collection of cone-shapes, one cone-shape for each point of I. A graphics engine can be used to render one such cone-shape, rooted at $z = 0$, for each point $i \in I$. The extent of each cone-shape is limited by the portion of the x, y-plane being used to view the cones, corresponding to the bounds of the $\Delta[x, y]$ array being computed. Most graphics engines render only polygons, which is not a problem for the L_1 or L_∞ norms. However, the L_2 cones must be rendered approximately, using a polyhedral approximation to a circular cone; generally, a polyhedron with a small number of sides (12 or 16) is sufficient for reasonable accuracy.

$\Delta[x, y]$ is the pointwise minimum, or lower envelope, of the cone-shapes rendered as described above. Consider the operations performed by a graphics rendering engine set up to perform orthographic (rather than perspective) projection, and set up to view this collection of surfaces from below. It can render the cones and perform visibility calculations quickly using a z-buffer. Suppose that location (x_0, y_0) in the z-buffer contains value d. Then the closest surface to the viewer which intersects the line $(x = x_0, y = y_0)$ is d away. This means that the lower envelope of the egg carton is at height d at (x, y), and so $\Delta[x, y] = d$. Thus, to generate the distance transform, simply render each of the cones described above into a z-buffer doing orthographic projection (i.e., with a view from $z = -\infty$), and read off the resulting z-buffer values. The running time of this method is $O(p)$, where p is the number of points in the set I. This is because each source point results in the rendering of a constant number of polygons (a single cone), and then the z-buffering operation is constant-time. With current graphics hardware tens or hundreds of thousands of polygons per second can be rendered in a z-buffer, and thus it is possible to compute $\Delta[x, y]$ in a fraction of second. Note that the only output desired from this rendering is the contents of the z-buffer, not the actual rendered pixels. Most graphics systems allow the z-buffer to be transferred into main memory after the rendering has been done; the resulting values may need to be scaled.

A.4 Computing the Box Distance Transform $\Delta'[x, y]$

Recall from Subsect. 5.5.3 that the box distance transform $\Delta'[x, y]$ is defined by

$$\Delta'[x, y] = \min_{\substack{0 \le x' \le d_x \\ 0 \le y' \le d_y}} \Delta[x + x', y + y'].$$

In other words, the value of $\Delta'[x, y]$ is the minimum value attained by Δ over a box $d_x + 1$ wide by $d_y + 1$ high, whose top left corner is at (x, y).

The array $\Delta'[x, y]$ can be computed for any given d_x and d_y in time proportional to the size of the array times $O(\log(d_x d_y))$. This is done using a prefix-based technique. Generally, the size of the array $\Delta'[x, y]$ is the same as that of $\Delta[x, y]$.

$\Delta'[x, y]$ can be computed in two passes: first compute

$$\Delta_1[x, y] = \min_{0 \le x' \le d_x} \Delta[x + x', y]$$

and then

$$\Delta'[x, y] = \min_{0 \le y' \le d_y} \Delta_1[x, y + y'].$$

The first operation works on each row of $\Delta[x, y]$ independently; the second one works on each column of $\Delta_1[x, y]$ independently. Both of these operations can be done using a single primitive transformation. Let $\delta[i]$ be a one-dimensional array. For any value d, define

$$\delta'_d[i] = \min_{0 \le j < d} \delta[i + j] . \tag{A.1}$$

As above, the array $\delta[i]$ can be considered to be padded with infinite values outside its bounds.

Now, $\delta'_d[i]$ can be computed in $\log(d)$ steps, each involving a pass over an array the size of δ. First, note that $\delta'_1[i] = \delta[i]$. Next, note that

$$\delta'_{d_1 + d_2}[i] = \min \left(\delta'_{d_1}[i], \delta'_{d_2}[i + d_1] \right) .$$

These two observations imply that $\delta'_{2^n}[i]$ can be computed in n steps, since

$$\delta'_{2^n}[i] = \min \left(\delta'_{2^{n-1}}[i], \delta'_{2^{n-1}}[i + 2^{n-1}] \right) .$$

A side effect of this process is the computation of the $n+1$ one-dimensional arrays $\delta'_{2^k}[i]$ for all $0 \le k \le n$.

Now, suppose that the binary decomposition of d is $d = d_1 + \ldots + d_n$, where each of the d_j are distinct powers of 2. There are $O(\log(d))$ such d_j for any d. Then

$$\delta'_d[i] = \min \left(\delta'_{d_1}[i], \delta'_{d_2}[i + d_1], \ldots, \delta'_{d_n}[i + d_1 + d_2 + \cdots + d_{n-1}] \right) .$$

Thus, the array $\delta'_d[i]$ can be computed using the $O(\log(d))$ arrays δ'_{2^k}: select those arrays whose indices are present in the binary decomposition of d. The overall process of computing the array $\delta'_d[i]$ thus consists of $O(\log(d))$ passes, creating those intermediate arrays, followed by one pass computing the final result; the total amount of work is $O(\log(d))$ times the size of the array $\delta[i]$.

Given this primitive operation, it is easy to see how $\Delta'[x, y]$ can be computed: compute the array $\Delta_1[x, y]$ by applying this operation, with $d = d_x + 1$, over each row of $\Delta[x, y]$, then applying it down each column of $\Delta_1[x, y]$, using $d = d_y + 1$. The total time taken for this is $O(\log(d_x) + \log(d_y)) = O(\log(d_x d_y))$ times the size of the array $\Delta[x, y]$.

A.5 Summary

The distance transform is of central importance to the efficient search of transformation space. In this appendix, I presented several different methods for computing the distance transform. Some of these methods are extremely fast, but have the disadvantage that for some norms they compute only an approximation to the true distance transform, while others compute the distance transform exactly, but pay the penalty of a constant factor in speed.

Bibliography

[ABB1]   H. Alt, B. Behrends, and J. Blömer. Approximate matching of polygonal shapes. *Discrete and Computational Geometry*, 9:267–291, 1993.

[ACH+1]   E. Arkin, L.P. Chew, D.P. Huttenlocher, K. Kedem, and J.S.B. Mitchell. An efficiently computable metric for comparing polygonal shapes. *IEEE Transactions on Pattern Analysis and Machine Intelligence*, 13(3):209–216, 1991.

[AF1]   N. Ayache and O. Faugeras. HYPER: A new approach for the recognition and positioning of two-dimensional objects. *IEEE Transactions on Pattern Analysis and Machine Intelligence*, 8(1):44–54, January 1986.

[AHU1]   A.V. Aho, J.E. Hopcroft, and J.D. Ullman. *Data Structures and Algorithms*. Addison-Wesley, 1983.

[AJ1]   T.D. Alter and D.W. Jacobs. Error propagation in full 3D-from-2D object recognition. In *Proc. Computer Vision and Pattern Recognition*, pages 892–898, 1994.

[AMWW1]   H. Alt, K. Mehlhorn, H. Wagener, and E. Welzl. Congruence, similarity, and symmetries of geometric objects. *Discrete and Computational Geometry*, 3:237–256, 1988.

[AST1]   P.K. Agarwal, M. Sharir, and S. Toledo. Applications of parametric searching in geometric optimization. In *Proc. Third ACM-SIAM Symposium on Discrete Algorithms*, pages 72–82, 1992.

[BGKW1]   H. Breu, J. Gil, D. Kirkpatrick, and M. Werman. Linear time Euclidean distance transform algorithms. *IEEE Transactions on Pattern Analysis and Machine Intelligence*, 17(5):529–533, May 1995.

[Bo1]   G. Borgefors. Distance transforms in digital images. *Computer Vision, Graphics and Image Processing*, 34:344–371, 1986.

[Bo2]   G. Borgefors. Hierarchical chamfer matching: A parametric edge matching algorithm. *IEEE Transactions on Pattern Analysis and Machine Intelligence*, 10(6):849–865, November 1988.

[BO3]   G. Borgefors and H. Olsson. Localizing and identifying objects: A method for distinguishing noise, occlusion and other disturbances. In *Proc. Second Nordic Workshop on Industrial Machine Vision*, Kuusamo, Finland, March 1992.

[Br1]   A.J. Briggs. *Efficient Geometric Algorithms for Robot Sensing and Control*. Ph.D. dissertation, Cornell University, January 1995.

[Br2]   R.G. Brown. *Localization, Mapmaking and Distributed Manipulation with Flexible, Robust Mobile Robots*. Ph.D. dissertation, Cornell University, January 1995.

[Br3]   T.M. Bruel. Fast recognition using adaptive subdivision of transformation space. Technical Report 1313, M.I.T. AI Lab, February 1991.

[Br4]   T.M. Bruel. Fast recognition using adaptive subdivision of transformation space. In *Proc. Computer Vision and Pattern Recognition*, pages 445–451, Champaign-Urbana, Illinois, 1992.

172

[BTBW1]   H.G. Barrow, J.M. Tenenbaum, R.C. Bolles, and H.C. Wolf. Parametric correspondence and chamfer matching: Two new techniques for image matching. In *Proc. Fifth International Joint Conference on Artificial Intelligence*, pages 659–663, Cambridge, MA, 1977.

[Ca1]   J.F. Canny. A computational approach to edge detection. *IEEE Transactions on Pattern Analysis and Machine Intelligence*, 8(6):34–43, 1986.

[Ca2]   T.A. Cass. Feature matching for object localization in the presence of uncertainty. In *Proc. Third International Conference on Computer Vision*, pages 360–364, Osaka, Japan, 1990.

[Ca3]   T.A. Cass. *Polynomial-Time Geometric Matching for Object Recognition*. Ph.D. dissertation, Massachusetts Institute of Technology, 1993.

[CGH⁺1]   L.P. Chew, M.T. Goodrich, D.P. Huttenlocher, K. Kedem, J.M. Kleinberg, and D. Kravets. Geometric pattern matching under Euclidean motion. In *Proc. Fifth Canadian Conference on Computational Geometry*, pages 151–156, Waterloo, Ontario, August 1993.

[CK1]   L.P. Chew and K. Kedem. Improvements on approximate pattern matching problems. In O. Nurmi and E. Ukkonen, editors, *Proc. Third Scandinavian Workshop on Algorithm Theory*, pages 318–325. Lecture Notes in Computer Science 621, Springer-Verlag, 1992.

[Cs1]   A. Csaszar. *General Topology*. Adam Hilger Ltd., Bristol, 1978.

[Da1]   P.E. Danielsson. Euclidean distance mapping. *Computer Graphics and Image Processing*, 14:227–248, 1980.

[DG1]   E. Dickmanns and V. Graefe. Dynamic monocular machine vision. *Machine Vision Applications*, 1:223–240, 1988.

[DJ1]   M.-P. Dubuisson and A.K. Jain. 2D matching of 3D moving objects in color outdoor scenes. In *Proc. Computer Vision and Pattern Recognition*, pages 887–891, Seattle, Washington, 1994.

[FHS1]   D. Fu, K. Hammond, and M. Swain. Vision and navigation in man-made environments: Looking for syrup in all the right places. In *Proceedings of the Workshop on Visual Behaviors*, pages 20–26, Washington, DC, 1994. IEEE Computer Society Press.

[Ge1]   D. Gennery. Tracking known three dimensional objects. In *Second National Conference on Artificial Intelligence*, pages 13–17, 1982.

[GH1]   W.E.L. Grimson and D.P. Huttenlocher. On the sensitivity of geometric hashing. In *Proc. Third International Conference on Computer Vision*, pages 334–338, Osaka, Japan, 1990.

[GH2]   W.E.L. Grimson and D.P. Huttenlocher. On the sensitivity of the Hough transform for object recognition. *IEEE Transactions on Pattern Analysis and Machine Intelligence*, 12(3):255–274, March 1990.

[GH3]   W.E.L. Grimson and D.P. Huttenlocher. On the verification of hypothesized matches in model-based recognition. *IEEE Transactions on Pattern Analysis and Machine Intelligence*, 13(12):1201–1213, December 1991.

[GHJ1]   W.E.L. Grimson, D.P. Huttenlocher, and D.W. Jacobs. A study of affine matching with bounded sensor error. In *Proc. Second European Conference on Computer Vision*, pages 291–306, Santa Margherita Ligure, Italy, May 1992.

[GLP1]   W.E.L. Grimson and T. Lozano-Pérez. Localizing overlapping parts by searching the interpretation tree. *IEEE Transactions on Pattern Analysis and Machine Intelligence*, 9(4):469–482, July 1987.

[Gr1]   W.E.L. Grimson. The combinatorics of object recognition in cluttered environments using constrained search. *Artificial Intelligence*, 44:121–165, 1990.

[Gr2]   W.E.L. Grimson with T. Lozano-Pérez and D.P. Huttenlocher. *Object Recognition by Computer: The Role of Geometric Constraints*. MIT Press, Cambridge, 1990.

[GTS1]   E. Grosso, M. Tistarelli, and G. Sandini. Active/dynamic stero for navigation. In *Proc. Second European Conference on Computer Vision*, pages 516–525, Santa Margherita Ligure, Italy, May 1992.

[HJ1]   D.P. Huttenlocher and E.W. Jaquith. Detecting moving objects with a moving camera by comparing edge contours. Technical Report 1405, Cornell University, Department of Computer Science, 1994.

[HJ2]   D.P. Huttenlocher and E.W. Jaquith. Computing visual correspondence: Incorporating the probability of a false match. In *Proc. Fifth International Conference on Computer Vision*, pages 515–520, Cambridge, MA, June 1995.

[HKR1]   D.P. Huttenlocher, G.A. Klanderman, and W.J. Rucklidge. Comparing images using the Hausdorff distance under translation. Technical Report 1211, Cornell University, Department of Computer Science, 1991.

[HKR2]   D.P. Huttenlocher, G.A. Klanderman, and W.J. Rucklidge. Comparing images using the Hausdorff distance under translation. In *Proc. Computer Vision and Pattern Recognition*, pages 654–656, Champaign-Urbana, Illinois, 1992.

[HKR3]   D.P. Huttenlocher, G.A. Klanderman, and W.J. Rucklidge. Comparing images using the Hausdorff distance. *IEEE Transactions on Pattern Analysis and Machine Intelligence*, 15(9):850–863, September 1993.

[HKS1]   D.P. Huttenlocher, K. Kedem, and M. Sharir. The upper envelope of Voronoi surfaces and its applications. *Discrete and Computational Geometry*, 9(3):267–291, 1993.

[HLO1]   D.P. Huttenlocher, R.H. Lilien, and C.F. Olson. Object recognition using subspace methods. In *Proc. Fourth European Conference on Computer Vision*, pages I.536–I.545, Cambridge, UK, 1996.

[HLR1]   D.P. Huttenlocher, M.E. Leventon, and W.J. Rucklidge. Visually-guided navigation by comparing two-dimensional edge images. Technical Report 1407, Cornell University, Department of Computer Science, 1994.

[HLR2]   D.P. Huttenlocher, M.E. Leventon, and W.J. Rucklidge. Visually-guided navigation by comparing two-dimensional edge images. In *Proc. Computer Vision and Pattern Recognition*, pages 842–847, Seattle, Washington, 1994.

[HNR1]   D.P. Huttenlocher, J.J. Noh, and W.J. Rucklidge. Tracking non-rigid objects in complex scenes. Technical Report 1320, Cornell University, Department of Computer Science, 1992.

[HNR2]   D.P. Huttenlocher, J.J. Noh, and W.J. Rucklidge. Tracking non-rigid objects in complex scenes. In *Proc. Fourth International Conference on Computer Vision*, pages 93–101, Berlin, Germany, May 1993.

[Ho1]   M.J. Hopcroft. *A Geometrical Approach to Model-Based Vision*. Ph.D. dissertation, Cornell University, January 1995.

[HR1]   D.P. Huttenlocher and W.J. Rucklidge. A multi-resolution technique for comparing images using the Hausdorff distance. Technical Report 1321, Cornell University, Department of Computer Science, 1992.

[HR2]   D.P. Huttenlocher and W.J. Rucklidge. A multi-resolution technique for comparing images using the Hausdorff distance. In *Proc. Computer Vision and Pattern Recognition*, pages 705–706, New York, NY, 1993.

[HU1]   D.P. Huttenlocher and S. Ullman. Recognizing solid objects by alignment with an image. *International Journal of Computer Vision*, 5(2):195–212, 1990.

[Ja1]   D.W. Jacobs. Optimal matching of planar models in 3D scenes. In *Proc. Computer Vision and Pattern Recognition*, pages 269–274, 1991.

[JR1]   J. Jennings and D. Rus. Active model acquisition for near-sensorless manipulation with mobile robots. In *Proc. IASTED International Conference on Robotics and Manufacturing*, Oxford, England, September 1993.

[Ka1]   A.V. Karzanov. Quick algorithm for determining the distances from the points of the given subset of an integer lattice to the points of its complement. *Cybernetics and System Analysis*, pages 177–181, April-May 1992. Translation from the Russian by Julia Komissarchik.

[KDTN1]   D. Koller, K. Daniilidis, T. Thórhallsson, and H.-H. Nagel. Model-based object tracking in traffic scenes. In *Proc. Second European Conference on Computer Vision*, pages 437–452, Santa Margherita Ligure, Italy, May 1992.

[LL1]   F. Leymarie and M.D. Levine. Fast raster scan distance propagation on the discrete rectangular lattice. *Computer Vision, Graphics and Image Proc.: Image Understanding*, 55(1):84–94, 1992.

[Lo1]   D.G. Lowe. Three-dimensional object recognition from single two-dimensional images. *Artificial Intelligence*, 31:355–395, 1987.

[Lo2]   D.G. Lowe. Robust model-based motion tracking through the integration of search and estimation. *International Journal of Computer Vision*, 8(2):113–122, 1992.

[LW1]   Y. Lamdan and H.J. Wolfson. Geometric hashing: A general and efficient model-based recognition scheme. In *Proc. Second International Conference on Computer Vision*, pages 238–249, 1988.

[Me1]   N. Megiddo. Applying parallel computation algorithms in the design of serial algorithms. *Journal of the Association for Computing Machinery*, 30:852–865, 1983.

[OH1]   C.F. Olson and D.P. Huttenlocher. Recognition by matching dense, oriented edge pixels. In *Proc. International Symposium on Computer Vision*, pages 91–96, 1995.

[Ol1]   C.F. Olson. Time and space efficient pose clustering. In *Proc. Computer Vision and Pattern Recognition*, pages 251–258, Seattle, Washington, 1994.

[Pa1]   D.W. Paglieroni. Distance transforms: Properties and machine vision applications. *Computer Vision, Graphics and Image Proc.: Graphical Models and Image Processing*, 54(1):56–74, 1992.

[PFT1]   D.W. Paglieroni, G.E. Ford, and E.M. Tsujimoto. The position-orientation masking approach to parametric search for template matching. *IEEE Transactions on Pattern Analysis and Machine Intelligence*, 16(7):740–747, July 1994.

[PS1]   F.P. Preparata and M.I. Shamos. *Computational Geometry*. Springer-Verlag, New York, 1985.

[RD1]   J. Rees and B. Donald. Program mobile robots in Scheme. In *Proc. IEEE International Conference on Robotics and Automation*, Nice, 1992.

[Ro1]   G. Rote. Computing the minimum Hausdorff distance between two point sets on a line under translation. *Information Processing Letters*, 38(3):123–127, May 1991.

[Ru1]   W.J. Rucklidge. Efficiently locating objects using the Hausdorff distance. *International Journal of Computer Vision*. To appear.

[Ru2]   W.J. Rucklidge. Lower bounds for the complexity of the Hausdorff distance. *Discrete and Computational Geometry*. To appear.

[Ru3]   W.J. Rucklidge. Lower bounds for the complexity of the Hausdorff distance. In *Proc. Fifth Canadian Conference on Computational Geometry*, pages 145–150, Waterloo, Ontario, August 1993.

[Ru4]   W.J. Rucklidge. Efficient computation of the minimum Hausdorff distance for visual recognition. Technical Report 1454, Cornell University, Department of Computer Science, 1994.

[Ru5]   W.J. Rucklidge. *Efficient Computation of the Minimum Hausdorff Distance for Visual Recognition*. Ph.D. dissertation, Cornell University, January 1995.

[Ru6]   W.J. Rucklidge. Locating objects using the Hausdorff distance. In *Proc. Fifth International Conference on Computer Vision*, pages 457–464, Cambridge, MA, June 1995.

[SHD1]   T.M. Silberberg, D.A. Harwood, and L.S. Davis. Object recognition using oriented model points. *Computer Vision, Graphics and Image Processing*, 35:47–71, 1986.

[TM1]   D.W. Thompson and J.L. Mundy. Three-dimensional model matching from an unconstrained viewpoint. In *Proc. International Conference on Robotics and Automation*, pages 208–220, 1987.

[UM1]   N. Ueda and K. Mase. Tracking moving contours using energy-minimizing elastic contour models. In *Proc. Second European Conference on Computer Vision*, pages 453–457, Santa Margherita Ligure, Italy, May 1992.

[VGD1]   G. Verghese, K. Gale, and C.R. Dyer. Real-time, parallel motion tracking of three-dimensional objects from spatiotemporal image sequences. In Kumar et. al., editor, *Parallel Algorithms for Machine Intelligence and Vision*, pages 340–359, New York, 1990. Springer-Verlag.

[WZ1]   J. Woodfill and R.D. Zabih. An algorithm for real-time tracking of non-rigid objects. In *Proc. American Association for Artificial Intelligence Conference*, 1991.

[YC1]   X. Yi and O.I. Camps. Line feature-based recognition using Hausdorff dis-
            tance. In *Proc. International Symposium on Computer Vision*, pages 79–84,
            1995.
[ZBT1]   J.Y. Zheng, M. Barth, and S. Tsuji. Qualitative route scene description us-
            ing autonomous landmark detection. In *Proc. Third International Confer-
            ence on Computer Vision*, pages 558–562, Osaka, Japan, 1990.
[ZF1]   Z. Zhang and O.D. Faugeras. Building a 3D world model with a mobile
            robot. In *Proc. 10th International Conference on Pattern Recognition*,
            1990.

Index

Springer
and the
environment

At Springer we firmly believe that an
international science publisher has a
special obligation to the environment,
and our corporate policies consistently
reflect this conviction.
We also expect our business partners –
paper mills, printers, packaging
manufacturers, etc. – to commit
themselves to using materials and
production processes that do not harm
the environment. The paper in this
book is made from low- or no-chlorine
pulp and is acid free, in conformance
with international standards for paper
permanency.

Lecture Notes in Computer Science

For information about Vols. 1–1099

please contact your bookseller or Springer-Verlag

Vol. 1135: B. Jonsson, J. Parrow (Eds.), Formal Techniques in Real-Time and Fault-Tolerant Systems. Proceedings, 1996. X, 479 pages. 1996.

Vol. 1136: J. Diaz, M. Serna (Eds.), Algorithms – ESA '96. Proceedings, 1996. XII, 566 pages. 1996.

Vol. 1137: G. Görz, S. Hölldobler (Eds.), KI-96: Advances in Artificial Intelligence. Proceedings, 1996. XI, 387 pages. 1996. (Subseries LNAI).

Vol. 1138: J. Calmet, J.A. Campbell, J. Pfalzgraf (Eds.), Artificial Intelligence and Symbolic Mathematical Computation. Proceedings, 1996. VIII, 381 pages. 1996.

Vol. 1139: M. Hanus, M. Rogriguez-Artalejo (Eds.), Algebraic and Logic Programming. Proceedings, 1996. VIII, 345 pages. 1996.

Vol. 1140: H. Kuchen, S. Doaitse Swierstra (Eds.), Programming Languages: Implementations, Logics, and Programs. Proceedings, 1996. XI, 479 pages. 1996.

Vol. 1141: H.-M. Voigt, W. Ebeling, I. Rechenberg, H.-P. Schwefel (Eds.), Parallel Problem Solving from Nature – PPSN IV. Proceedings, 1996. XVII, 1.050 pages. 1996.

Vol. 1142: R.W. Hartenstein, M. Glesner (Eds.), Field-Programmable Logic. Proceedings, 1996. X, 432 pages. 1996.

Vol. 1143: T.C. Fogarty (Ed.), Evolutionary Computing. Proceedings, 1996. VIII, 305 pages. 1996.

Vol. 1144: J. Ponce, A. Zisserman, M. Hebert (Eds.), Object Representation in Computer Vision. Proceedings, 1996. VIII, 403 pages. 1996.

Vol. 1145: R. Cousot, D.A. Schmidt (Eds.), Static Analysis. Proceedings, 1996. IX, 389 pages. 1996.

Vol. 1146: E. Bertino, H. Kurth, G. Martella, E. Montolivo (Eds.), Computer Security – ESORICS 96. Proceedings, 1996. X, 365 pages. 1996.

Vol. 1147: L. Miclet, C. de la Higuera (Eds.), Grammatical Inference: Learning Syntax from Sentences. Proceedings, 1996. VIII, 327 pages. 1996. (Subseries LNAI).

Vol. 1148: M.C. Lin, D. Manocha (Eds.), Applied Computational Geometry. Proceedings, 1996. VIII, 223 pages. 1996.

Vol. 1149: C. Montangero (Ed.), Software Process Technology. Proceedings, 1996. IX, 291 pages. 1996.

Vol. 1150: A. Hlawiczka, J.G. Silva, L. Simoncini (Eds.), Dependable Computing – EDCC-2. Proceedings, 1996. XVI, 440 pages. 1996.

Vol. 1151: Ö. Babaoğlu, K. Marzullo (Eds.), Distributed Algorithms. Proceedings, 1996. VIII, 381 pages. 1996.

Vol. 1152: T. Furuhashi, Y. Uchikawa (Eds.), Fuzzy Logic, Neural Networks, and Evolutionary Computation. Proceedings, 1995. VIII, 243 pages. 1996. (Subseries LNAI).

Vol. 1153: E. Burke, P. Ross (Eds.), Practice and Theory of Automated Timetabling. Proceedings, 1995. XIII, 381 pages. 1996.

Vol. 1154: D. Pedreschi, C. Zaniolo (Eds.), Logic in Databases. Proceedings, 1996. X, 497 pages. 1996.

Vol. 1155: J. Roberts, U. Mocci, J. Virtamo (Eds.), Broadbank Network Teletraffic. XXII, 584 pages. 1996.

Vol. 1156: A. Bode, J. Dongarra, T. Ludwig, V. Sunderam (Eds.), Parallel Virtual Machine – EuroPVM '96. Proceedings, 1996. XIV, 362 pages. 1996.

Vol. 1157: B. Thalheim (Ed.), Conceptual Modeling – ER '96. Proceedings, 1996. XII, 489 pages. 1996.

Vol. 1158: S. Berardi, M. Coppo (Eds.), Types for Proofs and Programs. Proceedings, 1995. X, 296 pages. 1996.

Vol. 1159: D.L. Borges, C.A.A. Kaestner (Eds.), Advances in Artificial Intelligence. Proceedings, 1996. XI, 243 pages. (Subseries LNAI).

Vol. 1160: S. Arikawa, A.K. Sharma (Eds.), Algorithmic Learning Theory. Proceedings, 1996. XVII, 337 pages. 1996. (Subseries LNAI).

Vol. 1161: O. Spaniol, C. Linnhoff-Popien, B. Meyer (Eds.), Trends in Distributed Systems. Proceedings, 1996. VIII, 289 pages. 1996.

Vol. 1162: D.G. Feitelson, L. Rudolph (Eds.), Job Scheduling Strategies for Parallel Processing. Proceedings, 1996. VIII, 291 pages. 1996.

Vol. 1163: K. Kim, T. Matsumoto (Eds.), Advances in Cryptology – ASIACRYPT '96. Proceedings, 1996. XII, 395 pages. 1996.

Vol. 1164: K. Berquist, A. Berquist (Eds.), Managing Information Highways. XIV, 417 pages. 1996.

Vol. 1165: J.-R. Abrial, E. Börger, H. Langmaack (Eds.), Formal Methods for Industrial Applications. VIII, 511 pages. 1996.

Vol. 1166: M. Srivas, A. Camilleri (Eds.), Formal Methods in Computer-Aided Design. Proceedings, 1996. IX, 470 pages. 1996.

Vol. 1167: I. Sommerville (Ed.), Software Configuration Management. VII, 291 pages. 1996.

Vol. 1168: I. Smith, B. Faltings (Eds.), Advances in Case-Based Reasoning. Proceedings, 1996. IX, 531 pages. 1996. (Subseries LNAI).

Vol. 1169: M. Broy, S. Merz, K. Spies (Eds.), Formal Systems Specification. XXIII, 541 pages. 1996.

Vol. 1170: M. Nagl (Ed.), Building Tightly Integrated Software Development Environments: The IPSEN Approach. IX, 709 pages. 1996.

Vol. 1171: A. Franz, Automatic Ambiguity Resolution in Natural Language Processing. XIX, 155 pages. 1996. (Subseries LNAI).

Vol. 1172: J. Pieprzyk, J. Seberry (Eds.), Information Security and Privacy. Proceedings, 1996. IX, 333 pages. 1996.

Vol. 1173: W. Rucklidge, Efficient Visual Recognition Using the Hausdorff Distance. XIII, 178 pages. 1996.

Vol. 1174: R. Anderson (Ed.), Information Hiding. Proceedings, 1996. VIII, 351 pages. 1996.

Vol. 1175: K.G. Jeffery, J. Král, M. Bartošek (Eds.), SOFSEM'96: Theory and Practice of Informatics. Proceedings, 1996. XII, 491 pages. 1996.

Vol. 1176: S. Miguet, A. Montanvert, S. Ubéda (Eds.), Discrete Geometry for Computer Imagery. Proceedings, 1996. XI, 349 pages. 1996.

Vol. 1177: J.P. Müller, The Design of Intelligent Agents. XV, 227 pages. 1996. (Subseries LNAI).